Celebrating

Insurrection

The Mexican Experience | William H. Beezley, series editor

Celebrating
Insurrection

The Commemoration
and Representation
of the Nineteenth-
Century Mexican
Pronunciamiento

Edited and with an introduction by
WILL FOWLER

University of Nebraska Press | Lincoln & London

Manufactured in the United States of America
∞

Library of Congress Cataloging-in-Publication Data

Celebrating insurrection: the commemoration and
representation of the nineteenth-century Mexican
pronunciamiento / edited and with an introduction
by Will Fowler.
p. cm. — (The Mexican experience)
Includes bibliographical references.
ISBN 978-0-8032-2541-1 (pbk.: alk. paper)
1. Revolutions — Mexico — History — 19th century.
2. Mexico — History — 19th century. 3. Political
violence — Mexico — History — 19th century.
4. Political culture — Mexico — History —
19th century. 5. Government, Resistance to —
Mexico — History — 19th century. 6. Legitimacy
of governments — Mexico — History — 19th
century. 7. Collective memory — Mexico. I. Fowler,
Will, 1966–
F1232.C36 2012
972'.04 — dc23   2012015375

Set in Adobe Garamond by Bob Reitz.

Contents

Preface

This book is about revolutions and fiestas. To be more specific, it is about a very particular kind of revolution: the nineteenth-century Mexican *pronunciamiento*, and how this intriguing insurrectionary practice was celebrated at the time and commemorated thereafter. It is also concerned with how the pronunciamiento was perceived, depicted, and represented by Mexicans and foreigners who witnessed and/or participated in one or several of them. Given that there were more than fifteen hundred pronunciamientos between the achievement of independence in 1821 and the pronunciamiento that brought Porfirio Díaz to power in 1876, their regular celebration paired with the ambivalent impact they had on the country merits careful consideration.

Unlike full-scale revolutions that occur once or twice in the history of a nation and arguably change it forever, displaying in so doing a clear and unambiguous legacy, the frequent and regular pronunciamientos that were staged in Mexico from 1821 to 1876 were, in contrast, full of contradictions and mixed signals. Many pronunciamientos were initiated to address genuine political concerns and to overcome concrete instances of injustice, and yet in adopting what amounted to a blatantly unconstitutional insurrectionary practice, *pronunciados* also contributed to Mexico's notorious chronic instability.

As becomes poignantly evident in this book, pronunciamientos were celebrated, commemorated, and yet condemned at the same time. The men who led them were likewise damned *and* venerated. Unlike the sanctified heroes of the U.S. and Mexican Revolutions of Independence (George Washington, Thomas Jefferson, Miguel Hidalgo y Costilla, José María Morelos) — whose unambiguous patriotism, selflessness, and righteousness continue to be celebrated to this very day on the Fourth of July and the Sixteenth of September in their respective countries, regardless of whether they were the wonderful individuals we have been led to believe they were — the commemorated pronunciados of nineteenth-century Mexico were characterized by their flawed heroism. They were the interpreters of the ignored and trampled will of the nation. But they were also outlaws who "pronounced" to gain power or promotion and to indulge in all forms of plunder. Studying the contradictory treatment pronunciamientos received reveals a number of crucial aspects of the pronunciamiento as an ambivalent revolution of sorts as well as of Mexican political culture. A key aim of this volume is precisely to decipher what the noted ambivalence tells us about the practice as a necessary yet problematic means of informing political change, and of the culture that reluctantly endorsed it, celebrating the pronunciamientos when they happened, rapidly forgetting them soon after.

Celebrating Insurrection provides at one level, and for the first time, a collection of individual yet interrelated studies on the role civic fiestas played in informing the Mexican people's collective response to these nineteenth-century revolutions "of sorts." How, for instance, did the celebrations that followed the triumph of most pronunciamientos sacralize and/or legitimize their role and that of their leaders in Mexican history? Did the fiestas that celebrated the victorious pronunciamientos and pronunciados contribute to the legitimizing of the pronunciamiento as an accepted metaconstitutional means of effecting political change? And if so, why were these celebrations ineffective in ultimately consecrating the role of the pronunciamiento as a force for good? There are chapters on the memory, representation, and influence of seminal pronunciamientos such as Rafael del Riego's 1 January 1820 pronunciamiento of Cabezas de San Juan, which forced King Ferdinand VII to restore the liberal 1812 Constitution; Agustín de Iturbide's 24 February 1821 pronunciamiento of Iguala, which brought about Mexican independence; and Porfirio Díaz's action of 2 April 1867, which signaled the end of the French Intervention. There are also essays on how the pronunciamientos and pronunciados of the 1820s–1840s were actually celebrated in Jalisco, San Luis Potosí, and Yucatán as well as during the Mexican-American War. These case studies eloquently describe what the fiestas entailed, highlight the thinking behind their organization and ceremonies, and analyze how the events that gave rise to them were manipulated by the authorities and the pronunciados' supporters with varying degrees of success. The mixed fortunes that flawed heroes such as Agustín de Iturbide, José Márquez, Joaquín Gárate, Santiago Imán, Ignacio Comonfort, Juan Bustamante, and Porfirio Díaz enjoyed *and* suffered as figures of both veneration *and* damnation in fiestas and historiographical texts are also researched in depth, providing valuable insights into the paradoxical nature of the pronunciamiento, a practice that was unlawful yet allegedly legitimate, as well as into the difficulty Mexicans had in overlooking the flaws of the pronunciamientos' heroes. Two chapters address contemporary historical representations of this phenomenon, focusing on how the Mexican intelligentsia of the early national period and the foreign travelers of the time understood the pronunciamiento, as it became part of past and present concepts of Mexican nationhood and political culture during the nineteenth century.

In the first of four volumes on the pronunciamiento of independent Mexico, *Forceful Negotiations: The Origins of the Pronunciamiento in Nineteenth-Century Mexico*— (2010), we established that the pronunciamiento was a phenomenon that became common in the Hispanic world in the nineteenth century. We argued that it was a practice (part petition, part rebellion) that sought to effect political change through intimidation and that was adopted to negotiate forcefully. We showed, moreover, that the pronunciamiento developed alongside Mexico's constitutions and formal political institutions and was resorted to, time and again, to remove unpopular politicians from positions of power, put a stop to controversial policies, call for a change in the political system, and promote the cause of a charismatic leader and/ or the interests of a given region, corporate body, or community. We concluded that the pronunciamiento became *the* way of doing politics. In the second edited volume of our pronunciamiento tetralogy, *Malcontents, Rebels, and Pronunciados: The Politics of Insurrection in Nineteenth-Century Mexico* (2012), we explained why this was the case. The process whereby the pronunciamiento went from originally being a military-led practice to one that was endorsed and employed by civilians, priests, indigenous communities, and politicians from all parties was traced through the study of a rich variety of pronunciamientos stretching from Tlaxcalan pueblo political activities in the late colonial period to a socialist *levantamiento* (uprising) with anarchist overtones in Chalco in 1868, with the stress being on individual and collective motivation.

In this third volume in the series we are interested in how Mexicans tried to come to terms with this practice, how they attempted to legitimize it by celebrating it and including it in their repertoire of civic fiestas, and how these fiestas came to reflect the ambivalence people felt toward the pronunciamiento. We provide an innovative and revisionist collection of essays, written by some of the leading authorities in the field, seeking to explain how pronunciamientos were celebrated, remembered, commemorated, and represented. What emerges is a striking interpretation of a phenomenon that was characterized by its duality and ambivalence, one that was experienced as a necessary evil, celebrated yet criticized, reluctantly justified, its heroes both damned and venerated. We hope this volume offers the reader a challenging collection of interpretations of and explanations for the reasons Mexicans, as individuals and members of given communities, celebrated yet struggled to commemorate the pronunciamiento, a practice they adopted, albeit with serious misgivings, as their preferred means of effecting political change during this turbulent period.

Acknowledgments

In June 2007 I was the recipient of a major Arts and Humanities Research Council (AHRC) research grant amounting to more than £610,000, which funded the three-year project on "The *Pronunciamiento* in Independent Mexico, 1821–1876" (2007–2010). It paid for the salaries of two research fellows and a database developer and covered the cost of two PhD studentships. It also funded the research team's travel expenses to and from Mexico, including the expenses that were incurred in the organization of three major conferences held at St. Andrews in June 2008, 2009, and 2010. This generous award allowed me to put together a vibrant research team focused on producing a major online relational database that includes transcriptions of over fifteen hundred pronunciamientos (see http://arts.st-andrews.ac.uk/pronunciamientos/) and publishing four volumes (three edited and one monograph) on different aspects of this phenomenon. The first of these volumes came out in 2010, addressing the origins, nature, and dynamics of this practice. The second was published in 2012 and concentrated on who adopted this form of insurrectionary politics and why, noting how it evolved from 1821 to 1868.

Needless to say, I am extremely grateful to the Arts and Humanities Research Council. Without the AHRC's funding, this extraordinary project would never have taken place. Thanks to the AHRC the third of three planned international conferences was held in St. Andrews, 11–13 June 2010, bringing together the St. Andrews–based research team and a formidable group of international scholars. This book contains the findings of a selection of the papers that were presented. I would like to thank St. Joseph's University, the Universidad Autónoma de San Luis Potosí, the Universidad Nacional Autónoma de México, the Instituto Mora, California State University at San Bernardino, and the Universities of Leeds and Warwick for the financial contributions they made toward the travel expenses of their respective speakers.

The conference went ahead (only after the delegates were allowed to watch Mexico play South Africa in the inaugural match of the 2010 World Cup) and was extremely lively, generating intense discussion. Thanks are due to the late Michael P. Costeloe, Paul Garner, Brian Hamnett, Francisco Parra, and Guy Thomson, all of whom kindly chaired the sessions and generously contributed their thoughts to the dialectics unleashed by the conference. Likewise I offer my sincere thanks to those speakers who, although not included in this volume, offered suggestive papers on different aspects of the memory, commemoration, and representation of the Mexican pronunciamiento, in particular Germán Martínez Martínez and Natasha Picôt.

As always, I would like to thank my colleagues in the Department of Spanish and the School of Modern Languages at the University of St. Andrews for their unwavering support and collegiality. I am indebted to our former student Elspeth Gillespie for her assistance during the conference and to our extremely diligent conference secretary, Barbara Fleming. Thanks are also due to Salvador Rueda Smithers and Hilda Sánchez at the Museo Nacional de Historia in Mexico City for providing us with a digital image the painting entitled *Discurso cívico en la Alameda* and for ensuring that the Instituto Nacional de Antropología e Historia authorized its use on the cover of the present volume. And my gratitude extends, as ever, to my wife Caroline and our children for being so incredibly patient and supportive.

Last but not least, I must thank Bridget Barry and her first class editorial team at the University of Nebraska Press, including Sabrina Ehmke Sergeant, Joeth Zucco, and Sally E. Antrobus. It was a real pleasure to work with Nebraska on my *Santa Anna of Mexico* (2007), *Forceful Negotiations* (2010), and *Malcontents, Rebels, and Pronunciados* (2012). I am delighted that we continue to work together. I thank Bridget, in particular, for believing in this project and for supporting the publication of the books it is generating.

Introduction

The Damned and the Venerated: The Memory, Com-memoration, and Representation of the Nineteenth-Century Mexican Pronunciamiento

After watching *Memorias de un mexicano* (1950), the extraordi-nary documentary Carmen Toscano produced with the footage from her father's historical archive, one is left with the vivid im-pression that in Mexico the passing of time was punctuated by the regular eruption of revolutions and the authorities' obses-sion with constantly organizing fiestas to celebrate them: as if the Mexican calendar were made up of seasonal revolutions and fiestas.[1] Salvador Toscano's coverage of most, not to say all, of the key events that unfolded in Mexico between 1897 and 1924, paired with his regular filming of the annual celebrations of in-dependence in the capital, provides an exceptional visual record of the first decades of the twentieth century, offering a narrative in which revolutions and fiestas followed one another with star-tling yet remarkable consistency.

In *Memorias de un mexicano* we actually see the 1904 parade that celebrated Porfirio Díaz's penultimate rise to the presiden-cy, the celebrations of 16 September 1908, those of the centenary in September 1910, Francisco Madero's revolution of 20 Novem-ber that year (following his feted journey by train from Ciudad Juárez to Mexico City), and the celebrations that were held af-ter his electoral victory and accession to the presidency. We wit-ness Emiliano Zapata's 1911 uprising in Morelos, Pascual Orozco's rebellion in Chihuahua, the battle of Bachimba, Félix Díaz's insurrection in Veracruz, and Madero's participation in the *fiestas patrias* of 1912. The *Decena Trágica* of February 1913 is followed by the 16 September celebrations of 1913 (now with Victoriano Huerta at the head of the government) with footage of a further military celebration to decorate Huerta's loyal officers, including General Aurelio Blanquet. Similarly, violent events such as the U.S. intervention in Veracruz, together with the mobilization of Francisco Villa's forces in the north and Zapata's in the south, are accompanied by footage of the short-lived president Francisco Carvajal hosting the ceremony of 18 July 1914 in the Hemiciclo Benito Juárez, of the parades that accompanied the Constitutionalist Army's entrance into Mexico City, of those that followed Villa and Zapata's arrival a few months later, and of the celebrations that marked Venustiano Carranza's presidential accession in 1917. After witnessing Amado Nervo's and Carranza's funerals, the film ends with the major celebrations of September 1920, now with Álvaro Obregón on the presidential balcony. The ostensibly cyclical pattern of fiestas and revolutions that features so prominently in the film serves as a powerful reminder of the extent to which the Mexicans' experience of their long nineteenth century, from 1810 to 1920, was characterized by political violence but also by civic fiestas, parades, and celebrations.

Mexico experienced two major revolutions in a period of just one hundred years, the 1810–21 War of Independence and the 1910–20 Revolution, with over fifteen hundred pronunciamientos launched in between, and has developed over the years a long-lasting tradition of celebrating and commemorating its insurrections, whether via the fiestas patrias of 15–16 September that commemorate Father Miguel Hidalgo y Costilla's 1810 *grito* (cry) of Dolores or the processions and parades that annually mark Madero's revolutionary 1910 Plan of San Luis Potosí on 20 November.[2] Not only do the street names of many Mexican cities conjure up a mental geography of insurgency and revolution — 16 de Septiembre, 20 de Noviembre, Insurgentes, Revolución, Hidalgo, Allende, Madero — but the commitment to celebrating these events remains strong: in 2010 the Mexican government did not allow even worldwide economic crisis to stand in the way of spending 45 million U.S. dollars on the eight-hour-long celebratory bicentenary extravaganza of 15–16 September. Mexicans take their partying extremely seriously. As Octavio Paz noted in his famous *El laberinto de la soledad* (1950), "The lonely Mexican loves his fiestas and public gatherings. Any pretext is good to interrupt the passing of time and celebrate men and events with parties and ceremonies. We are a ritual people."[3] The fact that Mexicans have acquired a reputation for hosting lively parties, spending whatever they have on fiestas and fireworks regardless of their dire straits, did not escape Aldous Huxley's attention in his 1934 travelogue of Guatemala and Mexico: "On nights of jollification, you may see, even in quite modest little towns, the most astonishing displays of pyrotechny. Indians are desperately poor, but they are always ready to spend their last centavo on something that goes off with a bang and a bright light."[4]

Viewed from a British perspective where Oliver Cromwell's 1642–46 Glorious Revolution is neither celebrated nor remembered, the idea of a government investing large sums of money, even in times of economic austerity, to commemorate rebellions and violent acts of insubordination is certainly intriguing. What does a disposition to celebrate revolutionary activity tell us about a given national culture or imagined community? And what impact does celebrating revolutionary activity on a yearly basis have? If revolutions are good (i.e., worthy of parades, fireworks, and jollities), how can an established government frown on anybody who takes up arms in the name of freedom? How can one condemn revolutionary activity (e.g., the Zapatista uprising in Chiapas of 1 January 1994), or deem it an aberration, when every year you parade, holiday, and proudly as well as patriotically celebrate revolutions from the past? Is the fact that Subcomandante Marcos named his Zapatista national liberating army after the commemorated Mexican revolutionary Emiliano Zapata not indicative of the extent to which a tradition of celebrating revolutions and revolutionary heroes has given past Mexican revolutionary actions a noteworthy resonance in the Mexican national psyche?[5]

Just as it is extremely difficult for any current Mexican government seriously to consider privatizing Petróleos Mexicanos (PEMEX) when every year Mexicans commemorate the 1938 nationalization of the oil industry on 18 March, it is possible to suggest that a regular celebration of revolutionary endeavors may have fostered a revolutionary culture. And yet one could also argue that the celebrations, in institutionalizing these revolutions, have served to sanitize them, de-revolutionize them, disempower their original values. They have assisted with the legitimizing of those in power, those who do the celebrating, who pay for the fiesta and make everybody happy with *panem et circenses*, "bread and circuses for the people," regardless of whether they actually believe in what the commemorated event or heroes actually stood for.

With these questions in mind, we endeavor in this volume to determine whether the constant celebration of the Revolution of Independence and the numerous pronunciamientos that ensued gave the nineteenth-century Mexicans' "right to insurrection" a certain respectability and legitimacy, transforming the actual threat of violence or revolutionary action into an acceptable, desirable, even admirable way of addressing issues of political injustice. Given the frequency with which Mexicans "pronounced," it would certainly appear to be the case that the pronunciamiento became the way to do politics from 1821 until 1876. Given the regularity with which Mexicans celebrated these "pronouncements," it also looks as though the pronunciamiento was a practice Mexicans deemed worthy of civic fiestas, which merited parades and public spectacles.

And yet the pronunciamiento, albeit enthusiastically celebrated, must not be mistaken for a full-scale revolution. Unlike the 1810 or 1910 revolutions, pronunciamientos did not involve mass participation and did not generally set out to overthrow the existing government and political system. They did not result in a dramatic change in the lives of great masses of people, nor did they bring about significant transformations in the organization and structure of Mexican society. Most pronunciamientos were, in fact, acts of insubordination staged to address very concrete grievances. As Miguel Alonso Baquer put it, rather than rebellions, they were "gestures of rebellion."[6] They contained an expressed intention on the part of the "pronounced ones" of rebelling or disobeying, of withdrawing their support or ceasing to recognize the authority and/or legitimacy of a given local or national government. They did so, however, in the hope that the challenged authorities would bow down to their demands before any threatened acts of violence were actually committed. In other words, the aim of the great majority of these "gestures of rebellion" was to force the government to listen and negotiate with the *pronunciados*, not to overthrow it.

Although the pronunciamiento is still defined in most diction-
aries and encyclopedias as a military uprising or coup, in reality
it was not always a military action, and it was generally *not* concerned with overthrowing the government.[7] As can be gathered
from Michael P. Costeloe's useful definition:

> The *pronunciamiento* in early nineteenth century Mexico is diffi-
> cult to define for practical purposes of analysis. Variable in size, ob-
> jective, cause and effect, it became an established and recognized
> means of seeking change. Often but not always accompanied by
> the threatened use of military force, it was used by leading politi-
> cians of all parties to demand change at the national political level
> but it also provided the opportunity for ambitious military officers
> to achieve promotion, dissatisfied merchants to obtain the repeal of
> laws, the poor to augment their income with loot, and bandits to le-
> gitimize their trade.[8]

In other words, the pronunciamiento, with its distinctive and
culturally unique expectations, formulistic and formulaic procedures, and easily recognizable generic-driven texts, was a nineteenth-century Hispano-Mexican extra-constitutional political
practice that was used by soldiers and civilians to lobby forcefully, negotiate, or petition for political change, both at a national
and at a local level.

For the sake of clarity it may be worthwhile to review how we
came to regard the pronunciamiento in the first volume we dedicated to the study of this political phenomenon, *Forceful Negotiations: The Origins of the Pronunciamiento in Nineteenth-Century
Mexico* (2010). Regardless of the pronunciamiento's evolution, it
was a remarkably formulaic and ritualistic practice. In this sense it
retained over time a number of characteristics that make possible

creating a taxonomy of the phenomenon, despite the difficulties of defining the pronunciamiento.

Given that there would have been a grievance shared or that could usefully be exploited by a number of officers and/or villagers, the initial stage of most pronunciamientos involved a conspiracy. The potential pronunciados sought to gain adherents and establish whether they would have sufficient support from key players in the community once their forceful protest was launched. During this preparation stage the pronunciados-to-be entered into so-called *compromisos* with potential backers. This involved promising rewards to officers, merchants, priests, etc., in exchange for their support. Once the aspiring pronunciados were persuaded that they could garner a meaningful following, a meeting was convened to discuss formally the grievance or matter at hand. In the original military-led pronunciamientos, this generally took place in the leading commander's quarters. Thereafter, and once the practice of the pronunciamiento was taken up by civilians, such a meeting went on to take place in the town council rooms (i.e., the *casas consistoriales*), the main square, the parish church, or even, in a few cases, in a particular individual's house. The holding of a supposedly spontaneous meeting in which grievances were openly discussed before the premeditated resolution of launching the pronunciamiento was taken became customary. At this point, a secretary was appointed who wrote down the minutes of the meeting, the *acta*, which would go on to outline the plan, petition, or *grito* that was formally and almost ritualistically *pronunciado*.

Most of the pronunciamiento texts thus began with a preamble explaining how it had come to pass that those concerned had been compelled to gather and discuss the stated grievances and how, in turn, they had resolved unanimously and as a corporate body (specific garrison, *ayuntamiento*, etc.) to "pronounce." In so doing they often claimed to represent an ignored or oppressed general or popular will. They outlined their demands in the petition that ensued and noted, in the more forceful cases, that they would unwillingly resort to violence if their grievances were not addressed. The pronunciamiento invariably carried the signatures of the pronunciados, who often claimed to represent the men under their orders (e.g., a specific artillery unit, all the sergeants of a given division). The text was then circulated as widely as possible, printed and distributed as a pamphlet or inserted and reproduced in the press. It was also read out to the community from where the pronunciamiento was launched, an event that could be celebrated (as the chapters in this book attest) with fireworks, tolling of church bells, music, and, in some instances a fiesta. If the pronunciamiento received a significant number of *pronunciamientos de adhesión*, and the pronunciados could hold the government to ransom by controlling a geopolitically important town, such as Veracruz, Guadalajara, or San Luis Potosí, its chances of success were indeed great.[9]

In Mexico the pronunciamiento texts developed into a genre in their own right. What is more, it is actually difficult to conceive of a pronunciamiento without a text. The importance of the text as a key element of the pronunciamiento cannot be overstated. The legalistic language employed is indicative in itself of how the pronunciamiento represented an alternative legality or bureaucracy that was on a par with the supposed constitutional order it was challenging.

It was also an appealing and addictive practice because it was ultimately a contained form of revolutionary action. The pronunciamiento was meant to be resolved without bloodshed. Its dynamic was one based on threats and counter-threats, in which rebels and government officials waited to see how much support the original pronunciamiento received before deciding whether negotiation would be necessary or whether one side or the other would have no choice but to back down. As Josep Fontana has argued, the pronunciamiento opened up the possibility of effecting a contained or controlled revolutionary action, namely one that — although employing a threat of violence — forced change without actually unleashing a bloodbath in the manner of the French or Haitian revolutions: "It consecrated a new political formula which allowed the political and military 'liberal' minorities to carry out a controlled revolutionary process."[10] The degeneration into violence or civil war was therefore an aberration.

It was an incredibly paradoxical practice. It was extra-constitutional, and yet it was regularly used to save the constitution from the abuses of those in power. It was unlawful, and yet its instigators often noted that they were taking up arms legitimately since the national will had been flagrantly ignored by the government. It was an act of insurrection, and yet it typically involved rigorously adhered-to bureaucratic procedures in which minutes of the initial revolutionary meeting were taken, and in which the pronunciados' demands were formulated in signed and counter-signed documents — the famous *actas* and *planes* (plans), — which were then circulated across the country in the hope that they would be supported by other garrisons and communities. It was illegal, and yet the language that was used in the pronunciamiento texts was tediously legalistic and formulaic. It was not part of the constitutional fabric of the republic, and yet national and state legislatures often ended up amending the law in response to pronunciamiento demands. At a time of constitutional crisis in which

Mexico's incipient institutions lacked authority, in many ways the pronunciamiento supplemented what was arguably a faulty constitutional process, in so doing correcting the constitution's own flaws and limitations. And yet the pronunciamiento was, by the same token, a force of chaos that prevented the constitution from being respected and from setting down long-lasting roots. It goes without saying that the pronunciamiento set a precedent for repeated unlawful political behavior and a context in which politics were decided, time and again, by pronunciamiento pressure rather than through the country's established constitutional institutions.

Therefore, it is fair to say that the pronunciamiento was a somewhat ambivalent phenomenon, one that the same individual could deplore and support, condemn yet practice. In this sense the 1831 *Catecismo de la Federación Mexicana* attributed to liberal thinker José María Luis Mora is quite representative. The answer to the question: "Have there been many pronunciamientos in the republic?" was: "Yes, much to its own misfortune, for apart from two or three at most, which after a thousand disasters have resulted in real and positive improvements, the rest, far from being useful, have caused it immense problems."[11] In other words, for Mora the pronunciamiento was a problematic practice that, while generally damaging, could nonetheless bring about "real and positive improvements." A temporarily reformed compulsive pronunciado such as José María Tornel would admit toward the end of his life, in 1853: "Now that we fix our sight on the road to perdition we have all followed; now that the patria harvests the sad fruits of our common errors, it is imperative that the hatreds and conflicts which were the cause of such harsh wrongs, disappear."[12] And yet he had not appeared to have such qualms when he collaborated with the 1832 pronunciamiento cycle and organized both the 1834 Plan of Cuernavaca pronunciamiento constellation and the 1842 Plan of Huejotzingo series.[13]

While Mora and Tornel and most of their contemporaries (as may be seen in Melissa Boyd's chapter on the intelligentsia's representation of the phenomenon) were capable of criticizing although reluctantly accepting the potential benefits offered by the pronunciamiento, a handful of Mexican politicians took a less ambivalent stance on the subject. Serial pronunciado Antonio López de Santa Anna was one of these.[14] Writing in January 1832, accepting the invitation to lead the Plan of Veracruz, he saw the pronunciamiento as a "right given to us in our own constitution to request as citizens and as the first proclaimers of the nation's liberty, what we consider conducive to the patria's happiness and decorum; [for which reason we are] happier as a result than those who, subject to an arbitrary regime, must indispensably conform themselves with the worst abuses of power."[15] In contrast, the 1835 *voto particular* against abolishing the 1824 Constitution issued by liberal and civilian politician José Bernardo Couto responded to the wave of pronunciamientos that called for such a move. He noted that "there is not a more equivocal and false way of finding out what the popular will is than through petitions or revolts which we have been given to dress up with the soft surname of pronunciamientos. . . . [Pronunciamientos] undermine the bases of our representative system, and replace it with the most unstable and turbulent form of democracy. . . . [To follow] the theory of the general will by pronunciamiento is to canonize the essential principle of true anarchy."[16] Although Santa Anna and Couto provide us with two opposite views of the pronunciamiento, most nineteenth-century Mexicans tended to view the practice in more ambivalent terms, being capable of lamenting their frequency while at the same time supporting a given insurrectionary wave.

Notwithstanding whether it was perceived as a necessary evil, a constitutional right, or a source of chronic instability, the pronunciamiento inspired numerous celebrations throughout the nineteenth century. To note just one example, from the perspective of the state legislature of Veracruz in the very particular context of 1829, Santa Anna's pronunciamiento of Perote of 16 September 1828 was recalled not just fondly but with festive awe. Santa Anna was declared "*benemérito del Estado* (hero of the state)" for having, in essence, refused to accept the results of the presidential elections and challenged the government with his troops. What is more, all the men who had accompanied him — "the chiefs and officers who loyal to their heroic pronunciamiento, accompanied the state hero, citizen and general, Antonio López de Santa Anna, in his last campaign" — were considered "worthy of the appreciation and consideration" of the state and, together with their soldiers, were awarded in a particularly elaborate ceremony a blue sash inscribed with the words: "The state of Veracuz, to proven patriotism."[17] As may be seen in Rosie Doyle's chapter on the fiestas that were staged in Guadalajara to celebrate the pronunciamientos of 1823 and 1832, and Pedro Santoni's study on the elaborate ceremonies that were organized after two of the numerous pronunciamientos that were launched during the Mexican-American War, regardless of the Mexicans' ambivalence toward the pronunciamiento, the Mexican authorities took great care, at both national and regional levels, in celebrating these acts of insurrection, time and again, when they were successful.

Damned or venerated, and at times damned *and* venerated, the pronunciado and the pronunciamiento have become, in a sense, emblematic of nineteenth-century Mexico. Huxley, cited earlier, described the region as "a land of pronunciamientos."[18] It is for this reason that it is important to study why they were damned and venerated, and by whom, and how this may have had a lasting impact on the way people have understood the pronunciamiento, then and now. As William Beezley has noted, "Independence celebrations during the nineteenth century reveal much about Mexican society, politics, and values — about what Mexicans thought Mexico was and what they wanted their country to become."[19] The same can be said about the celebrations that accompanied so many pronunciamientos. Studying them tells us a great deal about Mexican society, politics, and values, what Mexicans thought their country was and what they wanted it to become.

So how were pronunciamientos celebrated, condemned, represented, remembered, commemorated, memorialized? In answering this question the contributors in this book force us to reflect on why this form of insurrectionary politics was so popular and widespread in nineteenth-century Mexico. Did the celebration of certain pronunciamientos and pronunciados give them a long-lasting heroic glow of legitimacy? Sacralize them? Make them worthy of emulation? What these essays show is that the celebration of the pronunciamiento certainly went a long way toward doing so but also that this came hand in hand with its condemnation. Pronunciamientos were celebrated, but they were also represented as a constant source of instability, lawlessness, routine violence, and chaos. What lasting impact would such a view have in the minds of nineteenth-century Mexicans and in the subsequent historiography?

Not surprisingly, depending on who was in power, certain pronunciados and pronunciamientos were celebrated some years and condemned in others. Kerry McDonald's chapter on how San Luis Potosí's authorities celebrated the execution of two pronunciados, then venerated them as martyrs, only to forget them subsequently, highlights only too well how their damnation and veneration was tied to whether their political enemies or allies were in power at the time. Shara Ali's chapter on the condemnation, celebration, and eventual oblivion of Yucatecan pronunciado Santiago Imán similarly illustrates the extent to which those in power used fiestas to manipulate the political context to their advantage.

For all of this, the memory, commemoration, and representation of Mexico's pronunciados were equally characterized by ambivalence and duality. Our pronunciados, as a result, were viewed as troublemakers as well as defenders of the constitution, ambitious restless officers *and* representatives of the ignored will of the nation. It was not so much a case of "one person's freedom fighter is another person's terrorist" but rather that the same man could be seen as having done something noble while being ignoble, or of doing wrong with good intentions. Rafael del Riego may well have been the liberal hero who forced King Ferdinand VII to restore the 1812 Constitution with his 1820 pronunciamiento of Cabezas de San Juan; the authorities in Spain did not take long to ensure that the monarch was portrayed as the benevolent figure who had magnanimously and legitimately reinstated the Constitution by royal decree, wresting attention away from what Riego and his unlawful actions had achieved. Agustín de Iturbide's 1821 pronunciamiento resulted in the achievement of independence, but the fact that he went on to have himself crowned emperor and became associated with an eventually defeated conservative and Catholic Mexico led to his being forgotten in favor of the supposedly liberal and radical heroes who initiated the War of

Independence in 1810 — Hidalgo and colleagues. Ignacio Comonfort was celebrated for his involvement in the pronunciamientos and revolution of Ayutla in 1854–55, but then condemned subsequently for backing the 17 December 1857 pronunciamiento of Tacubaya, which annulled the 1857 Constitution and resulted in the closure of Congress. Juan Bustamante was likewise praised for his role in local politics when Benito Juárez's government resided in San Luis Potosí in 1867, yet two years later Bustamante was condemned for pronouncing against the state authorities. Porfirio Díaz's liberation of Puebla on 2 April 1867 was celebrated every year until he was forced into exile by the 1910 Revolution. Thereafter, the date and his persona would cease to be the motive of any more patriotic fiestas. We are dealing with ambivalent revolutions and flawed heroes, and how these in turn were validated, re-created, experienced, and internalized through civic celebrations as well as depicted in contemporary speeches, historical accounts, and foreign travelogues.

In chapter 1, Rodrigo Moreno Gutiérrez analyzes the memory and representation of Rafael del Riego's pronunciamiento in Mexico during 1820–21. He examines how the news of the constitution's reestablishment was spread; how public writers interpreted it; and how these commentators projected, reconstructed, and commemorated that political-military history on the eve of Mexico's independence, considering the role the memory of that pronunciamiento played in Iturbide's own pronunciamiento of Iguala. We learn how early pronunciados were remembered, commemorated, and celebrated in the press, in songs and pamphlets, and how the representation of Riego's pronunciamiento — notwithstanding the crown's attempt to attribute the restoration of the 1812 charter to its own magnanimity — decisively undermined the Ancien Regime's legitimacy and made way for other forms of political negotiation. Moreno thus eloquently illustrates the extent to which the memory and representation of Riego's successful pronunciamiento was instrumental in inspiring the subsequent waves of pronunciamientos in Mexico.

However, as becomes evident in chapter 2, while the pronunciamiento of Iguala, like that of Cabezas de San Juan, went on to be celebrated, commemorated, and duly venerated, the same cannot be said of its visible author and leader, Agustín de Iturbide. Richard Warren forces us to reflect on the importance of the question of selectivity and provides a fascinating study of how, in the case of a flawed hero like Iturbide, sanguinary royalist turned liberator-cum-emperor/tyrant, as the nineteenth century unfolded the establishment gradually found a way of erasing him from the picture, giving prominence to Miguel Hidalgo and the initiators of the 1810 independence movement, and celebrating the Plan of Iguala without mentioning the part Iturbide played in it, attributing the achievements of 1821 to "a general force" rather than a forceful general. Interestingly, Iturbide's unglamorous posthumous career was not due to the role he played in Iguala (the pronunciamiento itself remained worthy of praise and emulation) but to the way the actions he carried out after Independence were perceived as ignominious. That Iturbide became increasingly associated with a Catholic, conservative, monarchist, and arguably reactionary Mexico, and thus with no place in the pantheon of national liberal republican and revolutionary heroes, was in no small measure a consequence of the enduring counternarrative that his grandson Agustín Yturbide formulated at the turn of the century.

In chapter 3 Rosie Doyle focuses on how pronunciamientos were actually celebrated from the regional perspective of Jalisco. While the first two chapters show that the representation of Riego's pronunciamiento and the pronunciamiento of Iguala (without mention of Iturbide) glorified the practice, the third chapter explores the extent to which the fiestas organized to celebrate a successful pronunciamiento cycle (in this case the Casa Mata constellation of 1823 that resulted in Iturbide's abdication and the 1832 Veracruz corpus that eventually brought down Anastasio Bustamante's 1830–32 government) served to legitimize this form of insurrectionary politics in nineteenth-century Mexico. Doyle addresses questions such as why the *ayuntamientos* (city councils) in Jalisco chose to celebrate pronunciamientos, which were essentially extra-constitutional, subversive acts, with civic and religious celebrations; why they spent funds on these public events; and how this suited their political purposes. In analyzing the role that civic and religious fiestas played in legitimizing the pronunciamiento, informing the public of its achievements, making heroes of the military officers who launched it, and making the pronunciamiento a part of the lives of ordinary people, Doyle highlights both the importance fiestas were awarded at the time and the resonance they had in endowing the pronunciamiento with an unquestionable sense of legitimacy.

Chapter 4 adopts a similar approach from the perspective of San Luis Potosí, concentrating on the mixed fortunes pronunciados José Márquez and Víctor Gárate enjoyed after they were executed. Kerry McDonald thus explores how the pronunciados' bodies, as a site of political profit, were used by their contemporaries and to what extent this treatment, together with their participation in the pronunciamiento, influenced their reception within the traditional and current historiography. By focusing on the memory and representation of the political dead in the form of executed local pronunciados, McDonald also inquires as to why these actors have been all but forgotten, or perhaps intentionally side-stepped, by the regional historiography, drawing conclusions about the often ambivalent nature of the historical selection process involved in any act of patriotic reconstruction or commemoration. In the case of McDonald's executed pronunciados we discover that they were celebrated both as criminals and as heroic martyrs at distinct moments in time, only to be largely forgotten, depending on who was in power and what political gains could be drawn from condemning them, venerating them, or deliberately forgetting them.

Shara Ali's chapter on how the dangerous and flawed hero Santiago Imán and his pronunciamiento of Valladolid were coopted by the Mérida elite to legitimize and popularize their separate, albeit allegedly supportive local-based coup of 18 February 1840, highlights only too well how the authorities could (and can) manipulate a potentially dangerous and damaging insurrectionary movement to suit their own ends by taking over the revolution in the first instance and then pacifying its more radical leaders (in this case Imán) by turning them into part of the establishment as official figures of veneration. Having achieved their aim of controlling the revolution and silencing Imán, the Yucatecan elites, as happened with Iguala, would move to commemorate the pronunciamiento of Valladolid without mentioning the role Imán played in it. They thus went on to commemorate the participation of the Maya in the pronunciamiento, in such a way as to be able to claim to represent the popular classes and, in so doing, paradoxically stifle any insurrectionary tendencies they may have had. The elite would thus simultaneously remember the

Imán pronunciamiento as having served the needs of the masses, to uphold its validity in memory, while actively disregarding the demands of the lower classes. There would also be a conscious elite attempt to forget Imán, whom they saw as an undeserving example of a pronunciamiento head. By implication Ali suggests that the Yucatecan elite understood the pronunciamiento as a controlled gentlemanly insurrectionary practice or game that was reserved exclusively for members of the elite and could not be led by someone belonging to the dangerous classes.

Pedro Santoni concentrates on the fiestas and ceremonies that were staged to celebrate two triumphant pronunciamientos that took place on the eve of and during the Mexican-American War. It is indeed extraordinary not only that Mexicans went on pronouncing even when the country was at war, but that they continued to celebrate their pronunciamientos, paying such attention to detail in every aspect of the corresponding fiesta, regardless of the string of defeats the Mexican Army suffered at the hands of the invading U.S. forces. Like Doyle, McDonald, and Ali, Santoni finds that those in power, in this case in 1845–47, moved with determined energy to legitimize their pronunciamientos through rituals and ceremonies of varying intricacy and sophistication to inform the population of the rebellions' objectives. However, Santoni finds that such festivities, described in chapter 6 in meticulous detail, could not overcome the manifold political, social, and economic problems that afflicted Mexico and argues that despite the fact that pronunciamientos left an indelible stamp in the mindset of nineteenth-century Mexicans, neither elaborate ritual and popular support nor soaring patriotic rhetoric managed to cement loyalty to the regimes that emerged from the revolts of San Luis Potosí (December 1845) and the Ciudadela (August 1846).

In chapter 7 Melissa Boyd analyzes the manner in which the pronunciamiento was understood and depicted in the writings of a representative sample of leading nineteenth-century Mexican politicians and intellectuals, including Luis Gongaza Cuevas, José María Luis Mora, Mariano Otero, Lorenzo de Zavala, Manuel Crescencio Rejón, Melchor Ocampo, Valentín Gómez Farías, Manuel Gómez Pedraza, José María Lafragua, and José María Gutiérrez de Estrada. On the one hand, what becomes evident is that although their opinions alternated between support, condemnation, and a mixed verdict, the importance they gave the practice was unanimous. By studying their analysis of and constant references to the pronunciamientos, Boyd enables us to appreciate the ambivalence most Mexican intellectuals felt toward these "gestures of rebellion." Intellectuals discussed them in an attempt to obtain a better understanding of the events that had led to the revolts themselves and, in so doing, arrived in some cases at extremely perceptive conclusions on the nature of Mexico's problems following independence and what needed to be done to overcome them. However, given that most of Boyd's commentators were pronunciados at some point during their lives, their accounts also acted as a vehicle for justifying the actions in which the authors had actually taken part. They also wrote about pronunciamientos to keep them alive in the memory of the nation, so that Mexicans could learn from the past and avoid making the same mistakes in the future. Although most nineteenth-century politicians and leading intellectuals regretted the prevalence of the pronunciamiento syndrome, they endorsed those whose leaders or ideas they supported.

Given that most pronunciados participated in more than one pronunciamiento, their commemoration and historical memory could change drastically depending on what was entailed in the most recent pronunciamiento in which they were involved. In chapter 6 Santoni quotes the preeminent nineteenth-century cartographer Antonio García Cubas as having once cynically remarked that Mexico's "perfectly established system of pronunciamientos" transformed men once praised as "saviors, regenerators, or liberators" into "arbitrary, illegal, and despotic" actors. Vividly illustrating this point is Antonia Pi-Suñer Llorens's study of the treatment that flawed hero Ignacio Comonfort, both venerated and damned, received in the liberal accounts of his day and in the subsequent historiography of the events in which he played a key role (namely, the 1854–55 Revolution of Ayutla, his 1855–58 term in office as Mexican president, his involvement in the pronunciamiento of 17 December 1857, and the French Intervention). She shows how Comonfort's support for Félix Zuloaga's pronunciamiento of Tacubaya had the effect of obliterating and annulling, to a degree, the memory of the courage and democratic values he stood for during the Revolution of Ayutla. As Pi-Suñer tells us, Comonfort's greatest mistake, which became the tragedy of his life, was to abandon the road of legality—of which he had been the staunchest supporter—by accepting the Plan of Tacubaya. That this was not unusual at the time, or that Benito Juárez and Porfirio Díaz later adopted emergency powers and dictatorial measures, respectively, turns out to be irrelevant; and it highlights how those who were responsible for writing Mexico's official history had the final say in the way Comonfort has come to be seen. Like the Iturbide of Warren's chapter 2, Comonfort figures here as another ambivalent and flawed pronunciado, venerated, condemned, and ultimately forgotten.

The Porfirio Díaz of Verónica Zárate Toscano's chapter 9 is one who was also venerated and damned. Although he may not have been forgotten, the action of 2 April 1867, celebrated with insistence throughout the Porfiriato, certainly has been. Zárate Toscano, like Doyle, McDonald, Ali, and Santoni, provides us with a detailed overview of the manner in which 2 April was celebrated, commemorated, and memorialized between 1876 and 1910. Díaz, like Iturbide and Comonfort before him, undermined the celebratory memory of his early pronunciamientos by adopting dictatorial measures once in power. Specifically, Díaz made the mistake of overstaying in power. Given that his regime ended with a ten-year revolution, all that was remembered until very recently was the dictatorial actions of his final years in power.[20] Given that the celebration of 2 April was intimately associated with Díaz (unlike that of 27 September, celebrated without mention of Iturbide, or of 12 February, celebrated without invoking Imán), it ceased to be commemorated or to have any resonance once Díaz went into exile in 1911 — even though the event was in many senses far more meaningful in terms of its consequences than the Battle of 5 May 1862, which continues to be commemorated to this day.

In chapter 10, Flor de María Salazar Mendoza combines an analysis of the speeches that were given in San Luis Potosí during the fiestas patrias of September 1869 with a study of the troubled political career of *potosino* pronunciado Juan Bustamante. In so doing her essay builds on the work on patriotic and revolutionary fiestas presented here by Doyle, McDonald, Ali, Santoni, and Zárate Toscano, while engaging with the ambivalence with which Mexicans received and represented their flawed pronunciado heroes, as explored in the contributions by Moreno, Warren, Boyd, and Pi-Suñer. What becomes evident is the extent to which the commemoration of past insurrections could be used to address strictly present grievances and issues. Salazar Mendoza's analysis of the civic speeches that were delivered on 15 and 16 September 1869 allows us to understand how the authors, who ironically had been vehement supporters of Juan Bustamante and Benito Juárez only a few years earlier, idealized the figure of Miguel Hidalgo y Costilla, to portray Bustamante as a "tyrant, antidemocrat and representative of disorder," depicting Bustamante's pronunciamiento as an undemocratic act of aggression against the institutional life of the state.

The final chapter analyzes how European and U.S. travelers represented the pronunciamiento in their nineteenth-century travelogues, letters, and dispatches, with all their prejudices and, in some cases, imperialist ambitions. To the Western gaze the pronunciamiento was a farcical practice, comical yet intensely irritating, that was ridiculed to prove that the Mexican people were incapable of governing themselves. There is little ambivalence in these accounts. Most foreigners who wrote down their observations on the pronunciamiento phenomenon regarded it as the source of the country's chronic instability. On the one hand, such a view would be used to justify the U.S. and French interventions and would nurture Britain's arguable informal imperial approach to Mexico and Latin America. And on the other hand, it would inform to a great extent the subsequent historiographic portrayal of nineteenth-century Mexico as an age of chaos, a view that only started to be redressed thirty years ago.

This book, like the two that preceded it (*Forceful Negotiations* in 2010 and *Malcontents, Rebels, and Pronunciados in* 2012), provides a revised understanding of the pronunciamiento. The contributors show that the celebration and representation of the pronunciamiento captured its contradictions and complexities. It was both the reason why Mexico was backward *and* the tool Mexicans used to ensure that the constitution was not ignored, reflecting the genuine grievances of an exploited and disenfranchised people. It was a practice that became legitimized through its constant and enthusiastic celebration. It caused irreparable damage, and yet, to return to Mora's view, resulted in "real and positive improvements." Foreigners may not have grasped the subtler functions, dynamics, and nature of the pronunciamiento, dwelling instead on its potential for humor or to justify European/U.S. misgivings about Mexicans' ability to govern themselves; but there was definitely more to it than met their eyes.

The pronunciamiento was the desperate measure Mexicans adopted to confront desperate times. It was both good and bad. When it brought an end to a particular injustice and succeeded in addressing a given grievance, it was celebrated and commemorated. Its heroes were duly venerated. Because it prevented any government or constitutional system from settling long-lasting roots, however, it was a source of chronic turmoil and instability. Its heroes became tyrants, betrayed their followers, and joined pronunciamientos that overthrew the governments they had helped forge with earlier acts of insurrection, and the memory of their actions thus became selective and ambivalent. The pronunciamiento was an ambivalent revolution; its pronunciados were flawed heroes. As the essays in this volume show, nowhere was this more obvious than in the way pronunciamientos and pronunciados were celebrated, remembered, commemorated, and represented in the nineteenth century.

Notes

1. *Memorias de un mexicano* has been re-released on DVD by the Fundación Carmen Toscano I.A.P. Worthy of note is that the Ingeniero Salvador Toscano was the grandfather of Verónica Zárate Toscano, author of chapter 9 of this volume.

2. For an excellent collection of essays on the yearly celebration of 16 September 1810 see Beezley and Lorey (eds.), *¡Viva México!* Also see Plasencia de la Parra, *Independencia y nacionalismo.*

3. Paz, *El laberinto de la soledad,* 72.

4. Huxley, *Beyond the Mexique Bay,* 233

5. I do not think Subcomandante Marcos's reference to a number of Mexican insurgents and revolutionaries from the past in his Declaration of the Lacandón Jungle of December 1993 (i.e., Miguel Hidalgo, José María Morelos, Vicente Guerrero, Francisco Villa, and Emiliano Zapata) was in any way gratuitous. The Declaración is reprinted in Rovira, *¡Zapata vive!,* 77–80.

6. Baquer, *El modelo español,* 40.

7. Typical definitions of *pronunciamiento* include: "Alzamiento militar contra el Gobierno, promovido por un jefe del Ejército u otro caudillo" (*Diccionario usual de la Real Academia Española,* http://buscon.rae.es/drael/SrvltGUI BusUsual); and "Sublevación militar cuyo objeto es la consecución del poder o, cuando menos, la presión que obligue a la sustitución de la política gubernamental. Lo que busca de inmediato es el apoyo castrense y por supuesto político, mediante una acción militar puntual normalmente de carácter incruento" (Enciclopedia Microsoft Encarta Online 2007, http://es.encarta.msn .com/text_7651585458___0/Pronunciamiento.html).

8. Costeloe, "A Pronunciamiento in Nineteenth-Century Mexico," 245.

9. For other accounts of the processes entailed in launching a *pronunciamiento* see Carr, *Spain 1808–1939,* 124; Vázquez, "Political Plans," 21–23; Guerra, "El pronunciamiento en México," 18; Vázquez, "El modelo de pronunciamiento mexicano," 35.

10. Fontana, "Prólogo," ix.

11. Quoted in Tanck de Estrada, "Los catecismos políticos, 78.

12. Tornel y Mendívil, *Breve reseña histórica,* 210.

13. For Tornel see Fowler, *Tornel and Santa Anna.*

14. See Fowler, "Pronunciamientos of Antonio López de Santa Anna."

15. Antonio López de Santa Anna, "Manifiesto del general Santa Anna para aceptar la jefatura del movimiento del Plan de Veracruz, en que lo justifica en el derecho constitucional de petición," 7 January 1832, reproduced in Vázquez (ed.), *Planes en la nación mexicana: Libro dos,* 76.

16. Quoted in Acle Aguirre, "Ideas políticas de José Bernardo Couto y José Joaquín Pesado," 40.

17. *Colección de decretos correspondiente al año de 1829,* 78–81.

18. Huxley, *Beyond the Mexique Bay*, 73.

19. Beezley, "New Celebrations," 131.

20. Díaz benefited from a positive reevaluation in the 1990s. For a discussion of this view with its overtly neoliberal political overtones, see Paul Garner's discussion of "neo-porfirismo" in his *Porfirio Díaz*, 12–15.

Chronology of Main Events and Pronunciamientos, 1821–1910

1810–1821	WAR OF INDEPENDENCE
1821	
24 February	Agustín de Iturbide launches the Plan of Iguala (see chapters 1 and 2)
24 August	Iturbide and Viceroy O'Donojú sign the Treaty of Córdoba
27 September	War ends with the Army of the Three Guarantees' capture of Mexico City (see chapter 2)
1822–1823	FIRST EMPIRE
1822	
19 May	Iturbide becomes Emperor Agustín I
26 August	Iturbide imprisons nineteen members of Congress
31 October	Iturbide closes down Congress
2 December	Santa Anna launches Pronunciamiento of Veracruz
1823	
1 February	Plan of Casa Mata (see chapter 3)
2 February	Santa Anna joins the Plan of Casa Mata

23 February	Plan of Jalisco (see chapter 3)
19 March	Iturbide abdicates
1823–1824	THE TRIUMVIRATE
	The Federal Constitution is drafted; triumvirate is made up of generals Guadalupe Victoria, Nicolás Bravo, and Pedro Celestino Negrete

1823

5 June	Santa Anna revolts, launching the Plan of San Luis Potosí
1824–1835	FIRST FEDERAL REPUBLIC
1824–29	Guadalupe Victoria, president

1827

19 January	Arenas pro-Spanish Conspiracy dismantled
10 May	First anti-Spanish Expulsion Laws
20 December	Second Expulsion Laws
23 December	Plan of Montaño, General Nicolás Bravo joins Montaño's revolt

1828

7 January	Battle of Tulancingo; *escoceses* are defeated
September	The moderate General Manuel Gómez Pedraza wins presidential elections
16 September	Santa Anna "pronounces" in Perote, proclaiming Vicente Guerrero president
30 November	Revolt of La Acordada (see chapter 7)
4 December	Raid of the Parián Market

27 December	Manuel Gómez Pedraza escapes and goes into exile
1829	Vicente Guerrero, president
26 July	Isidro Barradas's expedition lands in Tampico to reconquer Mexico for Spain
11 September	Santa Anna defeats Barradas's expedition
6 November	Centralist pronunciamiento in Campeche (see chapter 5)
4 December	General Anastasio Bustamante leads the Revolt of Xalapa (see chapters 4 and 7)
31 December	Bustamante takes Mexico City
1830–32	Anastasio Bustamante, president (also known as the Alamán Administration)
1830	
17 November	José Márquez and Joaquín Gárate's pronunciamiento of San Luis (see chapter 4)
1831	
14 February	Vicente Guerrero is executed
1832	
2 January	Santa Anna launches Plan of Veracruz (see chapters 3, 4, and 11)
March–December	Civil War spreads across central Mexico
27 April	Plan of Lerma (see chapter 3)
5 July	Pronunciamiento of Veracruz and San Juan de Ulúa (see chapter 3)
10 July	Plan of Zacatecas (see chapter 3)
14 July	Plan of Guadalajara (see chapter 3)
December	Convenios de Zavaleta bring an end to Bustamante's regime

1833

January	Manuel Gómez Pedraza, president (as agreed in Zavaleta, Gómez Pedraza returns to complete his interrupted term in office while elections are held)
1 April	Santa Anna, president; however, he does not take up the post, leaving the Vice President Valentín Gómez Farías in charge (see chapter 6)
1833–34	Gómez Farías "Radical" Administration
26 May	Pronunciamiento de Morelia
1 June	Plan of Durán
8 June	Plan of Huejotzingo calling for an end to Congress's radical reforms and for Santa Anna to become dictator

1834

25 May	Plan of Cuernavaca, starts a series of pronunciamientos against the reforms of the Gómez Farías Administration; Santa Anna intervenes and annuls most of the reforms (see chapter 4)

1835

January	Gómez Farías is stripped of his vice presidential office
1835–36	Santa Anna, president; however, due to his absence the presidency is taken by Miguel Barragán
28 January	Miguel Barragán, president
February	Federalists revolt in Zacatecas against the rise of the centralists

11 May	Santa Anna quells the revolt in the Battle of Guadalupe
19 May	Pronunciamiento of Orizaba calls for change to centralism (see chapter 4)
29 May	Pronunciamiento of Toluca does so as well
22 June	Revolt in Texas begins (see chapter 5)
23 October	The Federal Constitution is abolished and Mexico becomes a central republic
1835–1846	THE FIRST CENTRAL REPUBLIC

1836

27 February	José Justo Corro, president (following Barragán's death)
6 March	Battle of the Alamo
21 April	Battle of San Jacinto (Santa Anna is taken prisoner the following day)
29 December	The Siete Leyes (creating the 1836 Constitution) consolidate a centralist political system and limit the suffrage
1837–41	Anastasio Bustamante, president

1837

April	Anastasio Bustamante, president (after winning elections)
February	Santa Anna returns from the United States in disgrace

1838

March	French fleet starts blockade of port of Veracruz
May	Santiago Imán revolt in Yucatán begins (see chapter 5)

27 November	French Pastry War begins with the bombardment of Veracruz
5 December	Santa Anna forces the French to retreat and loses one leg in battle

1839

April	José Antonio Mejía and José Urrea start federalist revolt in Tamaulipas
May–June	Santa Anna acts as interim president
3 May	Battle of Acajete; Santa Anna defeats Rebels; Mejía is executed
29 May	Pronunciamiento of Tizimín (see chapter 5)

1840

14 February	Pronunciamiento of Mérida (see chapter 5)
15 July	Federalist pronunciamiento in the Capital; Bustamante is taken prisoner in the National Palace (see chapters 7 and 11)
27 July	Revolt ends and Bustamante is restored to power

1841

August–October	Triangular Revolt (also called Revolución de Jalisco) overthrows Bustamante's regime (see chapters 7 and 11)
1841–1844	Santa Anna, president

1841

October	Bases de Tacubaya approved; Santa Anna has "almost absolute power"
22 December	Pronunciamiento of Valladolid (see chapter 5)

1842

9 December	Pronunciamiento in San Luis Potosí demanding closure of Congress
11 December	Pronunciamiento in Huejotizingo also demanding closure of Congress
18 December	Congress is closed down

1843

8 June	Bases Orgánicas; ultimate *santanista* constitution is accepted

1844

2 November	Pronunciamiento of Guadalajara is launched by General Mariano Paredes y Arrillaga against Santa Anna
6 December	Revolt of Las Tres Horas overthrows Santa Anna's regime in the capital
1845	José Joaquín Herrera, president
June	Santa Anna goes into exile to Cuba
14 December	Pronunciamiento of General Mariano Paredes y Arrillaga in San Luis Potosí leads to fall of Herrera's government (see chapter 6)
23 December	Pronunciamiento of Veracruz (see chapter 11)
1846	Paredes y Arrillaga's dictatorship
April	War with the United States begins
4 August	Plan de la Ciudadela overthrows Paredes y Arrillaga and replaces the Centralist Republic with the Second Federal Republic; Santa Anna returns, invited by the Federalists (see chapter 6)

5 August	Pronunciamiento of Toluca (see chapter 11)
August	José Mariano Salas, temporary president while elections are held
1846–1853	SECOND FEDERAL REPUBLIC
1846	
December	Santa Anna, president; however, due to the War with the United States, Valentín Gómez Farías acts as president again
1847	
February	Pronunciamiento of Los Polkos against Gómez Farías and anti-clerical measures (see chapters 6 and 7)
23 February	Battle of Angostura–Buena Vista
9 March	General Winfield Scott arrives in Veracruz
21 March	Santa Anna ends Gómez Farías's administration again
18 April	Battle of Cerro Gordo
August	Caste War begins in Yucatán (see chapter 5)
11 August– 15 September	Campaign of the Valley of Mexico
14 September	Government leaves Mexico City to become established in Querétaro
15 September	The U.S. Army takes Mexico City
September	Manuel de la Peña y Peña, president, forms new government
1848	
2 February	Treaty of Guadalupe Hidalgo grants half

	of Mexico's national territory to the United States
1848–51	José Joaquín de Herrera, president
1851–53	Mariano Arista, president

1852

26 July	Plan of Blancarte
13 September	Second Plan of Blancarte
20 October	Plan del Hospicio

1853

January–February	Juan Bautista Ceballos, president
February– April	Manuel María Lombardini, president

1853–1855	SANTA ANNA'S DICTATORSHIP

1854

1 March	Revolution of Ayutla begins (see chapter 8)
11 March	Plan of Acapulco (see chapter 8)

1855

8 August	Plan of San Luis Potosí; Santa Anna's last regime falls

1855–1876	REFORM PERIOD

1855

4 October	Juan Álvarez, president
22 November	Ley Juárez
1855–58	Ignacio Comonfort, president

1856

January	Six-day siege of Puebla
February–March	Siege of Puebla

11 April	Ley Iglesias
25 June	Ley Lerdo

1857

5 February	Federal Constitution published
17 December	Coup d'etat of Tacubaya (see chapter 8)

1858–1860	Civil War of the Reform

1858

11 January	Pronunciamiento in Mexico City (see chapter 8); Félix Zuloaga, president of Rebel Conservative Government (Mexico City)
4 May	Júarez becomes president of "Legitimate" Government (Veracruz)

1859

31 January	Miguel Miramón, Conservative president

1860

March	Armistice Plan between Juárez and Miramón
September	Santos Degollado's Plan de Pacificación
October	Armistice Plan between Zaragoza and Castillo
25 December	Liberal forces recover Mexico City

1861

March	Benito Juárez, president (after winning elections)
17 July	Government suspends payment on foreign debt

1862–67	The French Intervention (see chapters 8 and 9)
1862	
7 January	Allied fleets land in Veracruz (Britain, France, and Spain)
5 May	Mexican army succeeds in defeating the French at the Battle of Puebla (see chapter 9)
1863	
19 May	French take Puebla
9 June	Juárez's government flees to San Luis Potosí
10 June	French take Mexico City
18 June	Regency Council is formed with Nepomuceno Almonte, Bishop Pelagio Antonio de Labastida, and Mariano Salas
3 October	Maximilian accepts the throne at Miramar (Europe)
1864	
5 January	French take Guadalajara; Juárez's government flees to the north
10 April	Maximilian formally accepts Mexican crown
12 June	Maximilian and Carlota arrive in Mexico City
12 October	Juárez's government flees to Chihuahua
1865	
14 August	Juárez's government flees to Paso del Norte

| 5 September | Maximilian's Colonization Law |

1866

January	Napoleon III orders phased withdrawal of French troops
17 June	Juárez returns to Chihuahua City
September	Last stage of French withdrawal begins
30 November	Maximilian decides to remain in Mexico
26 December	Juárez arrives in Durango

1867

14 January	Republicans recover Guadalajara
5 February	French troops order evacuation of Mexico City
21 February	Juárez arrives in San Luis Potosí (see chapter 10)
2 April	Porfirio Díaz liberates Puebla (see chapter 9)
12 March	Last French troops leave Veracruz
15 May	Querétaro is taken; Maximilian and Miramón are captured
19 June	Maximilian and Miramón are executed
21 June	Porfirio Díaz enters Mexico City

| 1867–1876 | THE RESTORED REPUBLIC |

1867

15 July	Juárez arrives in Mexico City
October	Juárez, president (after winning elections)
18 December	Peasant revolts in central Mexico

1868

| 28 February | Pronunciamiento of Julio López Chávez |

8 May	Juárez obtains further extraordinary powers

1869

12 April	Manuel Lozada's circular for the defense of village lands is published
April	Agrarian rebellions start across central and western Mexico, 1869–1870
20 August	Pronunciamiento of Villa de Cedral (see chapter 10)

1870

June	*Jimenistas* seize control of Tuxtla, Guerrero
September	Gran Círculo de Obreros de México is formed

1871

February	Anti-*Juarista* rebellions in Nuevo León, Zacatecas, and Durango
June	Anti-Juárez rebellion in Tampico is quelled
12 October	Juárez, president (reelected)
8 November	Porfirio Díaz stages failed pronunciamiento of La Noria (see chapter 11)
21 November	Anti-Juárez revolt in Puebla begins

1872

29 February	Government troops retake Aguascalientes
2 March	Government troops retake Zacatecas
5 March	Government troops start siege of Puebla
17 May	Congress extends Juárez's extraordinary powers

9 July	Government troops retake Monterrey and end rebellion in Nuevo León
9 July	Juárez dies
18 July	Sebastián Lerdo de Tejada, president
1875	*Cristero* revolt starts in Michoacán and Jalisco
1876	Lerdo de Tejada, president (reelected); he is accused of electoral fraud; Porfirio Díaz launches the Pronunciamiento of Tuxtepec (see chapter 9)
16 November	Díaz takes Tecoac, Tlaxcala
19 November	Díaz takes Puebla
20 November	Lerdo leaves Mexico City
23 November	Díaz takes Mexico City and becomes president
1876–1910	THE PORFIRIATO

RODRIGO MORENO GUTIÉRREZ

One. The Memory and Representation of Rafael del Riego's Pronunciamiento in Constitutional New Spain and within the Iturbide Movement, 1820–1821

> Listen to what must inevitably take place: if Colonel [Iturbide] succeeds in pulling off his plan, he will be compared to Quiroga, if he fails to do so, he will be compared to Hidalgo or another [like-minded] insurgent leader. That is the way of the world. The winner is always applauded, the loser deplored. . . .
>
> Sr. Iturbide finds himself precisely in this exact situation. If he succeeds, [people will shout out] Long live our hero! The Quiroga of America! All will be [bells] pealing, salutes, hymns, marches and flattering songs; if he doesn't, he will be confined to oblivion and misfortune.
>
> —EL PENSADOR MEXICANO, 7 March 1821

On Thursday 1 June 1820 the *Gaceta del Gobierno de México* reproduced the Count of Venadito Viceroy Juan Ruiz de Apodaca's decree, issued in Mexico City the previous day, announcing the reintroduction of the 1812 Constitution in what was then still New Spain. It would be as a result of this disposition that New Spain would find itself subjected to a highly volatile political process ultimately culminating in the consummation of the colony's independence from Spain.

The reinstatement of the 1812 Cádiz charter in Spain and its remaining colonies had come about as a result of Lieutenant Colonel

Rafael del Riego's pronunciamiento of 1 January 1820 in the Andalusian village of Cabezas de San Juan, which, paired with the Spanish liberals' effective mobilization at the time, forced King Ferdinand VII to restore the constitution. It is worth recalling that after many setbacks, the government in Madrid had succeeded in organizing a large expeditionary army in the proximity of Cádiz with a view to reconquering those of its colonies that had become independent in Spanish America. Anti-absolutist masonic conspiracies, combined with the expeditionary troops' reluctance to embark to go to fight in the Americas, favored the liberal-constitutional drive that lay behind the cycle of pronunciamientos Riego's *grito* of 1 January 1820 unleashed. Notwithstanding the setbacks some of his friends had suffered in the summer of 1819, with a number of liberal leaders and conspirators having been arrested and imprisoned, Riego and his battalion proclaimed the return of the Constitution of 1812 in their pronunciamiento and reinstated the constitutional municipality of Cabezas de San Juan. Although Riego's movement was militarily erratic and almost failed, liberal networks across the Iberian Peninsula pronounced in support of Riego's call and forced Ferdinand VII to reinstate the constitution in March, restoring its values and institutions across the Spanish monarchy.[1] It was to be a little less than nine months after the 1812 Constitution had been reinstated in New Spain that creole royalist Colonel Agustín de Iturbide rebelled in the southern village of Iguala, on 24 February 1821, in favor of religion, independence, and union. Thus began the process whereby Mexico achieved its independence seven months later.

In this first chapter I propose to analyze the memory and representation of Riego's pronunciamiento in New Spain on the eve of the incipient country's independence from Spain. I examine how the news of the constitution's reestablishment spread; how public writers interpreted it; and how these commentators projected, reconstructed, and commemorated these recent political-military events in the hectic context of 1820 and 1821. I also consider what role the memory of Riego's pronunciamiento played in Iturbide's revolution.

To begin, it is useful to summarize the ideas Will Fowler put forward in a recent study on the impact Riego's pronunciamiento had in Mexico.[2] According to Fowler, Riego's pronunciamiento brought together a whole range of political-military practices that had begun to be used in the Iberian Peninsula between 1814 and 1819. He also argued that Riego's model traveled to Mexico, where it was adopted by Iturbide's movement of the Three Guarantees (Religion, Independence, and Union). Here began a political practice that was to become emblematic of nineteenth-century Mexican history.

It should be pointed it out that much historiographical ground has been covered in order to reach this interpretation. Even though it remains the case that we are still far from reaching a consensus on the issue of pronunciamientos — (What were they? Who carried them out and why?) — recent research has helped us appreciate that they were more than just a vehicle to attain power by force. Although the traditional Spanish historiography originally approached the subject of the pronunciamiento from a rather militaristic angle, recent studies have come to acknowledge the importance of civilian participation in the development and success of the pronunciamientos' published plans.[3] The principal proponents of the Spanish militaristic school of thought, historians such as Raymond Carr, José Luis Comellas, and Miguel Alonso Baquer, were subject to criticism more than twenty years ago by

Roberto Blanco Valdés, who dismissed their ideas as overly prae-torian and insisted that, on the contrary, the outcome of the po-litical events of the period was determined by "activities led by civilian groups, revolutionaries or counterrevolutionaries, as well as [by . . .] successive cycles of structural crisis."[4] These features are particularly noteworthy, according to Blanco, for the years 1808–23. Much more recently, Jaime Rodríguez radicalized this civilian-centered or political-based interpretation, categorically concluding: "It is clear that the people and their civilian political leaders restored the Constitution, not Riego."[5]

Meanwhile, in parallel, Mexican historiography has also un-dergone a process whereby the 1821 "Consummation of Inde-pendence" has come to be interpreted in many different ways. Usually portrayed as the result of a counterrevolutionary or con-servative movement, Iturbide's consummation of independence on 27 September 1821 has received scant attention from the tra-ditional nationalist historiography (which, for reasons Richard Warren explores in the following chapter, has become more con-cerned with the history of the origins of the independence move-ment that allegedly began in 1810). Neither has the consummation of independence been granted much importance in the studies of nineteenth-century politics, perhaps because nationalist his-torians see 1821 as a very late birthday for the *patria*. As a result, it would seem that the importance of such a fundamental mo-ment — that of the actual achievement of independence — has been underestimated by the traditional historiography, intent on presenting independence as an inevitable and linear process, as part of an epic narrative wherein Mexico always was a pre-con-stituted and liberated nation.

Nonetheless, a large range of interpretations about the

Moreno Gutiérrez

consummation does exist. Since the days when Iturbide was Emperor Agustín I (1822–23), his opponents (particularly Vicente Rocafuerte) went out of their way to depict his movement as a betrayal of true independence. This reading of the consummation as a counterrevolution, imposed by reactionaries solely concerned with safeguarding the permanence of long-held colonial privileges, has been reproduced consistently since then and for the last two hundred years. Slightly more complex interpretations (such as those Lorenzo de Zavala and Lucas Alamán wrote during the early national period and that were subsequently taken up in the twentieth century by historians such as William Robertson and Juan Ortiz Escamilla) see the 1821 *trigarante* process more as a large-scale compromise, a huge but fleeting alliance of elites. In addition, there is the nationalist version that Carlos María de Bustamante first propounded in the 1820s and that was later canonized in Vicente Riva Palacios's classic late nineteenth-century history *México a través de los siglos*, which developed the idea that the consummation of independence was the triumphant culmination of an eleven-year-long struggle for liberation. Finally, through the more recent works of historians such as Doris Ladd, Timothy Anna, Jaime Rodríguez, and Ivana Frasquet, the consummation of independence has come to be understood as the triumph of Mexico's radicalized autonomists; that is, the triumph of those political factions who united to a greater or lesser degree and persistently sought ways of giving the government in New Spain greater autonomy from 1808 onwards.[6]

However, this historiographical spectrum contains few studies documenting and analyzing in depth the inextricable relationship that existed between Riego's pronunciamiento and the restoration of the 1812 Constitution, on the one hand, and Iturbide's pronunciamiento and the establishment of the Mexican Empire, on the other. In most cases the prevailing perception is that the restoration of the constitution in 1820 aroused the New Spaniards' political tempers, opened Pandora's box and made possible the expected conclusion of the eleven-year-long independence struggle.[7] But for most historians it remains just as a simple precedent. Having said this, recent research has highlighted the need to understand the close relationship that existed between the restoration of the constitution and the consummation of Mexican independence.[8]

If we accept that in New Spain Riego's pronunciamiento was a *lesson* well learned, it becomes necessary to understand the memory and representation of this phenomenon in the viceroyalty. For Fowler, Riego's victory offered a tempting example: it demonstrated that through a "gesture of rebellion," a group of officers and soldiers could impose significant political changes. The time has come to analyze the many ways in which this example was present during Iturbide's revolution, and how it was interpreted, adapted, and projected.

The reactivation of the 1812 Constitution dramatically altered the political scene of New Spain, not only in institutional terms but also at the heart of political culture, in terms of the use of political language. Peninsular political events and their actors provided irreplaceable references that became part of New Spain's political language from 1820 to 1821. The rest of this chapter examines this process in detail.

The Official Version

The decree of the Count of Venadito that was inserted in the *Gazette* of Mexico on 1 June 1820 was only one in a crowded list of references to royal decrees and regulations that were first published in the *Gazette* of Madrid.[9] This confusing string of edicts explained the king's decision to swear allegiance to the Constitution of 1812 as well as explaining the measures that had resulted from this, such as the creation of a Provisional Junta; the summons for elections for the *Cortes ordinarias* (parliament) for the period from 1820 to 1821; the restoration of the Supreme Court, etc. Alongside these were a number of exhortations to guarantee peace and public order. In the text that followed Venadito's decree, the Mexican *Gazette* explained that His Excellency (Viceroy Juan de Apodaca) had taken the oath in conjunction with the *Real Acuerdo* (a select number from his advisory committee of judges, the *Audiencia*) with due solemnity and accompanied by 300 people "of the first distinction." Immediately the *ayuntamiento* (city council), the other tribunals, and the political and military corporations did the same, "[maintaining] the best order and public peace," according to the *Gazette*'s telegraphic statement.

The following number of the *Gazette* (3 June) contained the Madrid-based documents that Apodaca's decree had recounted so succinctly. All these decrees and manifestos came from Ferdinand VII himself and, as the *Gazette* related, had been signed by the "Royal Hand." In the first decree, dated in the palace on 7 March, the monarch specified that the parliamentary summons and his decision "to swear my loyalty to the Constitution" had been made in response to "the general will of the people."[10] His manifesto to the nation offered a slightly broader explanation, but the central argument reinforced the same ideas of the previous decrees. Ferdinand VII attributed his return to the throne in 1814 to the efforts of heroic Spaniards. It had been this same heroic Nation (capitalized) that had then persuaded him that its "almost general" vote was in favor of the resurrection of the "previous form of government" (i.e., the former absolutist monarchy that pre-dated the drafting of the 1812 Constitution). In that way, the collective desire had led him to repeal the liberal constitutional system. Now, with the restoration of the constitution in 1820, the king maintained that again he had listened to the popular will and was acting in accordance with it ("you have made me understand your wishes. . . . I have heard your petitions, and as a tender Father I have condescended [to grant] what my children consider conducive to their happiness").[11]

In all his publications the script is the same: Ferdinand, attentive and paternal, has granted the demands of his people. Even though other motives are mentioned, the king appears to be the ultimate cause for all political changes in the Spanish monarchy. The pronunciamiento is never referred to here; neither do these documents mention the liberals' mobilization that forced the monarch's hand, nor the individual protagonists who participated in Riego's movement. While it may be true that Ferdinand VII made use in his texts of modern terms such as *nation, people, general will*—conceived and given new meaning by the revolution—, the defining reason he employs to explain the transformations being enacted is his own sovereign determination.[12] The new implementation of the *Pepa* (the affectionate nickname given to Cádiz Constitution) was, strictly speaking, a royal order, and in that way the authorities of New Spain complied with it. But how did "public opinion" interpret this turnabout?

Opinions, Projections, Particular Interpretations
It is probably naïve for us to believe that Ferdinand VII reinstated the constitution voluntarily. We have to understand the dilemma

faced by contemporary political commentators in New Spain, bearing in mind the prevailing political culture. What was it possible to think and to say at that time? We must let the pamphlets themselves guide our response.

The *Gazette* was not the sole means of information in New Spain. With the constitutional restoration came the guarantee of press freedom. Almost automatically an avalanche of publications and newspapers invaded the viceroyalty's main city squares. Within this immeasurable, fascinating, and revealing wave of pamphlets, some other Spanish publications surfaced, offering a point of view different from that of the official *Gaceta de Madrid*. Writings by the protagonists of the liberal revolution were frequently reprinted in Veracruz, Puebla, Guadalajara, and Mexico City. In this way Ferdinand VII's voice was deafened by many other competing narratives that stated their case loudly, often forcefully, with clarity, conviction, and authority. It was possible to read reprints not only of Riego's or Quiroga's texts but also of Madrid-based newspapers with reports of the daily sessions of the Cortes.[13] Moreover, the combative pamphleteers of New Spain's public scene also discussed and interpreted peninsular events and publications on their own terms. Let us not forget that the Spanish American revolutions of independence created a context where public opinion became a legitimizing principle in political decision-making processes.[14] These and other elusive writers often presented themselves as the true interpreters and exponents of public opinion. A study of the pamphlets of these years cannot so much measure or gage true public opinion as it can help us understand and appreciate its value and resonance as a rhetorical device in the political culture of the time.

As we know, a great number of diverse topics as well as hotly contested controversies figured in the leaflets that circulated during these years. The peninsula's political events were present in multiple ways. With the aim of understanding the importance and development of these different forms of representation, we can distinguish at least three main discursive axes: the public reinterpretation of recent history; the creation of a new liberal pantheon; and (Hispanic) American exceptionalism or its differentiation in the current state of affairs.

It is difficult to gage what the 1820 restoration meant for New Spain's pamphleteers, given that they had been denied the opportunity to participate in any form of public debate for six years and that they retained indelible memories of what had occurred during the first constitutional period (1812–14). Probably, coming as it did after weeks of rumors, the viceroy's swearing of allegiance to the constitution aroused heightened emotions, from deep resentment and suspicion in some to an exhilarating sense of hope in others. However, all of them were obliged to rebuild public discourse, which meant significantly adjusting their relationship with the authorities as well as considering the manner in which they chose to represent this relationship. It is almost possible to say that overnight it became necessary to rewrite recent history in a new form: the liberal one. This does not mean to say that the past was not commemorated before but that in this process of rewriting the past, collective history was given a new meaning. How were these pamphleteers to explain what had happened before the restoration of the 1812 Constitution without transgressing the boundaries of the officially acceptable? How were they to refer to the absolutist coup of 1814 that resulted in Ferdinand VII's closure of the Cortes and the abolition of the constitution? How could they extol the abrupt end of this phase while celebrating the continuance of their given legal order and remonstrating their loyalty to the monarchy? Some excerpts from the patriotic song *La niña bonita* (The Pretty Girl) — originally printed in Cádiz and later published by Ontiveros's press in Mexico — show how this was achieved:

CHOIR

The girl is called
The *Constitution*
Whom Ferdinand
Gladly embraced.

A girl was fathered
By very good parents,
Lacking of malice,
Full of innocence.
Baptized in Cádiz
Her godparents were
The finest men
The Nation possessed.
On turning two,
Her face darkened,
And disappeared
From our region.
Her parents wept for her,
Although imprisoned;
Her supporters
Suffered in pain.
Six years was she hidden
Concealed in attics,
Enduring a thousand anxieties;

But she was resurrected.
Appearing in Las Cabezas [de San Juan]
Healthy and blushing
Just as a diamond shines
In the sunlight.

To the Island [León] they took her
Ten thousand defenders
Singing praises
For Her salvation:
Again they baptized her
This beautiful Girl,
And fixed the slab
Of her restoration.[15]

Therefore, after her ordeal, "the girl" — the Constitution — was resurrected in Cabezas de San Juan and was gladly embraced by Ferdinand. José Joaquín Fernández de Lizardi, *el Pensador Mexicano* (the Mexican Thinker, whose texts are essential for understanding these years) clarified this narrative further in the first number of his *Conductor Eléctrico*, the newspaper he created to educate the public on the benefits of the constitutional system once the decree authorizing freedom of the press had been passed. Here el Pensador undertakes the laborious task of explaining the *Manifiesto* in which the king ordered the changes mentioned. According to the writer, the monarch, along with the less educated among the nation's people ("who are the majority," he said), were deceived in 1814 by "detestable artifices" that saddled them once more with "the heavy yoke of infernal despotism." Everything returned to how it had been under the "mistaken system of 1808":

Science full of obstacles; the arts in a state of inertia; commerce lying idle; agriculture neglected; a nonexistent industry; a disdainful navy; the army, weak; education wearing a mask of kindness; religion, ridiculous and odious with its superstitions; legislation, nothing but vices. . . . In two words: despotism enthroned and all of us with our necks bent, suffering the most shameful humiliation under the weight of its yoke.

Such was the unhappy state of the nation six months ago; but, glory to the immortal Quiroga and his illustrious companions! Those enlightened men, those heroic Spaniards, those generous Galicians, who determined to promote the Patria's best interests, dared to raise their noble foreheads and, shaking their heavy chains, cried for freedom in both worlds.[16]

Note the relationship that Lizardi establishes between material progress and the political system. As soon as the colonial authorities allowed it, praise and acclaim were dedicated to the *pronunciados*. Events were personalized in a graphic and evident fashion, and the agents of liberation were glorified. Quickly, both colonels, Rafael del Riego and, more pronouncedly, Antonio Quiroga, were fixed in public writings as the principal enactors of the new state of affairs.[17] Their persons were firmly attached to the idea of freedom and the redemption of the patria, ciphers through which to interpret the constitutional reestablishment. Leaflets, a nutritious food for both written and collective memory, were emphatic to the point of exhaustion in underlining the generous heroism of the actors who "restored to this glorious nation the sweet and holy heritage of freedom, usurped six years ago by court intrigue." So declared Brigadier Castellar in a letter sent to Quiroga and published and circulated in Mexico as part of the pamphlet *Proclama dirigida al immortal Quiroga*.[18] Another example is *El Centinela de Noche-Bea*, which did not hesitate in exalting the reestablishment of the constitution over and above the war against Napoleon in order to crown it as the political and moral insignia of a regenerated Spanish nation.[19]

As we can see, the process was explained and publicized in a manner that was at once dramatic as well as suggestive and didactic. Symbols and allegories such as chains breaking, the resurrection of the nation, or the awakening of the patria offered readers clear and lasting images. Furthermore, the symbolic change in government provoked more specific expectations, such as those Lizardi suggested in the quotation "Science full of obstacles." In this way the previous system was associated with stagnation, decay, despotism, arbitrariness and even slavery, while the new one was coupled with freedom, vigor, justice, regeneration, courage, and bravery.

It is significant that despite these marked contrasts, the figure of the king was not treated badly, at least not openly. Ferdinand VII figured as the liberator king. Lizardi expresses it clearly again. Echoing the royal manifesto, el Pensador relates that the monarch awoke from a heavy lethargy after hearing the loud cries of his people calling for freedom and the constitution. As a result, His Majesty rightfully decided to swear allegiance to the charter and to restore the nation's sovereignty to his people (to whom it essentially belongs):

Yes, this is the legitimate Spanish King: Ferdinand, who only deserves glorious epithets such as King, Great, the liberator of the nation.

Eternal glory to such a brave Caesar! His memory will not perish with the passing of the centuries. Our children will say to future generations: you are citizens, you were born free. Then, they will tell them the story of our misfortunes; [so that] the children, utterly

Moreno Gutiérrez

amazed, will ask: who was the King destined by Providence for the glory of rescuing the nation from . . . our shameful servitude? Ferdinand VII, they will answer. This magnanimous monarch was the hero who, in eighteen hundred and twenty, pledged allegiance to the wise Constitution and restored the nation to its rights, who liberated it from the tyranny of despotism and respected the law, who turned his vassals into his loving children and restored the honor of his citizens. He was the nation's glory, the author of its happiness and the real father of his people.[20]

It would be slightly naïve to ignore in these and other resounding praises a subtle touch of ironic criticism for the monarch who finally woke up and heard the thunderous call of the nation. Lizardi's warning seems clear: the king has sworn allegiance to the constitution, and the nation is no longer made up of subjects but of free citizens. A new pact of subjection has been established that depends on the assent of both parts. For this same reason it is important to underline Ferdinand's alleged condescension and supposed magnanimity: if his pledge of allegiance was not forced but was an act of conviction, and a product of his dedication to his people (as was projected in the official discourse), then the voluntary agreement was legitimate, and respect for the charter was mandatory for all.

As I see it, this is the importance of the official version; that the Cádiz Constitution was reinstated by royal decree. In this sense the king managed to have the final say on the question of legitimacy. As an early conclusion, it might be argued that the official effort to deprive Riego's pronunciamiento and its revolution of the authorship of the reestablishment of the 1812 constitutional system facilitated the later loss of legitimacy for Iturbide's movement and its subsequent disqualification as an example of sedition or revolt. Thus, throughout the period in question, it is possible to observe a persistent effort to portray the constitutional restoration as a result of the king's and the nation's will.

Was this projection successful? Yes and no. Yes it was, because in 1820 the king's will continued to be the conditioning element in public discourse, and as a result publicists could not stop mentioning it as a principle of consensus in their explanations. Their discussions had to start from this accepted premise. But no it was not, because the mere enunciation of this principle contained within it the seed of its own destruction, turning it into a debatable issue.[21]

Away from the king, Spain's own political disorder allowed a new pantheon to be built. The personalization of heroism noted earlier led to a resonant narrative in which the story of prominent figures and events, previously exalted by the liberals, became widely disseminated. Quiroga was the first to be acclaimed, followed by colonels Riego, Felipe Arco Agüero, and Miguel López Baños; a quartet that inscribed itself in the upper parts of a collective memory stretching back to the popular revolution of 1808, celebrating the actions of Cádiz's deputies as well as of the leaders of the frustrated liberal uprisings that had occurred throughout the six years of absolutism (1814–20). Specifically, Quiroga, Riego, and Arco Agüero were linked to the names of the unfortunate Juan Díaz Porlier and Julio Lacy, both glorified as martyrs in the liberal struggle against despotism because of their respective failed pronunciamientos of 1815 and 1817.

In an amusing dialogue written by el Pensador Mexicano — whose characters, significantly, are called "Lacy" and "Don Servilio" — he highlights the content of this renewed heroic tradition. The participants represent two opposed political positions (that of the liberals and the conservatives, otherwise referred to as *serviles*); finding themselves in the afterlife, the characters debate the current situation in Spain. Don Servilio appears on the scene enraged by the restoration of the constitution, of which Lacy was not aware. General Lacy rushes to his friend and rival to demand details: "Has it been sworn in? Has it been reestablished? What has the King done? Who raised the sacred cry of liberty?" "Well, listen to me, [grumbles Don Servilio]. In short, four bewildered young men: Quiroga, Riego, Arco Agüero and López Baños; who knows how the hell [they did it, but] they gave the cry of liberty. They began to swear allegiance to the Constitution in several villages. They did their job well, because we defenders of the King opposed such out-and-out treason with all our strength; but . . . this damned system flatters the people so much."[22] The dialogue continues with a deliriously happy Lacy trying, to no avail, to convince Don Servilio of the virtues of the charter. The idea is clear. The pronunciados of the 1820s are part of the same liberal struggle. Their triumph has crowned the previous efforts of many others, all of whom are worthy of praise and gratitude.

The abundant references to Quiroga and Riego in New Spain's leaflets, consecrating them as liberators, show a series of patriotic, military, political, and moral values, most obviously those of glory, honor, bravery, and patriotic fervor (even to the point of sacrificing one's own life). These ideals, expressed in songs, ballads, and stories written on both sides of the Atlantic, fixed and projected the wishes of the liberal government, which found — in the pronunciados — the symbol of a revived Spain that looked to go beyond her borders. This is shown in the Mexican government's *Gazette,* which frequently inserted journalistic notes from other

European nations reporting Hispanic events in a praiseworthy manner. It is easy to imagine, for example, what the reactions of the Mexican readership were to the news published in the *Gaceta* that in celebration of the triumph of the Spanish Constitution, the French had ordered not only the engraving of a "great and beautiful medal in honor of His Majesty Don Ferdinand VII" but also that the silversmith, "Mr. Charpentier, has conceived the happy idea of engraving another medal in honor of the hero who brought about the happy and peaceful Spanish revolution. They say that the portrait of General Quiroga resembles him greatly and can be fixed on rings and jewelry of all kinds . . . [it] will be the fashion of the day; as a result, everybody will want to wear a Quiroga ring."[23]

The visible leaders of the 1820 pronunciamiento, in their heroic capacity, were transformed into figures of justice. They became role models and a liberal source of inspiration to the extent that not only were they regarded as bastions of rectitude and impartiality—they were invoked in the much thornier question of the Spanish American struggle for independence. This is demonstrated, for example, by the scandal provoked by the writing of Luis Gonzaga Oronoz, a Spanish American friar who had been involved with the insurgency and who remained imprisoned in a convent in Barcelona in 1820. From his cell he published a manifesto that originally appeared in the *Diario constitucional de Barcelona* in April 1820 and was later reprinted in Mexico. Demanding justice and equality for the Americas, Oronoz wrote: "I do not ask you to support my opinion but that of an impartial writer, such as our immortal Riego, who said in one of his manifestos that [Spanish] Americans were sacrificed 'because they want the same things that you do at present.'" The pamphlet was an

Moreno Gutiérrez

acid diatribe against Félix Calleja (ex-viceroy of New Spain and oppressor of the insurgency). In order to endorse the legitimacy of his words he concluded: "Will you still doubt the force of character of a disciple of the immortal Lacy, Porlier, and other heroes of our country? Will you distrust a patriot who, to avoid demeaning himself and his brothers with vile servitude, has put their existence before his blushes?"[24] In this way the friar, as a professed insurgent, tried to link his cause—the Spanish American cause—to the Spanish liberal revolution.

An outraged response to Oronoz's insolence came from the pen of "F. V." It is interesting to note here that one of the apoplectic writer's complaints was precisely the mention of the 1820 pronunciados: "Will the Quirogas, the Riegos, the Ballesteros, the Argüelles, the Minas, the *Empecinados* and holy wise men and brave warriors, who owe their whole being to Spain, tolerate such insults to their mother country?" For the author, it was offensive and unthinkable to compare the Spanish American revolution with the Spanish liberals' struggle:

> [Oronoz] wants to make us believe that the leaders of this insurrection defend the same cause as the enlightened Quiroga, Riego, Arco Agüero and Baños. . . . He makes the most infamous calumnies. . . . The author, a priest who wears the cord of Saint Francis, an insurgent who was later pardoned for [his rebellion], has the nerve to liken himself to Porlier and Lacy. . . . To compare crime with virtue! To compare factional leaders, who while demanding independence have only occupied themselves with theft and with sacrificing decent people's lives and properties on the altar of their private resentments, with these brave captains, whose humanity has been as great and vigorous with their own enemies as it was fighting his armies! What benefits has the insurgency brought to America?[25]

As we will see, this comparison was more relevant and appropriate than ever.

Subversive Appropriation of the Pronunciamiento

The Americas' place in the Spanish monarchy and the ongoing revolutions taking place across the region occupied a prominent space in New Spain's publications. Numerous leaflets portrayed the constitution as the end of despotism for the whole monarchy and, for that reason, praised the "immortal" Quiroga for banishing servility from the American hemisphere.[26] However, there were also documents that denounced the immobility prevailing in these lands. Pamphlets like *Don Antonio siempre el mismo, Dar que van dando*, and *Las zorras de Sansón* provide three clear examples of the demands that were being made in the public sphere. The central argument in all three texts is one and the same: Spain, thanks to Riego and Quiroga, has been liberated and is governed by the sacred constitution; but this liberty cannot be enjoyed in America, where the code is not being obeyed (or there is a marked reluctance to do so), and as a result despotism continues to reign. According to "Q. E. D.," the author of *Don Antonio*, the Spaniards "broke their chains and shook off their dreadful yoke with the cry from Quiroga the immortal, from Arco Agüero the illustrious, from Riego the brave, and from Castrillo and Ballesteros the virtuous (whose names will be respected by death itself). . . . They are free at last. . . . Only sad America still moans, oppressed under the enormous weight of arbitrariness."[27] Juan Nepomuceno Troncoso, the skillful and liberal priest, in his pamphlet *Dar que van dando*, invites readers to "compare the freedom that is enjoyed there [in Spain] with the one that we have here. How would men such as Quiroga and Riego have been treated here?"[28]

The anonymous text *Las zorras de Sansón*, one of the most incendiary of 1820, developed the argument one step further: "The benevolent hand of Quiroga has already communicated and indicated us the path of freedom from beyond the grave: let us follow his footsteps undaunted. Remorseful Spain already has freedom, thus America must have total freedom." Although for some people (such as Lizardi during many years) freedom was just a matter of constitutional observance ("with this beautiful charter every citizen is a free man"), for others, Quiroga's benevolent hand showed the way toward something more than just the constitution: independence.[29]

Vicente Guerrero, a long-standing insurgent, wrote the following in August 1820 to Carlos Moya, a royalist officer who had been chasing him but with whom he had entered into negotiations shortly before Iturbide pronounced: "As I consider you to be well informed about the liberals' revolution in the Peninsula, [and the actions of the] disciples of the great Porlier, Quiroga, Arco-Agüero, Riego and their colleagues, I will not spend too much time dwelling on this. Instead I shall tell you that this is the most precious time for Mexico's children, both legitimate and adoptive, to adopt their model, to be independent, not only from Fernando's yoke but also from that of the constitutionalist Spaniards [i.e., those Spaniards who supported the constitution]."[30]

Did Riego's pronunciamiento serve as a role model for Iturbide's Three Guarantees movement, the Trigarancia? To answer this question requires a much more detailed analysis than can be presented here. However, what can be pointed out through the study of the textual representations of Riego's revolt is that pamphlets and all kinds of newspapers containing references to the Spanish pronunciamiento circulated freely in New Spain, and that they were taken up again in a very similar manner during the Mexican independence movement of 1821. The commemoration given by many documents to the mechanics of the seconding of Riego's pronunciamiento as well as to its original declaration are among the ideas well represented in the texts chronicling Iturbide's movement. Other prominent themes are the values and virtues exalted in the narration of these events ("Constancy, courage, subordination, discipline and order, order above all," remarked Juan O'Donojú in Seville).[31] Even their objectives are relayed ("you gave us freedom and independence, fighting against Spain").[32]

Riego and Quiroga's shadows reached the Trigarancia, and the images of these men were employed to legitimize their struggle. "You are not less important than Quiroga," Vicente Guerrero wrote to Iturbide in January 1821. Guerrero, like Oronoz, understood that his cause was the same as the one championed in Andalusia and therefore was not willing to accept the pardon the viceregal government offered him. He asked: "So Quiroga, Riego, Arco Agüero, etc. are worthy of praise and prizes despite not having had to suffer the same evil and cruel sacrifices that we have had to. And all we deserve is a pardon and shame for pursuing the same goal?"[33]

As might be expected, the sanctification of the pronunciados created awareness among the rebels and the military of New Spain of their own potential for growth and access to power. The publication of the awards, public offices, and promotions rewarding many of those involved in the movement of 1820 made the idea of staging a parallel controlled revolution immensely tempting.[34] The glorification of its leaders, which started from the moment in which the constitution was reinstated, became a siren song that seduced the shrewd-minded.

Moreno Gutiérrez

The few—yet significant—references to these peninsular heroes that feature in the newspapers of the Army of the Three Guarantees (*El Mejicano Independiente* and *Diario Político Militar Mejicano*) reinforce the image of the trigarantes as the just liberators of the Mexican nation. The most ingenious writers were self-confessed Trigarancia supporters, like Troncoso, who suggestively compared Quiroga's movement with that of Iturbide, making it plain that the latter was superior. For Troncoso, Iturbide's revolution (which, in fact, was just starting) was more effective, more peaceful, more honest, and better organized than the peninsular one led by Riego.[35]

It is true that once the Plan of Iguala appeared, allusions to the Spanish pronunciamiento did not abound in the Trigarancia publications. The movement began to build its own tradition and its own particular legitimacy on the existing foundation of constitutionalism and its own references. The Andalusian pronunciamiento of 1820 had already performed the crucial task of making liberty and independence thinkable and noteworthy (debatable) aspirations.

Final considerations

The famous *Manifiesto al Mundo*—written by the priest Manuel de la Bárcena shortly after the Declaration of Independence of the Mexican Empire was signed—concluded: "Heroes of Spain, Quiroga, Riego, Arco Agüero, and you Argüelles, Flores, Herreros, torches and columns of the Spanish Constitution, you have taught us to be free, do not deny your doctrine now, do not contradict your own example, do not oppose our necessary and just independence."[36] In a book dedicated to the damned and the venerated, to the memory, commemoration, and representation of the pronunciamiento, we cannot avoid underlining the veneration of the Spanish pronunciamiento of 1820 that occurred in constitutional and trigarante New Spain, nor the historical (re)constructions that were built around its representation.

There is no question that the constitution of the Spanish monarchy served as the principal, even conditioning, element of public language and political sociabilities in New Spain after its reestablishment. In such a context, not many images contained as much political and discursive potential as those which referred to the heroic restorers of the constitution. The abundance and clarity of the documents analyzed here proves beyond doubt that the 1820 pronunciamiento was not perceived as a marginal event in New Spain.

Quentin Skinner recommends that the study of languages and their gradual innovations should not focus on the "language or traditions themselves, but rather on the range of things that in principle can be done with them in any given period"; in other words, the "speech-acts range."[37] At the beginning of this chapter I asked what could be thought and said in New Spain in 1820. To answer this question, I would affirm that insidious allusions to Riego's pronunciamiento, together with the way awareness was raised over the possibility of bringing about political change by the forceful enactment of people's will (whether that was the popular or the national will), opened up a whole range of thoughts, debates, and actions that ended up transforming New Spain's legitimacies. Liberating armies, immortal caudillos, the quest for freedom, and sacrifices for the patria were speech-acts and symbols that Quiroga and Riego sent to New Spain to awaken the New Spaniards' political imagination.

The events of 1820 altered the public discourse of the community and definitively destroyed existing consensus. Before these events, the referential and symbolic framework was the sovereignty of the king and his royal will; after them, despite efforts to maintain the royal will as the foundation of power, there was no way back. New fundamental agreements began to be articulated with new (or renewed) conventions and representations: the general or national will, representative regimes, and popular sovereignty.

Perhaps people did not know the details of the Spanish pronunciamiento's history. With a few exceptions, chronicles of the military events did not always circulate, nor were popular fiestas staged to celebrate these pronunciamientos, as would become the norm throughout the greater part of the nineteenth century in Mexico, as explored in several of this book's chapters. Nevertheless, every time allegiance was sworn to the constitution and every time someone adhered to the independence movement that started in Iguala, memorials were made to the movement that had originated in Cabezas de San Juan. And if there was no precise knowledge about the actions of those historical actors, their symbolism — in its abstract form — was more powerful. To mention Riego or Quiroga was to evoke freedom and how this freedom could be used to achieve, establish, and negotiate different goals.

Riego's pronunciamiento, the symbolic potency of which was multiplied in Mexico by Iturbide's pronunciamiento, conclusively altered the institutional agreements that had been in force until then. It made politics (forever) a field of contingency and discussion. Its memory, exaltation, and commemoration decisively undermined the Ancien Regime's legitimacy and unlocked other forms of political negotiation.

Somehow, within the Trigarancia's "genetic code" we can decipher the memory of Riego's and Quiroga's pronunciamiento and the collective construction of its representation in the dying days of New Spain.

Notes

This chapter has benefited from the comments and corrections made by Catherine Andrews, Sally Antrobus, Will Fowler, and Leticia Neria. The remarks of José Joaquín Fernández de Lizardi in the epigraph are from his *Contestación de el Pensador.*

1. Miguel Artola offers an account of the Riego conspiracy: *La España de Fernando VII*, 501–27. Alberto Gil Novales collected the movement documentation in *Rafael del Riego.*

2. Fowler, "Rafael del Riego."

3. The classic studies referred to here are Comellas, *Los primeros pronunciamientos en España*; Baquer, *El modelo español*; Cepeda Gómez, *Los pronunciamientos en la España*; and Fontana, *La quiebra de la monarquía absoluta.*

4. Blanco Valdés, *Rey, cortes y fuerza armada*, 474–76. Fowler also points out the importance of civil participation in his "El pronunciamiento mexicano del siglo XIX," 5–34.

5. Rodríguez E., "Los caudillos y los historiadores," 315.

6. I analyze in detail the different interpretations in Moreno Gutiérrez, "Nuestras ideas sobre la consumación."

7. This hypothesis (that the restoration was the main cause of the loss of the Americas) was spread by the peculiar Spanish texts of the late 1820s, such as José Presas's *Juicio imparcial*, Juan López Cacelada's journalistic articles, and Mariano Torrente's *Historia de la independencia.*

8. Contributions by Timothy Anna, Manuel Chust, and Ivana Frasquet to earlier volumes of this project on the pronunciamientos of independent Mexico start from this principle: Ivana Frasquet and Manuel Chust, "Agustín de Iturbide: From the Pronunciamiento of Iguala to the Coup of 1822"; and Anna, "Iguala: The Prototype."

9. *Gaceta del Gobierno de México*, 1 June 1820.

10. *Gaceta del Gobierno de México*, 3 June 1820.

11. Dated in Palace, 10 March 1820; *Gaceta del Gobierno de México*, 3 June 1820.

12. There is an ample historiography dedicated to the study of semantic and linguistic transformations during the Independence period, which was, in many senses, also a conceptual revolution. See, for example, works by Javier Fernández Sebastián, particularly "La crisis de 1808," 105–33.

13. For example, *Defensa del inmortal D. Rafael Riego*; *Proclama dirigida al inmortal Quiroga*; Quiroga, *Ejército nacional*; Quiroga, *Exhortación*; Riego et al., *Representación hecha al rey.*

14. Elías Palti is one of the authors who have studied this phenomenon more carefully; see his *La invención de una legitimidad*, 45–152; and his *El tiempo de la política*, 161–202. An excellent overview of the conceptual history of public opinion is Noemí Goldman's introduction, "Legitimidad y deliberación."

15. *Canción patriótica.*

16. Fernández de Lizardi, *Obras IV—Periódicos*, 264–65.

17. Quiroga was one of the leaders arrested by the conspiracy of 1819. Riego's movement released him and chose him as general of the pronounced troops.

18. *Proclama dirigida al inmortal Quiroga.*

19. *El Centinela de Noche-Bea.*

20. Fernández de Lizardi, *Obras IV—Periódicos*, 270–71.

21. This has already been demonstrated by Palti, *La invención de una legitimidad*, 23–44.

22. *Los diálogos de los muertos*, in Fernández de Lizardi, *Obras X—Folletos*, 245–49.

23. *Gaceta del Gobierno de México*, 19 October 1820.

24. Oronoz, *A la nación española*, 5.

25. F. V., *La Espada de la Justicia.*

26. For instance, *Las lágrimas del egoísmo*; or *La gratitud del ayuntamiento.*

27. Q. E. D., *Don Antonio siempre el mismo.*

28. Troncoso, *Dar que van dando.*

29. *Las zorras de Sansón*; Fernández de Lizardi, *Obras IV—Periódicos*, 258.

30. Document published by Lemoine, *La revolución de independencia*, 449–50.

31. *Proclama dirigida al inmortal Quiroga.* Juan O'Donojú, prominent liberal, was New Spain's last "viceroy" (although the constitutional regime prohibited the use of that title).

32. "Romance en alabanza a las heroicas tropas españolas, que componen el ejército nacional de la isla de León, y de sus ínclitos jefes Quiroga y Riego," in *Proclama dirigida al inmortal Quiroga.*

33. Transcription made by Epigmenio de la Piedra—known as "Padre Piedras"—who was commissioned by the colonial government to meet Guerrero. Document in Lemoine, *La revolución de independencia*, 449–50.

34. Fowler, "Rafael del Riego."

35. Troncoso, *Pascuas a un militar.*

36. Bárcena, "Manifiesto al Mundo," 126.

37. Skinner, "Algunos problemas," 237.

Two. The Damned Man with the Venerated Plan:
*The Complex Legacies of Agustín de Iturbide and
the Iguala Plan*

I n February of 1821 Agustín de Iturbide, a Mexican-born military
officer at the head of thousands of troops loyal to the Spanish
crown, issued the Iguala Plan, a schematic for achieving Mexican independence. The document is composed of two dozen articles that proclaimed Mexico's freedom from external domination, the right to citizenship of all inhabitants, and the primacy
of Catholicism. The *pronunciamiento* called for the formation of
an interim executive to preside over the nation during the delib-
erations of a new constitutional convention, which would ham-
mer out the details of a proposed constitutional monarchy, and
for the formation of an army to secure these principles. Distilled
to its essence, Iturbide's action rallied his troops to the cause of
"Three Guarantees": religion, independence, and union.

New Spain had been at war for over a decade by then. The mass
uprising initiated in September 1810 by the priest Miguel Hidalgo
with a call to arms in the town of Dolores had ebbed and flowed
according to a complex dynamic in which local grievances and
interests collided with trans-Atlantic geo-strategies and antago-
nistic principles of political philosophy. However, within months
Iturbide, who himself had fought for years against the insurgency, managed to mollify former enemies and to convince Spain's
highest ranking official in New Spain to sign a peace treaty. As a

result, on 27 September 1821, Iturbide marched into Mexico City at the head of the Army of Three Guarantees, by many accounts one of the more joyful and hopeful moments of the first half of the nineteenth century.[1]

Fast forward two centuries.

On 30 May 2010, as part of Mexico's Independence bicentennial celebrations, soldiers lined the streets of Mexico City as a funeral cortege with full military escort paraded up the Paseo de la Reforma. This honor guard transported the remains of twelve heroes of the era from their resting place at the foot of the Independence Monument to the National Museum of History, where preservation efforts were to be conducted on the heroes' remains. Before being returned to the Independence Monument, the urns containing these relics were placed on public display for a year in the National Palace.[2] The remains of Agustín de Iturbide did not make the trip. They stayed in a side chapel at the Metropolitan Cathedral, a few short miles from the Independence Monument, where they have been since 1838. However, while his worldly remains have enjoyed lengthy repose, of all the era's protagonists, Iturbide's place in Mexico's national saga has been among the most volatile, and he currently does not meet the Mexican state's definition of a hero of Independence. Explaining why this is so tells us many things about the struggle to define Mexican identity since Independence and the mechanisms that drive the damnation and veneration of the memories of historical actors and actions.

Iturbide's biography is complex. In addition to being a latecomer to the cause of Independence, within months of his triumphal march into Mexico City, Iturbide maneuvered himself into the role of emperor of a short-lived Mexican monarchy. Later exiled and denounced as a traitor, he ultimately returned to Mexico in 1824 as a self-styled political savior, only to be executed within days of setting foot in his homeland again. As a result, Iturbide does not fit easily into the republican, nationalist mythmaking that generally characterizes modern Mexico.[3] Yet as the architect of the Iguala Plan, the road map to end a decade of warfare, and as leader of the Army of Three Guarantees, which secured victory over the Spanish in 1821, Iturbide must be acknowledged somehow in any narrative about the achievement of Mexican Independence.

The complexities of Iturbide's role and legacy emerged from the very beginning of state builders' efforts to construct through public ritual and discourse a meaningful story of Mexico's path to Independence. During his brief reign, official celebrations to mark the achievement of Independence occurred on 27 September, to recognize the day in 1821 when the Army of Three Guarantees marched into Mexico City. However, anti-Iturbide politicians and polemicists promoted Miguel Hidalgo's 1810 uprising as the principal act in the Independence saga.[4] After Iturbide's regime toppled in 1823 and republicans gained control of the national government, the new congress declared over one dozen people "national heroes" and began the process of transferring their remains to the capital, beginning on 16 September 1823.[5] Yet even with Iturbide in exile and disgrace, the elaborate ceremonies of reburial that sanctified Hidalgo, Morelos, and others still culminated with a solemn ceremony on 27 September remembered as a day when "all were one."[6]

Amidst an intense struggle for political supremacy among the republican factions that had overthrown the Iturbide regime, and as part of a strategy for igniting popular political enthusiasm and nationalist sentiment, radical federalists aggressively promoted the annual commemoration of Hidalgo's call for mass uprising, known as the "grito de Dolores." It was during the mid-1820s, then, that 16 September, the day of this call to arms, emerged as the date most closely associated with Mexican Independence, akin to 4 July in the United States of America, and it remains so. Yet rather than simply attempting to erase Iturbide from national creation myths, this generation instead broke down his biography into distinct episodes. During the time of his exile and in the aftermath of his ill-fated return to Mexico, which led to his execution in 1824, vilification of Iturbide focused on his decisions after the achievement of Independence, especially to create a monarchy and take the throne for himself. Celebrations of 27 September continued, for example in 1826, and the events of 1821 were still recollected on the other Independence Day (16 September), but orators were generally circumspect in their references to Iturbide, if they mentioned him by name at all.[7] They might refer to the "celebrated Plan of Iguala" but attribute the achievements of 1821 to "a general force" rather than a forceful general.[8] Authors who did praise Iturbide by name could feel compelled to clarify their sentiments, like the poet who, in an ode to Independence, added a footnote to explain that he admired only "Iturbide, liberator of the country, not Agustín I, Emperor of Mexico."[9]

Partisan conflict culminated in armed struggle that nullified the results of the first republican presidential succession in 1828. Over the next decades, often in rapid succession, governments formed and fell as disputatious factions competed for control of the national state. Among the bitter divides were disagreements on the amount of power to invest in the central government, the nature of economic development and fiscal policy, the meaning of political participation, and the continued value of colonial institutions and structures. Given the rancorous, at times violent nature of these disputes, it is no surprise that competing factions sought to root their claims in an authentic *mexicanidad* associated with the nation's birth and thus positioned themselves in some relationship to the Iguala Plan, if only in adopting the form of this prototype pronunciamiento, and to its promulgator, if only to condemn him or some of his actions. Rather than fade into oblivion, then, the Iturbide/Iguala legacy was batted around by competing factions in ways that defy easy categorization. In the 1830s those seeking to create a stronger central government and those who would come to be called conservatives by later generations conjured the "Three Guarantees" of the Iguala pronunciamiento—with their emphasis on compromise, continuity, unity, and authority—as prudent, judicious political genius. The high point of Iturbide's rehabilitation came in 1838, as a centralist government orchestrated elaborate plans to transfer Iturbide's remains from the small town of Padilla (the place of his execution) to the capital's Metropolitan Cathedral, with the support of the Church hierarchy, relieved that the anticlerical firebrands of the early 1830s had been turned out of office by the current administration. Government sources claimed that four hundred coaches joined the procession through the capital, as an honor guard of saluting troops lined both sides of the route to the cathedral, welcoming the return of the Liberator.[10]

Editorials in the official government newspaper made explicit for readers the regime's interest in rehabilitating Iturbide as a symbol of unity, whose brilliant pronunciamiento and willingness to negotiate with former enemies brought Independence in a matter of months after ten years of civil war.[11] Some in the opposition did not respond with their own rhetoric of unity. One newspaper columnist sarcastically noted that since Iturbide's ashes had arrived finally in Mexico City, surely the government would now also bring to the capital the remains of Vicente Guerrero, the long-term insurgent who marched at Iturbide's side on that triumphant day in 1821 and later served his own controversial term as head of state. Savvy readers did not need this editorialist to point out explicitly that members of the sitting government stood accused of complicity in Guerrero's 1831 assassination.[12]

While this *puro* ("pure" or more radical) strain of federalism remained an important ingredient in Mexico's post-Independence political stew, the partial redemption of Iturbide as the genius behind Iguala remained a feature of national political life through the 1840s and into the 1850s. Celebrations of both 16 and 27 September, known together as the *"fiestas patrias,"* became a common feature of the holiday calendar. In addition to the more conservative, centralist motivations already described, many moderate liberals, particularly during the great peasant unrest that characterized the 1840s, also rediscovered an important message in the Iguala Plan and encouraged their coreligionists to "forget the Iturbide of the Spaniards and the Iturbide of 1822, and remember only the hero of September."[13]

In the aftermath of Mexico's devastating war with the United States (1846–48), individuals and groups sought to place blame for the ignominious loss of vast amounts of territory and to map out a path to preserve the nation itself, which appeared to teeter on the verge of collapse. At the center of the ideological scrap, political figures in the capital used their newspapers to present competing interpretations of the meaning of Independence and the worthiness of its various protagonists, and the gulf between Hidalgo and Iturbide grew again. At this critical moment the conservative *El Universal* published a series of opinion pieces that not only extolled Iturbide and the Three Guarantees but also called Hidalgo a failure and his movement a disaster. Liberals in the national congress attempted, but failed, to impose sanctions against the newspaper for such political heresy.[14]

Exemplary of the political confusion and desperation that marked these years, Antonio López de Santa Anna, who had played the roles of both hero and goat numerous times in his long career, returned to national power one last time from 1853 to 1855, as an authoritarian "serene highness." *Santanistas*, as they had before, revised the national foundation myth by adding a third day to the September fiestas patrias: 11 September, to commemorate the day in 1829 when Santa Anna defeated a Spanish invasion force at Tampico.[15] This construction placed Santa Anna in the center of Mexico's national origin myth, as Hidalgo had set fire to nationalist sentiment and Iturbide had designed the strong pillars of a new state based on unity and religion, but only Santa Anna had finally been able to vanquish the threat of Spanish reconquest and thus complete the long birth process of the new nation. Other symbolic acts reinforced this connection. The title "serene highness," bestowed on Santa Anna by his obsequious Council of State, had been a title associated most closely with Miguel Hidalgo until that time. Further, despite the conflicts that characterized their personal relationship during Iturbide's lifetime — Santa Anna joined the Plan of Casa Mata that toppled the Emperor Agustín — over the course of his career, Santa Anna had developed a sense of the Liberator's symbolic potential and an appreciation of his ritual panache. In 1854 Santa Anna commissioned a new national hymn, which contained laudatory lyrics about Iturbide. Further, his Serene Highness declared that the day of Iturbide's execution was to be a national day of mourning. Finally,

Santa Anna revived the honorific Order of Guadalupe, which had been founded by the Emperor Agustín.[16]

Santa Anna's regime fell to an uprising led by champions of the liberal reform movement that culminated in the 1857 Constitution. Santa Anna's place in a trinity of Independence heroes fell with it, never to emerge again. While the victors compared their movement to that of the virtuous Hidalgo, they continued, at least sporadically, to celebrate the Iguala incarnation of Iturbide as well, adopting a device by then familiar in Mexico. Supporters of the liberal regime wrote that while the Iguala Plan should inspire unity and reconciliation, the subsequent actions and fate of Iturbide himself served as sufficient warning to those who would promote solutions to Mexico's problems that were too conservative or authoritarian.[17] This strategy, coupled with the rhetorical bifurcation of Iturbide's life into distinct stages—first as the genius of Iguala riding in triumph at the head of the Army of Three Guarantees, only later to fall as a hubristic overreacher—might have secured him a more enduring place in the official pantheon of Mexico's Independence heroes were it not for the dramatic reentry of his descendants into Mexican politics beginning in the 1860s.

Machinations of Mexican conservatives to seek external assistance for their political plans dovetailed with a decision in 1861 by the liberal regime to suspend foreign debt payments. First came threats of European military intervention, and later a full-blown French invasion to prop up a new Mexican monarchy, with the Hapsburg Archduke Maximilian on its throne. During this period Iturbide, the self-proclaimed emperor, lost all currency with liberals, who initiated another rhetorical shift in their framing of the story of Independence, moving from appeals to unity and reconciliation to an emphasis on the incomplete nature of Mexico's

Independence and Mexicans' liberty.[18] Maximilian, too, deployed the trope of incompleteness. While the regency that set the stage for his arrival placed equal weight on both 16 and 27 September as national holidays, during his first year in Mexico, Maximilian chose to deliver an Independence Day speech in Hidalgo's home town, declaiming upon the affinity he felt for Mexico and asserting that he had come to assure that the goals of Hidalgo finally would be achieved.[19] On the other hand, he also decided to transfer Iturbide's remains yet again; however, this time it was to be only an upgrade in accommodations (to a bronze sarcophagus) rather than a change of location, as the Liberator remained in the Metropolitan Cathedral.[20] Finally, the childless royal couple made the dramatic decision to designate one of Iturbide's grandchildren, whose name happened to be Agustín, as the heir to the emperor's throne.[21]

The Empire, fiercely resisted by liberal republicans and increasingly left to its own devices by the French, did not last long. Empress Carlota returned to Europe to seek aid, and allegedly suffered a mental breakdown. Emperor Maximilian faced a firing squad outside Querétaro. In the decade after the collapse of this second imperial experiment since Independence, Porfirio Díaz, a military officer who had fought against the French (see chapter 9), emerged to build a stable state that was, in theory, based on the liberal republican principles of the 1857 Constitution. In reality, the Porfirian state relied on repression and deal making fueled by impressive amounts of foreign investment and economic growth to cement Díaz's control over the executive branch for more than thirty years. One of the keys to understanding the success of the regime was its equal-opportunity approach to authoritarian nation-state construction. "Old liberals died off or were harassed into

silence or grew fat on the spoils of office; the Church was concil-
iated and allowed, tacitly, to recover some of its old importance,
political, social, and economic."[22] In an apparent paradox, however, during the Porfirian Peace, the national state never reinte-
grated Iturbide into the pantheon of Independence heroes, despite
his symbolic value in certain circles, especially among Catholic
elites. To understand why this was so, one must return to the overlooked living legacy of the Liberator — his family.

The baroque melodrama that surrounded Maximilian and Carlota's designation of an Iturbide heir to the throne — including
remuneration (Iturbide family members received a pension in
return for leaving Mexico), regret (both of young Agustín's parents were still alive), and international scandal (the boy's mother was a U.S. citizen who attempted to nullify the deal) — is often the last one reads of the Iturbide family in the historiography
of Mexico: young Agustín leaves Mexico to be reunited with his
father and mother and then fades into oblivion. Indeed, one of
the best known historical reference works in Mexico summariz-
es the post-Empire life of this Agustín Iturbide in four brief sen-
tences, concluding that as an adult, "he did not maintain proper behavior and in the end, joined a monastery, where he died."[23]
Yet there are further twists and turns in the family history and its
relationship to powerful political actors, which continued to influence not only the construction of the Liberator's place in state-
centered accounts of Independence, but which also contributed
mightily to an enduring counternarrative that still places a symbolically united Iguala Plan and Iturbide at the center of an alternative national identity.

Contrary to the account of a quick descent into obscurity as
described earlier, in fact "Prince Yturbide," off and on throughout

his life, was a highly visible media darling, public intellectual, dissident, and polemicist.[24] In the early 1880s he completed his education at Georgetown College and entered cosmopolitan high society. Important power brokers in the U.S. and Mexican governments, as well as the Catholic Church, advised Yturbide, as they negotiated with and cajoled each other in trying to shape his fate and Mexico's future. Some of this maneuvering took place in public, with interviews, news, and opinion pieces published in various media outlets in the United States and Mexico. Readers of the *New York Times*, the *New York Herald*, the *Washington Post*, and *Harper's Monthly*, among others, could bear witness to the angst over what role the former poster child of Catholic monarchy in Mexico would play now that he was a man.

During these years Manuel González, a close ally of Porfirio Díaz with a similar military background and political outlook, was president of Mexico. The González regime continued its predecessor's efforts to consolidate a stable national political system and to accelerate economic development based on liberal models of foreign investment and private property. A boom in railroad construction occurred; a national banking system put down roots; and by 1883–84 the Department of Development, an executive branch agency, claimed over one-third of the federal budget. Yet the González administration stumbled. Budget deficits mounted, efforts to introduce a new currency sparked protests, and the resolution of a long-standing diplomatic impasse with Great Britain backfired, as critics in the press excoriated the regime for its lack of nationalist backbone. By the end of 1883, as the González administration came under increasing assault, Porfirio Díaz returned to salvage the liberal development project and to heal political rifts that had begun to fester.[25] By October 1883 Mexican

newspapers were printing articles in support of Díaz, and a growing number of conservative elites joined Díaz's liberal core con-
stituency in the opinion that he had become Mexico's necessary
ruler. By the following summer's elections, there really were no
other serious candidates. The formal announcement of his reelection elicited wide, though by no means complete, approbation on
both sides of the border.[26]

One of the dissonant voices belonged to the young Yturbide.
During the fall of 1884, in the months between Díaz's second election and his inauguration, Agustín gave a series of interviews to
U.S. reporters in which he promised that he would soon return
to Mexico to work for the reestablishment of a legitimate political order, since the Mexican people wanted to move beyond the
"atheistic" liberal party that Díaz exemplified. The Mexican le-
gation in Washington, which maintained a watch on Yturbide's
comings and goings, forwarded clippings of these articles to the
secretary of foreign relations, along with their dutiful condem-
nations of Yturbide's sedition. Soon after their appearance in the
U.S. press, parts of these interviews were republished in Mexico.[27] A little more than two years later Yturbide again criticized
Díaz in the U.S. press and suggested that "there is imminent danger of a revolution." In addition he concluded that he might have
his own claim to national authority: "Should the people declare
for the dynasty of Maximilian I would succeed to the throne."[28]

Yet over the course of the next year Yturbide and Díaz achieved
an agreement, brokered by Agustín's long-time patron, the powerful
Bishop Ignacio Montes de Oca, who had been imperial chaplain
to the court of Maximilian.[29] In August 1888 Yturbide accepted
an officer's commission in the Mexican military. While this may
appear a surprising turn of events, one might also contextualize

it as evidence of the growing rapprochement between conservative Catholics and the liberal republic in its wily Porfirian incarnation. As it turned out, the rapprochement lasted less than two years, as Agustín was court-martialed for alleged attempts to undermine the regime. He spent months in jail at the beginning of the 1890s and then the rest of his life in the United States.

In exile Yturbide continued to interpret Mexican affairs for audiences in the United States and Mexico, both as a college instructor and, perhaps more important, as what we would today call a public intellectual. Even as a much younger man, Yturbide already knew that he wanted to write about Mexican history, particularly about his grandfather. He had noted to a family friend that he thought a comparison of George Washington, Simón Bolívar, and his grandfather would prove to be an interesting study. The friend's response provides insight into the mindset of the Liberator's family and supporters: "I judge that you are correct that Yturbide [sic] is worth more than Washington; and I judge that Bolívar is worth less than the other two."[30] Now Yturbide had a chance to spread this interpretation to the public. He wrote a number of articles for the *North American Review* and other periodicals, in which he consistently lamented Mexico's wrong turn in its rejection of an authentically independent, hierarchical, Catholic national destiny, embodied in the principles of his grandfather's home-grown Iguala pronunciamiento, in favor of foreign abstractions.[31]

The Díaz regime did not take kindly to this turn of affairs with Yturbide and the Liberator's legacy. Here, after all, was a highly cosmopolitan, media-savvy member of one of the better known families in Mexican history, who continually criticized the Díaz regime as oppressive, corrupt, and engaged in a financial Ponzi scheme that would ultimately bring down the Mexican economy and the foreigners who invested in it. Thus, while Díaz did manage to reach a more comfortable modus vivendi than his liberal predecessors with many conservative elements of Mexican society, including the Catholic Church hierarchy, his regime did not do the same with the Iturbide legacy. While the Catholic press extolled Iturbide, and the Sociedad Patriótica Agustín de Iturbide organized solemn masses for 27 September, little reconciliation with the Porfirian state occurred. The Díaz regime chose instead to strengthen the symbolic connections between Hidalgo (for a long time the liberal national state's preferred Independence icon), Benito Juárez (the most revered of liberal reformers and, like Díaz, a Oaxaca native), and Díaz himself, through construction projects like the Independence Monument on the Paseo de la Reforma and the Benito Juárez Monument on the Alameda Central. Time also presented the Porfirian regime with a gift and a challenge: the centennial of the outbreak of the Independence War would occur in 1910, at a time when the regime showed no signs of relinquishing its grip after decades in power.

As part of the elaborate celebrations held throughout the month of September 1910, an Iturbide actor took his place alongside those representing Vicente Guerrero, Manuel Mier y Terán, Guadalupe Victoria, and Anastasio Bustamante in a recreation of the Army of Three Guarantees' entrance into the city, part of a larger public spectacle reviewing the entirety of Mexican history.[32] Yet at the same time, the *porfiristas* scrubbed the lyrics to the national anthem, which dated to 1854. The fourth verse, a shameless paean to Santa Anna, the "serene highness" at the time of its composition, was eliminated entirely. More subtly, the third line of the seventh verse was rewritten, with the word "patria" substituting for the word "Iturbide," so as to eliminate a "dangerous confusion" about Mexico's past caused by the "uncertain figure" of Iturbide.[33]

During the years between the outbreak of the revolution in 1910 and the militant Catholic rebellion of the 1920s known as the Cristero Rebellion, the relationship between Mexican politics and Iturbide/Iguala legacy remained complex and fluid. In the early years of the revolution, pro-Church forces pressed their interests and chose among competing factions, but the triumphant coalition that emerged after 1915 counted among their number some strong anticlerics, who triumphed in the debates that led to the 1917 Constitution.[34] In the lengthiest article that he would ever write for a U.S. audience, published in two parts in the *Records of the American Catholic Historical Society* in the midst of these pitched battles, Agustín Yturbide distilled down to a few basic factors his vision of Mexican history and the way his family legacy had been marginalized and betrayed. He wrote:

> The polemics attaching to Iturbide's memory are as live a subject, still, as in that day. The reason is obvious:
>
> the Masonic party is busy with its work of decatholicization and the consolidation of Jacobin institutions and policies, with the help of the United States.
>
> Liberals, through international solidarity, denigrate Iturbide in works of reference, travel books and the press generally.

He concluded that his grandfather had been fundamentally a man of religion "governed by the principle that his countrymen should seek their national prosperity in the legitimate development of their own customs, traditions and character, and not in the importation of political institutions of which they knew nothing more than that some prosperous alien people had adopted them."[35] For

the grandson, Mexican national identity and political legitimacy remained rooted in the Iguala Plan. During the height of revolutionary upheaval, Yturbide and others promoted as a potential
president of Mexico a living embodiment of the Iguala/Iturbide
legacy, his cousin Eduardo Iturbide, a general in the Mexican army
who had served as governor of the Federal District during the brief
military regime of Victoriano Huerta, which lasted from February
1913 until July 1914. With the aid of U.S. officials, General Iturbide crossed the border to escape almost certain death when the
Constitutionalist army drove Huerta from power. He remained a
figure of hopeful speculation about Mexico's future leadership for
those who condemned the likes of Pancho Villa, Emiliano Zapata, and Venustiano Carranza as dangerous radicals.[36]

It was not without irony, then, that in 1921 the administration of President Álvaro Obregón, who had been a general in the
Constitutionalist army, organized commemorations of the consummation of Independence in an effort to build support for the
revolutionary regime and to send a message that a more tranquil
nation was emerging after a decade of bloodshed. In the contre-
temps unleashed by this decision, radical legislators wailed that
Iturbide's name should be removed from the Gallery of Illustrious Men in the congress building, while conservative elites argued
that true national reconciliation could be aided at this time by restoring a more holistic understanding of Iturbide and his legacy to
its proper and enduring place in the Mexican national story. Although he had been invited, Agustín Yturbide refused to attend
the ceremonies because he felt that neither he nor his grandfather
would in fact be given this appropriate respect by the Obregón regime.[37] In the end the ceremonies in 1921 harkened back to earlier
fiestas patrias but ended with a new twist, no doubt insulting to

conservatives and delighting the more radical factions of the new regime. Solemn ceremonies, allegorical parades, balls, and beauty contests continued through the month of September, while the annual celebration of the grito de Dolores maintained its central ritual position in the calendar. The government named streets in the capital after early Independence War leaders Miguel Hidalgo and Ignacio Allende. Finally a special ceremony was held on 27 September, but this time the regime identified the "Consummator of Independence" as Vicente Guerrero, the popular long-term insurgent who marched at Iturbide's side into Mexico City on that day in 1821, rather than Iturbide himself.[38]

The Catholic Church hierarchy played no role in planning these public celebrations, a telling sign of Church-state relations, and at this moment Catholic opponents of the new regime responded with their counternarrative, holding a thanksgiving mass to honor Iturbide.[39] Three years later, members of the Knights of Columbus, the Damas Católicas, and the Catholic Young Men's Association organized a memorial for the centenary of Iturbide's death. A U.S. journalist noted drily, "Official Mexico was conspicuously absent" from the services. The reporter concluded, "To the Mexican conservatives and clergy to-day Iturbide is *the* liberator, the others a shabby lot, and the issue is thoroughly alive. It has been presented to me with as much heat as if it dealt with contemporary figures. Deep is the cleft which divides Mexico."[40] This would be the last such ceremony of which Iturbide's grandson might possibly be aware, for he died in Washington in March of 1925. Later that same year revolutionary state builders turned again to the Independence era for ritual mojo, as President Plutarco Elías Calles presided over the transfer of the remains of twelve Independence era heroes and heroines to a new home beneath the

Independence Monument on the Paseo de la Reforma. And what of Iturbide, whose remains had rested for decades within steps of the others in the Metropolitan Cathedral? President Calles remarked, "I left Iturbide there among his kind, where he belongs."[41]

And there he remained through the end of the twentieth century. Historians, novelists, and playwrights regularly rediscovered Iturbide, but the contemporary Mexican state, in the secular, liberal tradition inherited from the revolutionary era, generally ignored him. Meanwhile, Catholic publications continued to offer a counternarrative of Mexican history embodied in the writings of his grandson.[42] It flowed through the overheated prose of books with titles like *Blood-Drenched Altars* and *Mexican Martyrdom*, both published just after the Cristero Rebellion to explain the sweep of Mexican history to U.S. Catholics.[43] Thirty years later, in a collection of "historical essays for the general reader" that received the Church's imprimatur as "free of doctrinal error," Paul V. Murray wrote, "With all his faults, Iturbide undoubtedly was the consummator of Mexican Independence and well deserves the title of Liberator. Throughout most of the past century he was so honored, but since the triumph of the Revolution of 1917, he has been banished from the list of Independence heroes and, as a victim of sectarian passion, strongly tinged with Masonic feeling, is excoriated at every turn."[44] As recently as 1999, an article in the *Catholic Standard and Times*, the newspaper of the Archdiocese of Philadelphia, reported that Iturbide "is compared to our country's George Washington." The author further stated that in following the design of the Iguala Plan, "the emperor attempted to introduce a form of democratic government, to give both rich and poor a voice in the government" and that "the nouveau-riche revolutionaries who had helped put Iturbide in power quickly became dissatisfied with his rule, because they wanted to maintain sole power of the new government."[45] It would be an understatement to note that this is not the consensus interpretation among professional historians about Iturbide and his regime.

The new millennium brought new challenges and opportunities. The World Wide Web provides a vast territory for the proliferation of *iturbidista* sites and information, from monarchy fetishists to organizations founded to enlighten Mexicans on their "true" history to the "Agustín de Iturbide" values-based investment fund. Dozens of homages to Iturbide and *iturbidismo* may be found on YouTube. Several years ago the archbishop of Guadalajara called for the national state to give Iturbide the "place he deserves in our national history."[46] Indeed, one might have thought that as the clock ticked down to 2010, Iturbide might be reclaimed by the state. The dominant Partido Revolucionario Institucional (PRI), which arose from the Revolution to dominate national politics for seven decades, had resumed diplomatic relations with the Vatican in the 1990s. Further, the executive branch of the government since 2000 has been controlled by the Partido de Acción Nacional (PAN), which had since its inception in 1939 attracted Catholic opponents to the anticlerical PRI. Finally President Felipe Calderón (2006–12) was quoted years ago as saying that *panistas* do, in fact, shout, "Viva Iturbide" on Independence Day "because Mexico cannot be the product of a partial history, of a history of some against others."[47] Yet, in 2010, the Liberator remained in his chapel while his contemporaries were paraded through the streets. One wonders, though, what the ceremonies might be like in 2021.

Yet we need to consider that history is always "partial" in so much as it consists of our own relationship to the past and is

Warren

therefore always a story of "some against others." Let us then end this essay with one final demonstration of the complex relationships among Iturbide, Iguala, and Mexican nationhood, which suggests that the Liberator may remain in his chapel. The Catholic University of America holds in its archive a rare hand-written version of the Iguala Plan, contemporaneous with the pronunciamiento itself, and therefore a precious touchstone of Mexican history, which had been passed down through three generations of the Iturbide family. Agustín Yturbide's widow donated it to the university, stipulating that the document could never be returned to Mexico because the family refused to let the Mexican state separate the memory of the document from the memory of its maker. Monsignor James Magner, a university administrator, author on Latin American affairs, and confidant of Mrs. Yturbide, wrote in his memoirs, "I understood, however, the reason supporting this decision, namely, the disgraceful treatment which Agustín I received from his political enemies and their successors in the nation to which he brought Independence."[48]

Notes

1. For a description of the Iguala Plan and its place in the history of Mexican pronunciamientos, see Anna, "Iguala: The Prototype." For the reception of the plan, events leading to the triumphant march into Mexico City, and the rise of Iturbide to emperor, see Anna, *Mexican Empire*, 1–26; Archer, "Death's Patriots," 82–88; and Ivana Frasquet and Manuel Chust, "Agustín de Iturbide: From the Pronunciamiento of Iguala to the Coup of 1822," in Fowler, *Forceful Negotiations*, 22–46.

2. "Encabeza presidente homenaje a Héroes de la Independencia," Mexico Bicentennial Commission, accessed 6 August 2010, http://www.bicentenario.gob.mx/.

3. Anna, *Mexican Empire*, is the best scholarly analysis available in English of the rise and fall of the Iturbide regime.

4. Vázquez de Knauth, *Nacionalismo y educación*, 32–39.

5. Archer, "Death's Patriots," 92; Costeloe, "The Junta Patriótica," 23.

6. These lines, attributed to a public oration on that day, are quoted in Bustamante, *Cuadro histórico de la revolución*, 6:181.

7. Archivo General de la Nación, Mexico City (henceforth cited as AGN), Gobernación, Seguridad Pública, Leg. 1586, Exp. 2 (1826); Tornel, *Oración*.

8. See, for example, *Oración patriótica que en la plazuela principal*.

9. *El grito de libertad en el pueblo de Dolores* (Mexico City: Imp. Ontiveros, 1825). Colección Lafragua, Biblioteca Nacional de México (henceforth cited as CL-BNM), vol. 220.

10. *El Diario de Gobierno*, 26 September 1838.

11. *El Diario de Gobierno*, 16 September 1838.

12. *El Cosmopólita*, 27 September 1838.

13. *El Siglo XIX*, 27 September 1844.

14. Rodríguez Piña, "Conservatives Contest the Meaning of Independence," 116–24.

15. An earlier iteration of this construction is found in *Discurso pronunciado por el ciudadano Antonio Pacheco Real en la capital de la República Mexicana al 16 de setiembre de 1835 aniversario del glorioso Grito de Dolores proclamado la independencia nacional* (Mexico City: Imp. Ignacio Cumplido, 1835), CL-BNM, vol. 132.

16. Fowler, *Santa Anna of Mexico*, 301, 144; AGN, Gobernación, Casa Amarilla, Leg. 1039, exp. 4.

17. Parra, *Independencia y nacionalismo*, 99–100.

18. See, for example, the official program for the 1862 fiestas patrias, Archivo Histórico del Distrito Federal (henceforth cited as AHDF), Leg. 1068, exp. 52.

19. Arrangoiz, *México desde 1808*, 594.

20. Archer, "Death's Patriots," 95.

21. Duncan, "Political Legitimation," 59–60.

22. Knight, *The Mexican Revolution*, 1:15.

23. *Diccionario Porrúa*, 817.

24. This spelling of the family name was common in reference to this member of the family, especially in the United States, so I use it here to distinguish him from his grandfather.

25. Coerver, *Porfirian Interregnum*, 205, 230.

26. Coerver, *Porfirian Interregnum*, 282; Beezley and Maclachlan, *El Gran Pueblo*, 92; *New York Times*, 27 December 1883, 15 July 1884, 18 November 1884.

27. Archivo de la Secretaría de Relaciones Exteriores (henceforth cited as

SRE), Mexico City, I-197, 29 November 1884, with newspaper clippings from the *Evening Critic* (Washington) and *Baltimore American*, dated 28 November 1884.

28. "Dreaming of a Crown: Prince Yturbide Talks about Mexican Politics," *New York Times*, 30 August 1887.

29. Tapia Méndez, *El Diario de Ipandro Acaico*, 81.

30. Miguel Martínez to Agustín Yturbide, 18 December 1884, Archives of the Catholic University of America, Kearney-Iturbide Papers (henceforth cited as CUA-KI), box 2, folder 1.

31. See, for example, Yturbide, "Mexico under President Diaz," and his "Mexican Haciendas."

32. Tenorio, "1910 Mexico City," 185.

33. AGN, Gobernación, Festividades, 907-3-1, 24 November 1909.

34. See Niemeyer, "Anticlericalism in the Mexican Constitutional Convention."

35. Iturbide, "Don Agustín de Iturbide, Continued," 43–44.

36. Correspondence between the cousins may be found in the CUA-KI, boxes 2 and 3. For Eduardo de Iturbide's escape from Mexico, see Quirk, "Cómo se salvó Eduardo Iturbide," *Historia Mexicana* 6, no. 1 (July–September 1956): 39–58. A good example of the efforts of conservative Catholics to shape outcomes in Iturbide's favor is "Gibbons Stirs Speculation: New Leader for Mexico Thought by Some to Be Yturbide," *New York Times*, 15 March 1915. The Gibbons in the headline was the cardinal archbishop of Baltimore at the time.

37. A letter confirming these sentiments, addressed to Agustín Yturbide and dated 16 September 1921, may be found in CUA-KI, box 3, folder 2.

38. Lacey, "1921 Centennial," 213.

39. Lacey, "1921 Centennial," 226, n. 32.

40. Zárate Toscano, "Agustín de Iturbide," 23; Lacey, "1921 Centennial," 213–14; Gruening, *Mexico and Its Heritage*, 80.

41. Gruening, *Mexico and Its Heritage*, 80.

42. A recent attempt to "correct" some of the record is Morales Córdova, "Agustín I." Recent fictional treatments of Iturbide and his heirs include Beltrán, *La corte de los ilusos*, and Mayo, *Last Prince*.

43. Kelly, *Blood-Drenched Altars*; Parsons, *Mexican Martyrdom*.

44. Murray, *Catholic Church in Mexico*, 1:97–98.

45. McCullough-Friend, "Mexican Empress."

46. Zárate Toscano, "Las perviviencias de Iturbide," 120.

47. Quoted in Zárate Toscano, "Las perviviencias de Iturbide," 122.

48. Magner, *My Faces and Places*, 3:240–41.

Three. *Refrescos, Iluminaciones,* and *Te Deums*: Celebrating Pronunciamientos in Jalisco in 1823 and 1832

When, on 1 March 1823, Miguel Ignacio Castellano, the military commander of Tepic, Nueva Galicia, seconded the Plan of Jalisco drafted in the provincial capital of Guadalajara, he marched his officers straight to the municipal buildings, where the city council was in session, to arrange for three days of celebrations to mark the launching of his *plan de adhesión* (supporting pronunciamiento). He informed the governor and military commander of the state, Luis Quintanar:

> We agreed that the pronunciamiento should be declaimed following a parade of the troop and that when that was over there should be a Te Deum laudamus in the parish church . . . and it was decided that this night there will be street lighting throughout the town, tomorrow a thanksgiving mass and tonight and tomorrow night serenades with military music.[1]

Why did the *ayuntamientos* in Jalisco choose to celebrate pronunciamientos, which were essentially extra-constitutional, subversive acts, with civic and religious celebrations? Why did they spend funds on these public events and how did it suit their political purposes? This chapter addresses these issues by focusing on the celebration of the pronunciamientos that took place in the state of Jalisco in 1823 and 1832. I analyze the role that civic and religious fiestas played in legitimizing the pronunciamientos, informing the public of these newly legitimized historic events, making heroes of the military officers who launched them, and making the pronunciamientos a part of the lives of ordinary *tapatíos* (citizens of Jalisco).

The phenomenon of the pronunciamiento originated in Spain as a liberal form of effecting political change and challenging absolutism in what was quite evidently a context of contested authority following King Ferdinand VII's abolition of the 1812 liberal Cádiz Constitution when he returned to power in 1814. As has been argued in the first two volumes of Will Fowler's tetralogy on the subject, it became the political tool of choice of the Mexican political class in the early independence period.[2] As a result, the pronunciamiento played a significant role in the political and everyday life of Nueva Galicia/Jalisco between 1821 and 1852. Pronunciamientos, which have been referred to as revolts, are better understood as political movements in which petitions or plans were drafted and circulated by coalitions and networks of military and civilian actors who, with military backing and making use of threats of insubordination and violence, aimed to negotiate forcefully with the existing authorities when these were perceived to act arbitrarily or were seen to abandon the constitutional path. More often than not, the hope was that violence would not be resorted to, and that those in power would listen to the demands that were made in the given political plans.[3]

Pronunciamientos thus emerged in Mexico at a time of political crisis and uncertain legitimacy or, as Rodrigo Moreno Gutiérrez argues in chapter 1, a time when the origins of political sovereignty and legitimacy had been significantly called into question. The nascent governments and institutions of early independent

Mexico, together with the accepted political discourse and therefore the texts of the pronunciamientos themselves, were inspired by liberal constitutionalism. It was a time when the popular or national will paired with concepts of popular sovereignty started to be seen as the true source of legitimacy. However the power of, and people's loyalty to, a number of key colonial institutions and corporations—such as the church, provincial deputations, and ayuntamientos (with their new powers afforded by the 1812 Cádiz Constitution as representatives of popular sovereignty)—did not disappear overnight and were also powerful sources of political legitimacy.

Pronunciamientos, with their lists of grievances and political plans, were acts of insubordination but they were so commonly used in the public sphere that they became one of several means, alongside elections and the legislation proposed by nascent congresses and institutions, of promoting political ideologies, of defending and opposing constitutions and political systems, and of negotiating power. In Nueva Galicia and the state of Jalisco between 1821 and 1853, for example, pronunciamientos were used to lobby state and national governments into changing the law; to make proposals for new laws, constitutions, and political systems; to circulate pseudo-constitutional demands for new laws issued by the state authorities; to overthrow state and national governments; and to "elect" the members of those new governments.[4] Pronunciamientos in Jalisco were so closely intertwined with the legislative, representative, and civil activities of the state governments, church councils, and ayuntamientos that the line between extra-constitutional and constitutional acts, pronunciamiento and state decree, was not always clear.[5] This said, *pronunciados* (participants in pronunciamientos), who included most political actors of the day, needed to find ways to legitimize the pronunciamiento as a practice, given that it was essentially unlawful.[6] They did this by using discourses of representation of the people and soliciting the support of the ayuntamiento and the church. The town council, thanks to the 1812 Constitution of Cádiz (implemented in Mexico in 1813–14 and 1820–22), was seen as representative of the people and part of the new liberal legitimacy. The church was representative of the national religion, according to the Mexican constitutions of 1824, 1836, and 1843, but was also a powerful institution and corporation benefiting from the legitimacy that comes with time and tradition.

One way of publicly demonstrating the support of these institutions was through civic and religious fiestas. While pronunciamientos claimed to represent the will of the people, it is questionable and difficult to prove the extent to which ordinary Mexicans and tapatíos took an active part in the conspiratorial stages, signing, or launching of pronunciamientos. However, one way in which elite political actors could convey the appearance of popular support but also in which ordinary tapatíos were able to participate in the experience of the pronunciamiento was precisely through the celebration of them in civic fiestas and public events.

From independence and throughout the nineteenth century civic fiestas were used to legitimize the new regimes and institutions and to develop a sense of national identity based on the commemoration of the historic events of the newly independent nation.[7] Regional and national governments as well as different political factions used these fiestas to develop a civic calendar celebrating heroes and events that represented their ideas and helped propagate their contending ideologies.[8] These civic celebrations were "invented traditions" designed to establish and legitimize institutions or relations of authority and, in so doing, to institutionalize new political cultures such as the pronunciamiento.[9] The use of civic and religious fiestas for the celebration of pronunciamientos is particularly interesting. In the colonial period fiestas were designed to be demonstrations of power and wealth. In the early independence period they were used to create a calendar of historical events and to legitimize new institutions. Pronunciamientos at once challenged *and* served to install some of those new institutions that the fiestas served to legitimize. The pronunciamiento was part of a new political culture that was subversive and revolutionary and yet that aimed to be peaceful: a "happy revolution," as one *jalisciense* described the 1823 Casa Mata series of pronunciamientos.[10] As a revolutionary practice it evidently carried the threat of violence. However, civic and religious fiestas were used to institutionalize this new political culture so as to "sanitize," "derevolutionize," and "disempower" the subversive ideas that were contained in their original texts.

Some pronunciamientos, notably those supported or even instigated by regional and national authorities, were marked with civic and religious celebrations alongside the fiestas that were held to rejoice over battle victories, independence, and other events of the civic calendar. The 1821 Plan de Iguala, for example, the pronunciamiento that consummated Mexican independence (see chapters 1 and 2), was celebrated in towns and cities throughout the country, including Guadalajara. Such was the case, also, with two pronunciamientos that took place in Jalisco in 1823 and 1832. Both had the support of the state legislature and the municipal authorities of Guadalajara as well as that of other cantons in the state. In the case of the 1832 pronunciamiento this was actually instigated by the local authorities themselves. The following analysis of the civic and religious celebrations arranged by the ayuntamientos for these pronunciamientos shows how public events helped to legitimize particular pronunciamientos and the ideologies they supported. The celebrations also simultaneously legitimized the pronunciamiento as a political practice and the actions of new regional governments and institutions.

The Plan of Jalisco of 23 February 1823, which seconded the Acta de Casa Mata of 1 February, was one of the first pronunciamientos to be launched in Jalisco. The Acta de Casa Mata protested against Agustín de Iturbide's dissolution of Congress on 31 October 1822, but upheld the three guarantees of the Plan de Iguala that had brought about Mexico's independence: religion, independence, and union.[11] Iturbide, an ex-royalist officer and one of the signatories of the Plan de Iguala, had been crowned emperor following the pronunciamiento in the capital of 19 May 1822. Congress and the emperor could not agree on the division of powers, among other issues, and Iturbide dissolved Congress at the end of October.[12] The Acta de Casa Mata called for a new constituent congress, argued that sovereignty lay with the nation, and vowed that the army would make no attempt on the person of the emperor.[13] The provinces had seen in the proposed constituent congress an institution that could represent them, and the plan was seconded in most provinces, including Nueva Galicia. It led to the abdication of the emperor and established de facto federalism in Mexico.[14]

The Plan of Jalisco was launched from the garrison at Guadalajara and signed by officers on behalf of several regiments from Guadalajara and Colotlán.[15] It had the full support of the governor and military commander of the province, Luis Quintanar, who immediately issued proclamations addressed to the public and the soldiers applauding the heroism of the pronunciados, who he declared had "imitated the commendable virtues of the most worthy and distinguished heroes."[16]

The city council of Guadalajara also backed the pronunciados and the governor in their challenge to the emperor and the call for a new congress. They demonstrated their support by celebrating the actions of their pronunciados with three days of civic fiestas and religious ceremonies, including a mass, a *Te Deum* in the cathedral, a concert, and street lighting.[17] When Castellano's garrison in Tepic seconded the Plan of Jalisco on 1 March, the town council there hastily prepared a similar three-day celebration for the plan at the behest of the military commander who had made the organization of the processions, masses, and fanfares such a priority.[18] The fact that after launching his pronunciamiento, Castellano went immediately to the ayuntamiento to arrange the fiestas was an indication that he considered this type of official reception to be important. It was important because it gave the extra-constitutional act of the pronunciamiento official status. The civic fiestas gave the pronunciamientos in both the capital and the provincial city the endorsement of the ayuntamientos, the representatives of "the people" according to the constitution of Cádiz, the de facto constitution at the time.[19] The reception with a mass and a Te Deum also gave the pronunciamiento the sanction of the church and the Roman Catholic faith defended in the Plan of Casa Mata. The pronunciamientos thus had the triple sanction of "the people," the state, and the church.

Civic and religious rituals of this kind, in which the civil authorities entered the religious space and made solemn, pseudo-religious processions through the public space, did not start at independence. These rituals involving masses, processions, the proclamation of edicts, and street lighting—designed to demonstrate the "mutual recognition of civil and church authorities"—were similar to the vice-regal ceremonies of the colonial period.[20] Those ceremonies had displayed the spiritual, economic, and political power of the elites involved in them.[21] During the Mexican War of Independence (1810–21) similar celebrations commemorated the swearing of allegiance to Ferdinand VII and the claiming or reclaiming of cities by both insurgents and royalists. Tepic itself was the site of fiestas involving the civil and ecclesiastical authorities when it was taken by the forces of the insurgent leader José María Mercado.[22] Independence, consummated through the Plan de Iguala, was celebrated in Guadalajara in a similar way on 23 June 1821. The commander general and the *jefe político* (intendent) of Nueva Galicia, the ayuntamiento, corporations, and troops processed from the government palace toward decorated platforms in four of the city squares, to the accompaniment of the pealing of church bells, music, and a military salute. The mayor, Benito Domínguez, read the proclamation of independence, and they proceeded to the cathedral for a thanksgiving mass.[23] The authorities and the Junta Patriótica (patriotic committee) of Nueva Galicia, established on 22 September 1821, also organized fiestas in October 1821 for Ferdinand VII's birthday and in 1822 for the coronation of Iturbide as emperor.[24] The adaptation of these older traditions into the "invented traditions" of the post-independence period provided historical continuity to legitimize the new regimes and political practices.[25] The celebration of these early pronunciamientos in Jalisco as historic events gave these pseudo-constitutional acts a place in the historic tradition of the state and invested them with the trappings of institutional power.

For the political, religious, and mercantile elite who were the principle actors directly involved in pronunciamientos in Jalisco, the pronunciamiento was fast becoming an accepted political practice, albeit one that was considered a necessary evil. For these actors the celebration of a successful pronunciamiento put the seal on the particular occasion, and the repeated celebration of pronunciamientos over time legitimized the "institution" of the pronunciamiento as a political practice. However, the solemn ceremonies arranged by these political elites to celebrate pronunciamientos were above all aimed at legitimizing them in the eyes of ordinary tapatíos, while distracting people from the subversive ideas that could be found in their texts. The celebration of pronunciamientos would help to legitimize and "sanitize" — in the eyes of ordinary tapatíos or "the people" in whose name the pronunciamientos were launched — their subversive ideologies and the extra-constitutional demands of the state governments, regional authorities, and political actors who backed and launched the plans, as the following detailed arrangements for the fiestas and ceremonies for an 1832 pronunciamiento demonstrate.

This plan was launched in Guadalajara on 14 July 1832 and was led by Colonel José de la Cuesta of the Fourth Jalisco regiment and inspector of the civil militia. It was a plan de adhesión that supported the cycle of pronunciamientos initiated by Antonio López de Santa Anna's Plan of Veracruz of 2 January.[26] Santa Anna's federalist pronunciamiento unleashed a year-long civil war in which the pronunciados confronted President Anastasio Bustamante's government, which was perceived to be centralist for having dissolved a number of state congresses. The Jalisco state legislature conspired with that of Zacatecas, providing funds to Ignacio Inclán to launch the Plan of Lerma of 27 April 1832, in which he demanded the reestablishment of the constitutional order and the return of ousted President Manuel Gómez Pedraza, elected but overthrown before he could take up office in 1828.[27] Inclán's Plan of Lerma was followed by more than thirty-two federalist pronunciamientos throughout the republic, and its demands were repeated by Santa Anna's second Plan de Veracruz on 5 July.[28] On 13 July the state legislature of Jalisco issued decree 450, recognizing Pedraza as the only legitimate president. It was passed by the interim governor José Ignacio Herrera at a time of political crisis in the state caused by the conflict between the supporters of the moderate liberal governor José Ignacio Cañedo and the former governor, radical *yorkino* Juan Nepomuceno Cumplido.[29] The decree was seconded the following day by Cuesta's pronunciamiento.[30]

Like many pronunciamientos in Jalisco in the early independence period, this one involved the active participation of the state legislature. The garrison in Guadalajara and the civil militia were invited to pronounce to second the extra-constitutional state decree. Cañedo, who had returned to the governorship to deal with the unrest, opened the session of the state legislature of 14 July with the motion that "Pedro Anaya and the other officers of the garrison be invited to second the pronunciamiento of the state legislature recognizing the constitutional president Manuel Gómez Pedraza," which, after some debate, was approved.[31] Both the decree and the pronunciamiento were extra-constitutional but were afforded official recognition by the ayuntamiento of Guadalajara and the state government in the form of civic and religious ceremonies and the awarding of medals to the pronunciados. The fiestas served simultaneously to legitimize the pronunciamiento, the decree, and the ideology of the state government of Jalisco in contention with Bustamante's national government.

On the day that the pronunciamiento was launched the city council of Guadalajara was already making plans and selecting a committee to arrange the celebration of the decree and the reception of the *beneméritos pronunciados* (worthy *pronunciados*) with a *mesa de refresco* (a traditional drinks reception), street decorations, and street lighting.[32] The selection of a committee to ensure the smooth running of the events was a typical procedure in the preparation of civic fiestas.[33] For Independence Day celebrations, juntas patrióticas were elected by the ayuntamientos.[34] For the 1832 pronunciamiento, as with Castellano's 1823 plan, ostensibly spontaneous events, the celebrations were planned at short notice and the committees were made up of members of the ayuntamiento. The *regidor* (city councilor) José Castillo Negrete and "Citizen Castro" were delegated to draw up a budget.[35] The costs involved were to "purvey to the public some form of distraction to solemnify the recognition of the legitimate president Colonel [sic] Manuel Gómez Pedraza by the legislative assembly of the state."[36]

The concept of "solemnifying" an event was often expressed in documents related to the celebration of pronunciamientos. Castellano, the military commander of Tepic, had expressed a similar motive when, in the wake of his pronunciamiento, he took his troops to the meeting of the ayuntamiento "with the intention that together we determine how the proclamation of the aforementioned decree should be solemnized with the fitting order, decorum and splendor."[37] These ritualized celebrations were political acts. They were "public mirrors" meant to reflect images of power.[38] The municipal authorities, through arranging the celebrations, "officialized" the decree and the pronunciamiento by creating the trappings and performances of power. This solemnification meant that the decree and pronunciamiento appeared to be part of the constitutional political system. The spectator at such formal, ritualized displays—that is, *el pueblo* (the people) celebrating in the street—would have no reason to believe that the pronunciamiento was not constitutional. The reception of these extra-constitutional acts with the formal pomp and ritual of military parades, civic processions, and religious masses solemnized the plan and decree through the sanction of the church, the state, and the people, making the extralegal (or the pseudo-legal) legitimate.

The attention to detail with which the ayuntamiento of Guadalajara planned the mesa de refresco and the Te Deum to welcome the pronunciados of 14 July 1832 shows the importance that was afforded to the ritual reception of this pronunciamiento. The council minutes contain plans for highly ritualized procedures, processions, and pageantry that served to legitimize the pronunciamiento through the performance of power. All of the authorities, corporations, civil servants, and municipal employees would be invited to gather at five o'clock in the municipal assembly rooms. At the same time the third mayor, José María Díaz Arrango, councilor for schools Domingo Arrango, and Castro would go to the state palace to bring the members of the state government to the municipal buildings. Castillo, councilor for prisons and hospitals Dr. Pedro Tames, and Gregorio del Muro would accompany the commander and the officers. Once all were assembled they would process to the cathedral, where a Te Deum would be sung. As soon as they returned, councilor for police and hospitals Rafael Becerra, Tames, and Castro would each accompany an officer of the division to the *sala de refresco* (drinks reception room) to be received by the mayor, Jesús Camarena, second mayor Joaquín González, and fifth mayor Nicolás Echauri.[39]

It was common for spending on fiestas of this sort to exceed the projected budget, and the issue of overspending on the celebrations for the 1832 pronunciamiento and decree provides revealing insight into why the ayuntamiento regarded spending on the fiestas to be an important use of municipal funds.[40] In the wake of the pronunciamiento the Guadalajara City Council agreed how the fiestas would be paid for. The *mayordomo de propios* (superintendent of properties and finances) would make four hundred pesos available to "Citizen Rubio" and the councilor for public parks and street lighting, Nicolás de la Peña, to be spent on a mesa de refresco for the officers of the troops who had pronounced and on street lighting and decorations. A license would be requested from the mayordomo de propios to issue the money, and Echauri, Becerra, and Francisco Garibay would organize the lighting.[41] The celebrations clearly cost somewhat more than planned, however, as the issue reappeared in the town council minutes of 5 and 13 October.[42] The minutes of 5 October also contained a discussion of plans for the fortification of the city for protection from the ongoing civil conflict, albeit lower down the agenda than the vital issue of how to pay for the fiesta. The minutes mentioned that the *junta cantonal* (regional council) had not allowed the payment of 122 two pesos to cover the total cost of the refresco for the officers and agreed that Peña and Rubio should deal with it.[43] When the junta cantonal's objection to the use of funds for the fiestas in excess of four hundred pesos was raised once again on 13 October, the council minutes went some way to explaining why this expense was deemed necessary by the regidores of the Guadalajara ayuntamiento:

It was felt that although the expense appeared exorbitant to said junta, it had to be agreed that it was a necessary expense when one takes

Doyle

into account the fame the refresco enjoys among all those attending and its notorious abundance.[44]

It was agreed that permission would be asked for seventy-three pesos to be taken from the municipal coffers to cover the costs of the refresco, "and for the 175 pounds of coconut oil that was taken to get up the street lighting."[45]

In the midst of a civil conflict, the directives of the state government regarding the fortification of Guadalajara were put aside and the works suspended, yet funds were still found for the celebration of a pronunciamiento.[46] This suggests that the ayuntamiento had vital political reasons for spending money on the fiestas, which can be explained in part by the concept of a "ritual expense" or *derroche* (excess or squandering), as discussed by Octavio Paz:

> Wasting money and expending energy affirms the community's wealth in both. This luxury is a proof of health, a show of abundance and power. . . . The fiesta's function, then, is more utilitarian than we think, waste attracts or promotes wealth, and is an investment like any other. . . . What is sought is potency, life, health.[47]

The concept of abundance was expressed in the city council minutes and linked to the fame or celebrity of the refresco. This suggests that one of the purposes of the celebrations was to win the hearts and minds of the tapatíos. The fiestas were an exercise in propaganda and morale boosting at a time of political uncertainty; they were designed to develop a sense of community and patriotic identity.[48] In the context of civil conflict and the political crisis in Jalisco, the pronunciamiento would be associated in the minds of the people celebrating in the streets with opulence and times of plenty. *El pueblo* attending the fiestas, consciously or subconsciously, would associate that abundance with the call for the return of Gómez Pedraza. The rituals were not only "cognitively graspable" in that people were aware of what they were celebrating, in this case the state decree recalling Pedraza to the presidency, but also "emotionally livable" in that people danced, sang, and experienced the spectacle of the festivities.[49] These ceremonies were not only mirrors of power; they were also mirrors that reflected the self in the collectivity.[50] The experience of the fiesta propagated a sense of belonging, community, and identity that was vital in times of crisis and uncertainty.[51] The fiestas meant that the pronunciamientos were experienced as an everyday event and part of the cultural life of ordinary tapatíos. Ordinary people were involved not only in the celebration but also in the preparation of the fiestas. Artisans and members of the public would prepare the decorations and stages for the rituals, the refresco, and the food, and people would decorate their houses.[52]

The experience of the fiestas made the political impact of the pronunciamientos at once more powerful and less dangerous than the simple declamation of a political manifesto in a public place.[53] One of the purposes of the civic fiestas, like that of the communications media today, was to keep people informed of "the most pressing national issues of the day: . . . the evolution and resolution of social conflicts."[54] The celebration of a pronunciamiento was one of a range of media used to inform the public of the event. The plans were also printed in pamphlets and newspapers, which were posted in public places and read aloud by *voceadores* (town criers) in the streets of towns and cities. Civic fiestas as a means of informing the public about pronunciamientos were more powerful and less likely to cause political unrest than these other forms of communication. The political motivations of the creole elite on the city councils arranging these elaborate means of informing the people about pronunciamientos may have been to inspire in an indifferent populace a sense of regional or national identity, civic pride, and an interest in the political events of the day. Alternatively, the motivation may have been to provide some "distraction" from the subversive ideas of the pronunciamiento, allowing "the people" to experience the event through cheering the heroic soldiers, watching the processions, and enjoying a sense of community rather than taking up arms and taking an active part in the pronunciamiento. Some of the people attending the fiestas may have been indifferent to the nature of the event they were celebrating, intending simply to enjoy the spectacle and take the rare opportunity of seeing the elites who represented them. However, while historians have no data regarding the opinions of ordinary people in Jalisco at the time, it should not be assumed that the majority of those attending the celebrations were oblivious to the ideas expressed in the pronunciamientos and took no interest in the often violent political events that affected their everyday lives. The elites on the ayuntamiento organizing these fiestas were keen to control the "dangerous" classes and were aware of the potentially explosive nature of putting the subversive ideas in pronunciamientos in the hands of "the people."

A report in the *Gaceta del Gobierno de Guadalajara* regarding the celebrations of the 1823 pronunciamiento suggests that the intention of the governing elite was to inform the public of the heroic acts of the pronunciados but not to "empower" them with the ideas in the plan, belying the will to contain the masses while simultaneously creating a display of popular support for the pronunciamiento. The report stated that the City of Guadalajara had celebrated the historic event of the pronunciamiento of 27 February 1823 with "manifest enthusiasm" and that "the citizens and all the people had carried themselves with their customary conviviality without neglecting their duties of submission to calm and tranquility."[55] The presence of the people in the street created the appearance of popular support for the pronunciamiento, affording it legitimacy through evidence of the direct support of the people beyond their representation by the ayuntamiento. Pronunciamientos often claimed to represent the "good of the nation," the "popular will," or in the case of the 1823 pronunciamiento, "national independence" and the "opinion of the provinces."[56] This pronunciamiento, like most that took place in Jalisco in the early independence period, was led by the creole political and military elite, who identified themselves as the best placed representatives of the *opinión de la provincia*. They represented "the people," who were expected to be submissive and quiet in the celebration of the achievements of their representatives. The celebration of pronunciamientos with civic fiestas helped create a passive regional and patriotic identity.

The promotion of military heroes through the celebration of pronunciamientos also contributed to the creation of a passive patriotic identity. The council minutes of 19 July 1832 recorded the intentions of the ayuntamiento in investing in the celebration of the pronunciamiento: "In line with the patriotic sentiments that abound in this corporation it seems most fair and appropriate that it display its gratitude by presenting an offering to the worthy soldiers."[57] The fiestas and the recognition of the pronunciados as *beneméritos de la patria* (worthy citizens of the nation) demonstrated to the wider public that the pronunciados (and in this case also the state legislature) had acted in favor of "the good of the nation," thus legitimizing the pronunciamiento and the decree. The formal mesa de refresco and the studied ritual by which the worthy pronunciados were escorted through the streets of Guadalajara by the municipal officials was an elaborate display for the public of state and church recognition of the pronunciados as heroes. The state congress also agreed to award medals to the pronunciados.[58] Through the celebration of military heroes and their deeds, the creole élite hoped to create and institutionalize symbols of patriotism. They perhaps thought individual leaders and heroes had more tangible resonance with the people than did the abstract ideas contained in the pronunciamientos. A more likely scenario is that the celebration of the glorious attributes of the heroic soldiers was intended to detract from the dangerous, subversive ideas they represented. The civic fiestas aimed to inform the public of the deeds of great men and events rather than the subversive ideas that might incite them to rebel. The joyous, passive celebration of these pronunciamientos was a controlled way of involving "el pueblo" in this pseudolegal form of politicking and preferable to encouraging their active participation.

It has been suggested that fiestas celebrating pronunciamientos in the provinces were a symptom of boredom.[59] In the words of Octavio Paz, for "The solitary Mexican . . . any excuse is fine to interrupt the passing of time and celebrate great men and events with festivals."[60] However, the celebration of great pronunciados and historic pronunciamientos in Jalisco seen here shows that for the councilmen who organized them, civic and religious fiestas had much more utilitarian political aims than simply passing the time and alleviating the monotony of life in the provinces. The elite on the ayuntamientos of Jalisco in 1823 and 1832 used these fiestas to celebrate the pronunciamientos they supported in order to promote their ideology and that of the state governments in contention with the national governments of the day. They introduced these subversive acts into the civic calendar of historic events, the celebration of which helped develop a sense of regional and national identity. The celebrations informed the public of the patriotic deeds of the pronunciados while distracting them from the subversive ideas of the pronunciamiento and gave the pronunciamientos the official sanction of the ayuntamientos and the church as representatives of the people and the holy Catholic faith. The presence of "el pueblo" at the celebrations gave the pronunciamientos the direct endorsement of the people. The adapted use of these traditional civic and religious ceremonies with their solemn ritual and pomp invested the pronunciamientos with historic legitimacy and the trappings of officialdom and power. These fiestas thus earned pronunciamientos a place in the political and cultural life of the state of Jalisco and its citizens. Ordinary tapatíos experienced and celebrated these pronunciamientos alongside other events on the civic calendar as part of everyday life, probably oblivious to the fact that they were outside the law. The public celebration of specific pronunciamientos helped to establish the phenomenon of the pronunciamiento as a parallel institution that had the consent of the people and was perceived to be part of the constitutional order. Civic fiestas, a classic tool of Mexican governments at a national and regional level to promote patriotism and regional and national identity, were used by the city councils in Jalisco to celebrate pronunciamientos, extra-constitutional institutions, and to legitimize them in much the same way that they were used to legitimize the nascent regional and national institutions of the early republic.

Doyle

Notes

1. Biblioteca Pública del Estado de Jalisco (henceforth cited as BPEJ), Miguel Ignacio Castellano, comandante de las armas de la ciudad de Tepic, to Luis Quintanar, Tepic, Nueva Galicia, 3 March 1823, in *Gaceta Extraordinaria del Gobierno de Guadalajara*, Guadalajara 7 March 1823, microficha 128 (my translation).

2. See Fowler (ed.), *Forceful Negotiations*, and *Malcontents, Rebels, and Pronunciados*.

3. For a complete discussion of the nature and origins of the Mexican pronunciamiento see the collection of writings in Fowler (ed.), *Forceful Negotiations*. For a definition of the pronunciamiento as a military revolt see *Diccionario de historia de España* in Zoraida Vázquez, "Political Plans and Collaboration," and Carr, *Spain 1808–1939*, 124.

4. The first pronunciamientos used to lobby for a change in the law and to propose new laws were those backing anti-Spanish decrees and outlines of laws of exile for Spaniards; see, for example, Plan de Descoyotar, 7 August 1837. This pronunciamiento text and all those mentioned in this note, unless otherwise stated, can be found in the Jalisco section of the database "The Pronunciamiento in Nineteenth Century Mexico" of the University of St. Andrews and the Arts and Humanities Research Council, http://arts.st-andrews.ac.uk/pronunciamientos/regions.php).

The Acta de Jalisco launched in Guadalajara on 24 February 1823, which seconded the Acta de Casa Mata (Veracruz, 1 February 1823), was seen as a source of legitimacy for the provincial deputation to establish itself as the highest authority in the province and call for a federal system of government in Mexico. For the texts of these pronunciamientos see the St. Andrews database. For the decrees and *manifiestos* calling for a federal system issued by the *ayuntamiento* of Guadalajara and the Provincial Deputation, see Muría, *El federalismo en Jalisco (1823)*, 29–49. The Pronunciamiento de la Guarnición de Jalisco of 20 May 1846 called for a return to republican government and the reinstatement of the 1824 federalist constitution. The Acta y Proclama de la Guarnición de Jalisco of 1 November 1844 backed and circulated the iniciativa de la asamblea departamental de Jalisco of 30 October 1844, which was a proposal for a new law that would make the president accountable to congress and cede some concessions to the regions. The text of the pronunciamiento purported to be constitutional as the constitution of the time, the Bases Orgánicas, had a provision by which state governments could propose laws. The Blancarte series of pronunciamientos, which have been analyzed in detail in Doyle, "The Curious

Manner," called for renewal of and succeeded in overthrowing both the state and national governments, but the first pronunciamiento in the state to call openly for the renewal of both the state government and the ayuntamiento of Guadalajara was the Pronunciamiento de los barrios principales y suburbios de Guadalajara of 12 June 1834. This pronunciamiento led to the creation of a junta de notables, who established a system by which they could legitimately elect the new state and municipal authorities. For the full text of the plan describing the electoral procedures, the "Acta celebrada por la junta que se instaló en ésta capital, a consecuencia del pronunciamiento de la misma por el plan de Cuernavaca, para la elección de Gobernador y Vice-gobernador del Estado, y renovación del Ayuntamiento de Guadalajara," see Pérez Verdía, *Historia Particular*, 274–76.

5. For a full discussion of the legitimacy, uses, and experience of pronunciamientos in Jalisco see Doyle, "The Pronunciamiento in Nineteenth-Century Mexico," chapters 3, 4, and 5.

6. I am using Seymour Martin Lipset's concept whereby political legitimacy is related to "the capacity of the system to engender and maintain the belief that political institutions are the most appropriate and proper ones for the society." Lipset, *Political Man*, 64.

7. Zárate Toscano, "Las conmemoraciones septembrinas." For a case study see Duncan "Embracing a Suitable Past."

8. Zárate Toscano, "Las conmemoraciones septembrinas," 130–32, and Beezley and Lorey, "Introduction," ix–xviii. See also Beezley et al., *Rituals of Rule*.

9. Eric Hobsbawm defines an invented tradition as "a set of practices normally governed by overtly or tacitly accepted rules and of a ritual symbolic nature which seek to inculcate certain values and norms of behavior by repetition which automatically implies continuity with the past," occurring when "a rapid transformation of society weakens or destroys the social patterns for which 'old' traditions had been designed," and argues they are highly relevant to nation building. Hobsbawm, "Introduction: Inventing Traditions," 1–15.

10. Open letter to Agustín Iturbide signed by Luis Quintanar, Political Chief of New Galicia, and deputies Antonio Gutiérrez y Ulloa, Juan Cayetano Portugal, José Casal y Blanco, José de Jesús Huerta, Urbano Sanromán, and Domingo González Maxemín y Pedro Veléz, Guadalajara, 12 May 1823, reprinted in *Iris de Jalisco*, 9 June 1823.

11. Acta de Casa Mata, Casa Mata, Veracruz, 1 February 1823, http://arts.st-andrews.ac.uk/pronunciamientos/database/index.php?f=y&id=747&m=2&y=1823,

and Plan de Iguala, Iguala, The South (Guerrero), 24 February 1821, http://arts.st-andrews.ac.uk/pronunciamientos/database/index.php?f =y&id=740&m=2&y=1821, both accessed 10 August 2010.

12. Anna, *Forging Mexico*, 95.

13. Acta de Casa Mata, Casa Mata, Veracruz, 1 February 1823.

14. Benson, *Provincial Deputation*, 78–81.

15. Acta de Jalisco, Guadalajara, Jalisco, 26 February 1823, http://arts.st-an drews.ac.uk/pronunciamientos/database/index.php?f=y&id=748&m=2&y=1823, accessed 10 August 2010.

16. BPEJ, "El capitán general de la provincia de Guadalajara a sus conciudadanos" and "El capitán de Nueva Galicia a las tropas de esta Guarnición," *Gaceta del Gobierno de Guadalajara*, 5 March 1823, microficha 128; Archivo Municipal de Guadalajara (henceforth cited as AMG), "Contestación al bando/pronunciamiento de Luis Quintanar," Impreso 29.

17. AMG, Acta de Cabildo de Guadalajara, 27 February 1823; BPEJ, *Gaceta del Gobierno de Guadalajara*, 5 March 182, microficha 128.

18. BPEJ, Castellano to Quintanar, 3 March 1823 (see note 1).

19. Constitución de Cádiz de 1812, Título VI, Capítulo I: "De los ayuntamientos," http://www.cervantesvirtual.com/servlet/SirveObras/02438387547132507754491/index.htm, accessed 10 August 2010.

20. Cañedo Gamboa, "First Independence Celebrations."

21. Zárate Toscano, "Las conmemoraciones septembrinas," 132.

22. Comments of Rodrigo Moreno at the conference "The Damned and the Venerated: The Memory, Commemoration and Representation of the Nineteenth-Century Mexican *Pronunciamiento*," University of St. Andrews, 12 June 2010.

23. Acta de la Diputación Provincial, 14 June 1821, in Pérez Verdía, *Historia particular*, 171–72.

24. Pérez Verdía, *Historia particular*, 192–93.

25. Hobsbawm, "Introduction: Inventing Traditions," 7–8.

26. Acta de Veracruz sobre la remoción del ministerio, Veracruz, 2 January 1832, http://arts.st-andrews.ac.uk/pronunciamientos/database/?f=y&id=988 &m=1&y=1832, accessed 10 August 2010.

27. Plan de Lerma, Lerma, Estado de México, 27 April 1832, http://arts.st-an drews.ac.uk/pronunciamientos/database/index.php?f=y&id=816&m=4&y=1832, accessed 10 August 2010.

28. Acta de la guarnición de Veracruz y de la fortaleza de Ulúa, Veracruz, 5

July 1832, http://arts.st-andrews.ac.uk/pronunciamientos/database/?f=y&id =824&m=7&y=1832, accessed 10 August 2010.

29. Olveda Legaspi, *La política de Jalisco*, 142–44.

30. Pérez Verdía, *Historia particular*, 265; Olveda Legaspi, *La política de Jalisco*, 142–51.

31. Archivo del Congreso del Estado de Jalisco, Sesión del día 14 de Julio de 1832, Actas del Congreso del Estado de Jalisco, Libro 7.

32. AMG, Sesión extraordinario del día diez y nueve de Julio de 1832, Acta de Cabildo, 19 July 1832, F26-267.

33. Zárate Toscano, "Las conmemoraciones septembrinas," 149–50.

34. See Costeloe, "16 de septiembre de 1825," and Salazar Mendoza, *La Junta Patriótica*.

35. In the minutes the Cabildo de Guadalajara did not give the first names of those attending but referred to them as "citizen Garibay," etc. All the people named in this chapter as organizers of the celebrations were citizens of Guadalajara who attended the city council meetings, and some are indicated by surname only. José Castillo Negrete was the *regidor* (city councilor) responsible for schools, public spaces, and the civil militia. The full names and positions of the city councilors were found in López, *Guadalajara y sus mandatarios*.

36. AMG, Sesión ordinaria del día 14 de Julio de 1832, Actas de cabildo, Guadalajara, 14 July 1832, Leg. 163 A-4-832 GDL/ 163 (my translation).

37. BPEJ, Castellano to Quintanar, 3 March 1823 (see note 1).

38. Muir, "Images of Power."

39. AMG, Sesión extraordinario del día diez y nueve de Julio de 1832, Acta de Cabildo, 19 July 1832, F26-267 (my translation).

40. Zárate Toscano, "Las conmemoraciones septembrinas," 30.

41. AMG, Sesión extraordinario, 19 July 1832.

42. The municipal archives in Guadalajara contained no records of council meetings between 11 September and 5 October 1832.

43. AMG, Sesión ordinaria del día cinco de octubre de mil ochocientos treinta y dos, Acta de Cabildo, Guadalajara, 5 October 1832, F 59 Año 1823, Leg. 163 A-4-832 GDL/ 163.

44. AMG, Sesión ordinaria del día trece de octubre de mil ochocientos treinta y dos, Acta de Cabildo, Guadalajara, 13 October 1832, F 59 Año 1823 Leg. 163 A-4-832 GDL/ 163.

45. AMG, Sesión ordinaria, 13 October 1832.

46. AMG, Sesión ordinaria, 13 October 1832.

Doyle

47. Paz, *El laberinto de la soledad*, 75, and *Labyrinth of Solitude*, 50.

48. Jarman, *Material Conflicts*, 74–75, 79.

49. Handelman, *Models and Mirrors*, 16.

50. Handelman, *Models and Mirrors*, 41–42.

51. Fowler, "Fiestas santanistas."

52. Zárate Toscano, "San Ángel."

53. Jarman, *Material Conflicts*, 71.

54. Beezley and Lorey, "Introduction: The Functions of Patriotic Ceremony," xi.

55. BPEJ, *Gaceta del Gobierno de Guadalajara*, 5 March 1823, microficha 128 (my translation).

56. Acta de Jalisco, Guadalajara, Jalisco, 26 February 1823, http://arts.st
-andrews.ac.uk/pronunciamientos/database/index.php?f=r&id=748&rid=13
&m=02&y=1823, accessed 10 August 2010.

57. AMG, Sesión extraordinaria 19 July 1832.

58. Archivo del Congreso del Estado de Jalisco, Sesión del día 21 de julio de 1832, and Sesión del día 23 de julio de 1832, Actas del Congreso del Estado de Jalisco, Libro 7.

59. Staples, "The Clergy and How It Responded to Calls for Rebellion before the Mid-Nineteenth Century," paper given at the conference "Politics, Conflict and Insurrection: The Experience and Development of the Pronunciamiento in Nineteenth-Century Mexico," University of St. Andrews, 21 June 2009.

60. Paz, *El laberinto de la soledad*, 72 (my translation).

KERRY MCDONALD

Four. The Political Life of Executed Pronunciados:
*The Representation and Memory of José Márquez
and Joaquín Gárate's 1830 Pronunciamiento of
San Luis*

> To commemorate the dead is part of human culture. To commemo-
> rate the fallen, those violently killed who died in battle, in civil war
> or war is part of political culture.
>
> —REINHART KOSELLECK and MICHAEL JEISMANN

A s was the norm for the majority of successful *pronunciamientos* in San Luis Potosí, they ended in celebratory
acts which included *Te Deums*, ceremonial lighting of the
streets, and *repiques*, the pealing of church bells. Indeed it is the
political importance of post-pronunciamiento fiestas and celebrations that is the focus of several chapters in this volume.[1] The other outcome of the pronunciamiento practice, and the focus of this
chapter, was failure. In that case the general trend was the peaceful yet forceful negotiation and pacification of the *pronunciados*.
However, in San Luis Potosí on 17 November 1830 the pronunciamiento deviated somewhat from the norm, ending in two executions, around one hundred imprisonments, and at least one
self-imposed exile. Despite the pronunciamiento's failure, it nevertheless went on to provide a celebratory act of sorts. And it is from
the fatal outcome of this particular pronunciamiento that I draw
my line of inquiry, specifically the political lives of the two executed pronunciados or, more bluntly, the dead bodies of Colonel

José María Márquez and Lieutenant Colonel (and former deputy) José Joaquín Gárate.

Dead bodies, as several scholars have suggested, are potentially loaded sites of political profit and thus are especially useful and effective symbols for revising the past.[2] In the modern age, the Christian meaning of death subsided, making way for meaning to be established in purely social and political terms.[3] In this vein, like so many dead bodies, they can become more virulently politically charged than are the living, being used and manipulated in a variety of ways, including their use as effective political symbols, whereby they are called into the service of a given polity.

Given that crises in political authority often led to the seizure of politicized corpses as symbolic capital, it is important to bear in mind that postcolonial, independent Mexico was going through a tumultuous period of marked transformation, reconfiguration, and change, of which the practice of the pronunciamiento was a manifestation.[4] The political profit gained from the commemoration of corpses also lent itself to the process of establishing political legitimacy during these periods of upheaval.

Using the theoretical framework of dead body politics, in the chapter I explore first how the bodies, as a site of political profit, were used by their contemporaries, and second to what extent this treatment, together with their participation in the pronunciamiento, influenced their reception within the traditional and current historiography. By focusing on the memory and representation of the political dead in the form of executed local *pronunciados*, I also enquire as to why the actors who partook most heavily in this practice have almost all been forgotten, or perhaps intentionally sidestepped, by the regional historiography, and draw conclusions about the often ambivalent nature of the historical selection process of these actors.

How the Dead Bodies Came to Be: The Historical Context

In the first decade of Independence Colonel José María Márquez was the most notorious and active pronunciado of San Luis Potosí. Although it is far from certain whether he instigated every pronunciamiento, his military participation is clear. His consistent political goal in partaking in the pronunciamiento was federalism, albeit of a more progressive strand, but the consistent outcome was failure. Not one of his original pronunciamientos was successful, yet Márquez never found himself exiled (for long) from the state, nor severely punished, but rather in ever more favorable situations, thanks to the local government's willingness to negotiate with and placate him.

The explanation for the executions can be found in the historical context in which they took place, reflecting the attitudes and political turmoil of the late 1820s and early 1830s. It was a time of unparalleled fright in the history of the nascent independent country as the threat of social dissolution, experienced in the populist War of Independence, was echoed in the Acordada rebellion and the Parián riot of 1828, which brought Mexico's first mestizo and radical president to power, Vicente Guerrero. This national swing also ensured that at the local level, San Luis Potosí maintained its radical federalist governor, Vicente Romero, who had achieved his position through an initiative to impeach the first constitutionally elected governor. Finally, the Plan of Jalapa (4 December 1829) led by General Anastasio Bustamante put an end to this populist form of government and excessive liberalism, purging the states of their civic and military authorities and restoring the country to "constitutional law and order" under a *hombres de bien* form of government. As a result, the *jalapistas* were not short of opponents. The main national opposition movement was led by Guerrero in the War of the South (1830–31) and had spread throughout the country.[5] In San Luis the local movement was led, but perhaps not instigated, by Márquez.

On 17 November 1830 at 7:00 a.m, Márquez, the former inspector of the state militia, and Gárate, former lieutenant colonel of the first battalion of national militia of San Luis Potosí, led the former second battalion of the local militia in arms against the capital's authorities. Although a plan has not yet been found, the state government and neighboring states were certain it was a pronunciamiento against the general government of Anastasio Bustamante and in favor of Guerrero, suggesting the existence of a written document. Nevertheless, the pronunciados' own interpretation of the pronunciamiento was not to be heard, as the former royalist and state military commander, General Zenón Fernández, ended the pronunciamiento in a matter of hours. Said to have surrendered without a shot being fired, the troops were transferred to the state capital with the exception of their leaders, Márquez and Gárate, who were executed.[6] According to one account the execution squad did not wait for the order to shoot, and Márquez died with the first bullet, but the other five soldiers continued to fire upon the body. One of the bullets hit a dog that always accompanied Márquez and had rushed toward its master when it saw him fall. Gárate was not killed by the first shot but was finally given the coup de grace.[7] They were among the first in a series of leading pronunciados to be executed. By all accounts, it was an exceptional outcome to what, until then, had been a practice confined to a nascent form of legitimate political petitioning albeit it with the unlawful threat of force. While not wanting to underplay the threat of violence inherent in the pronunciamiento, I should note that research has suggested bloodshed was never the intention, and in this respect the treatment of these pronunciados was exceptional.[8]

Treatment by Their Contemporaries

As resources for creating meaning and legitimacy in moments of political contention, the executed pronunciados were invaluable—more so than the celebratory acts of a successful pronunciamiento. They could even be invoked in politically oppositional causes, in this case both conservative and radical. As Katherine Verdery has argued, "remains are concrete, yet protean. . . .They can be evaluated from many different angles and assigned perhaps contradictory virtues, vices, and intentions. While alive, these bodies produced complex behaviors subject to much debate that produces further ambiguity. [In short,] it is easier to rewrite history with dead people."[9] And each side went about doing just that. The more conservative federalists who carried out the execution used the executed pronunciados as a tangible warning (1) about joining a subversive pronunciamiento act, and (2) of the potential anarchy that could be unleashed should they not act decisively to rein in the radical faction. For radical federalists, on the other hand, the executed served as martyrs of the federalist and liberal cause. Reflected in this polarized political treatment by their contemporaries were the localized shifts in politics.[10] As concisely summed up by Lyman L. Johnson, "disputes over bodies are disputes about power, power over the past and power in the present."[11] As such, their legacies were reassessed by the latter political group in order to rewrite the past events, legitimize the present, and create a future memory in accordance with current local political thought.

The executions themselves were carried out by the party of order (supporters of Anastasio Bustamante and the hombres de bien); they were declared a necessary spectacle, and the ashes promptly swept under the proverbial carpet. The cremation appeared to be an attempt to eliminate the bodies' materiality or concreteness, which would have been critical to their symbolic efficacy.[12] Without the bodies on display, the governing authorities were congratulated on their quick resolution, and the soldiers of the capital's garrison were thanked for their act of pacification with a financial reward from the city's merchants in the form of a donation.[13] Thus the capital's interpretations and justification of events were promptly published on behalf of the state and the country in the national newspaper, *El Sol*. These so-called hombres de bien were the first to express their views openly on the pronunciamiento and, to a great extent, have influenced if not dictated the pronunciados' treatment in popular memory with views that continued to taint the traditional historiography.[14] The state governor, Manuel Sánchez, claimed there was no support for the pronunciados, and indeed that there existed a general loathing and hatred of them, the reason for which the capital saw in less than ten hours the birth, progression, and conclusion of a revolution without the usual disruption. He concluded that the pronunciados had "only served to prove the sentiments of their fellow residents who, faced with the horror of a pronunciamiento which they detested, experienced a victory received with acclaim."[15] Moreover, the gravity of the "monstrous anarchy" that could have been unleashed by the pronunciados was hammered home to the residents of San Luis Potosí in an address by the governor.[16]

> You do not have to fear any more as the storm has dissipated, because this truly paternal government protects your interests. Your wives will not be snatched from your side to satisfy the passions of some

despicable men, of whom the worst can only be expected. Neither must your wives have to mourn their widowhood, because the parricidal sword has sacrificed their husbands; nor do their young sons and daughters have to be subjected to a miserable orphanhood. Give thanks to Providence that protects all of us, and that the horrors of anarchy in which a few rebels tried to plunge us have vanished in a moment. Remain as you have done until now, loyal observers of the law and gathered in spirit around your government.[17]

In this address, the caliber of the pronunciados and their followers was that of immoral barbarians and was juxtaposed with the paternal and law-abiding state authorities. Their suggestion of the potential outcome of events led by the pronunciados had the state authority not stepped in further legitimized their authority as the keyholders of law and order. The later justification for the executions similarly tried to forge legitimizing of official actions and policies. The executed themselves were merely subjected to a piece of legislation to which they, as former civil servants and citizens, had agreed. Article one of Decree 64 of 10 December 1827, on public security measures, stated: "Every person of any class who directly conspires in the state to disrupt the public tranquility will be punished with the death penalty."[18] This final vilification of the executed as mere criminals in clear breach of state law was an attempt to bring any notion of heroism crashing to the ground.

However, one man's villain is another man's hero, and the fortunes of the executed pronunciados took a turn after the 1832 Civil War (discussed in the previous chapter). Ignited by the pronunciamiento series of Veracruz, and realigned by those of Zacatecas and Jalisco, this upheaval finally made Bustamante step down. After Manuel Gómez Pedraza's temporary installation to complete the term (cut short by Vicente Guerrero's anti-constitutional rise to the presidency), Antonio López de Santa Anna began his presidency with the interim leadership of Valentín Gómez Farías and his radical congress in April 1833. At a local level, Vicente Romero returned to state governorship in San Luis Potosí in the aftermath of the bloody battle of El Gallinero (18 September 1832). With this new political shift came a political reevaluation of the deceased in the form of new rhetoric and state legislation, the first aim of which was to restore the heroic status of those involved in the struggle for liberty.

By placing the names of Márquez and Gárate together with those of the other national heroes who died in a similar fashion, Romero's state administration was able to manipulate their death to serve his own cause.[19] Márquez and Gárate were firmly included among "the illustrious victims" Vicente Guerrero, Francisco Victoria, Juan Nepomuceno Rosains, and the liberals of Morelia who were claimed to have defended "the cause of liberty with their weapons in their hands."[20] Márquez, a former royalist, an inspector of the state militia, and ranked only as colonel, was essentially given the same standing as General Guerrero, the insurgent hero and former president. Moreover, Márquez was imbued with the same traditional Latin American heroic qualities of Guerrero, such as being portrayed as a problem solver in times of difficulty and holding liberal, progressive ideas.[21]

Lorenzo de Zavala's interpretation of Márquez's convictions was similarly indicative of the moral high ground on which he was placed during this period: "Márquez disapproved of the way in which his friend [Bustamante] seized power and even more so of having associated himself with people who had not provided the country with any guarantee of their love of independence or liberty, and of having converted himself into an instrument of a tyranny thus far unseen in the country under the national government."[22] From his interpretation we are led to believe that Márquez died in his attempt to correct Bustamante's unconstitutional seizure of power and to prevent a tyrannical government; in short, he died with the interest of the nation at heart. Not only did this interpretation call into play the intangible forms of political profit that could be extracted, the "something more," here in the form of morality, but it also afforded his politics further legitimacy.[23]

This representation of the memory of Márquez in particular as a hero is further facilitated when we look at the conclusions drawn by several scholars on how to become a Latin American hero.[24] At the top of the list was the fact that defeat is often more memorable than triumph, partially explaining why one of the most valuable attributes of a hero is a dramatic death, and preferably one that can be represented as a martyrdom for the benefit of a national community.[25] Similarly, as William Sater has observed, self-sacrifice is a virtue that officials in the public sector rarely display, and hence dying in a way that reflects sacrifice for a larger cause helps make clear the contrast between oneself and the state (or the political status quo).[26] Furthermore, it was observed that many of them died violently in ways that evoked concepts of tragedy, self-sacrifice, and betrayal, having fought so steadfastly for the good of the many against powerful elites. José Márquez certainly ticked all these boxes, if we are to believe the Zavala line of interpretation. Márquez was allegedly betrayed by his friend and the state military commander, Zenón Fernández. Fernández was rumored to have pushed Márquez for information and was suspicious of his secret meetings and aware of his plan six days before the pronunciamiento was launched. He was also rumored to have promised Márquez to come out in support of the pronunciamiento in favor of Guerrero.[27]

Alongside the development of the hero cult and to back up the rhetoric, new legislation was rushed through upon Romero's return to the governorship, understanding that unlike notions such as "liberty," a corpse could be moved around, displayed, and strategically located in specific places. Thus official commemorative acts were carried out in the state under Decree number 5 of the state legislature, 31 January 1833:

> Art 1° The government decrees that the esteemed ashes of the virtuous citizens, General José Márquez and Lieutenant Colonel Joaquín Gárate, are transferred to the parish church of the city and buried in a preferential location in a covered tomb with the respective marble gravestone engraved with an inscription of gold letters analogous to their virtues and the circumstances of their death.
>
> 2° This funereal function will be carried out with utmost solemnity and magnificence.
>
> 3° The government will reach an agreement with the ecclesiastic and military authorities with the end of resolving any difficulty and to ensure that everyone cooperates with the greatest effort to the complete magnificence of that act.
>
> 4° In the site where such a horrific sacrifice was made a monument will be erected that commemorates for posterity the gratitude and just appreciation of the *potosinenses*.
>
> 5° Their portraits will be hung as soon as possible in the chamber of the honorable congress with the inscription on each: sacrificed for the liberty of the country on 17 November 1830.
>
> 6° The government is authorized to use state funds to cover as many costs as necessary resulting from the accomplishment of this decree.[28]

This decree reflects one scholarly observation that the death of a soldier not only serves a political purpose, but its remembrance is also put to political service.[29] Part of their remembrance constituted the first lavish civic reburial of San Luis Potosí's first federalist martyrs. It was a poignant affair for many of the inhabitants and, more cynically, one that served as a vehicle for promoting political legitimacy and state formation through the public commemoration of the cult of heroes, not to mention the purported hero who buried them, namely Vicente Romero.[30] With this decree, the politically charged state burial that Colonel Márquez and Lieutenant Colonel Gárate had been denied by the previous state government was spectacularly overridden. The ashes took the place of bones as important political symbols able to transcend time and were to be returned to their material form through their transferral and reburial in a special place within the city's parish church, in a covered tomb with a marble tombstone.

This grand repositioning of their ashes and restoration of their honor was a clear marker of the change in social visibilities and values, which signaled a transition in the political landscape.[31] Reburial ceremonies, as has been widely acknowledged, are part of the body of public rituals that are of utmost importance to the governing authority in symbolizing and recreating their hegemony. This ceremony served both political and didactic ends: used to forge legitimacy for his second state leadership, it was also a visual and aural display for the citizens, a mirror on the society's hierarchy. Furthermore, the elites were able to inform and establish the moral values on which their authority rested through such ceremony. These demonstrative acts also served to shape interpretations of the society's past, here to emphasize the tyranny of Bustamante's administration; and to mask social divisions by seeming to unite disparate groups in shared ritual, to which article three of the decree alludes.[32] It was after all, Romero's report on the executions that leveled blame not only at the national administration but at several local clergymen and army officials. By decreeing the involvement of all sectors of authority in this ritual, Romero would have hoped to forge a display of unity and popularity.

Despite not having any written manifesto of the pronunciados' intentions or ideology for this particular pronunciamiento, Romero's own take on their virtues and events, to be inscribed on the tombstone, provided an opportunity to present the official interpretation of such historical events to the general public. In sum, through the manipulation of their past political life and death, Romero was able to provide himself and his state administration with a promotional political platform from which to add legitimacy to his faction.

Not content with a reburial ceremony of solemnity and magnificence, the state congress also decreed the erection of a monument and the inscribed portraits of the pronunciados (articles four and five) to be hung in the salon of the state congress — perhaps to serve as a symbol of unity in this often divided entity. The memorial to Márquez and Gárate commemorated violent death and thus provided a means of identification for both the deceased and the survivors. In this case the deceased were identified with the political struggle between tyranny and freedom/democracy, between the more progressive faction and the colonial privileged faction; and the survivors were effectively asked to choose their side.[33]

Remembrance also evoked the question of the justification of this death — the question of what they died for. The state administration took it upon itself to act on behalf of the "potosinos," who it decreed would erect this monument for posterity as a token of its gratitude and appreciation for their sacrifice; that sacrifice was made explicit in the inscription of the portraits ("sacrificed for the Patria's liberty on 17 November 1830"). The meaning with which such inscriptions are imbued is an action of the survivors in order to establish a common identity between those who died and those who remained.[34] The common identity that Romero's 1833 administration wanted to share with those heroic ashes was that of "liberty" from what they perceived as the shackles of the old aristocracy and Spanish domination. The final article of the decree, article six, is further indicative of this intention to cement this common identity and common cause between the dead and the current state government and its inhabitants, namely the financing of both the memorial and the reburial ceremony. The state's coffers were to foot the bill at any cost, despite the financial hardship in the aftermath of a civil war. Romero understood when it came to praising his flock of liberal fighters and supporters that the cost was never too great. He also authorized pensions for the widows of José Márquez and Joaquín Gárate as well as those potosinos (militiamen and their families) who fought on the side of liberty in the battles of El Pozo, El Gallinero, and within the capital.[35]

Due to the rapid political shifts and the frankly dizzying amount of legislation churned out to alter, amend, or annul previous legislation, this decree may not have been carried out in full. If a monument was erected, it does not appear to have survived in the present capital; in the course of time it has vanished and, with it, its political and social identifications, which had been intended to capture and sustain the cause.[36] Assuming it was erected, I suspect that it was quickly taken down in 1834 as the political order once again took a swift political swing away from radicalism when the Plan of Cuernavaca of 25 May 1834 was launched. This shift in defense of the *fueros* (legal exemptions or privileges) and religion paved the way for the 1835 call for a stronger centralist national government, which put an end to Romero's governorship.[37] Based on Reinhart Koselleck's observation that "memorials are taken down when they are felt to be a threat or when a tradition that is still living is intended to be suppressed," it is almost certain that the hombres de bien, wanting to silence the national and local radicals decisively, would have removed all visible symbols of their values.[38]

Treatment by the Current Historiography

The ambivalence or lukewarm stance of the traditional historiography toward the "lamentable" execution of Márquez and Gárate was presumably a result of their political afterlives. Their heroic commemoration was sponsored by Romero's generous administration and thus intimately linked to the radical politics perceived as being of one man, Vicente Romero.[39] Historians have appeared to uphold the derogatory view of Romero held by his opposition. A clear outsider in every respect (his status as a *fuereño* originally from Jalisco; his progressive/radical politics), Romero and his followers were easily viewed as the quintessential upstarts, Jacobins, embodying all the *yorkino* characteristics so despised by the more conservative federalists of San Luis who had held sway since the late colonial period.[40]

Therefore the link of the political lives of the executed pronunciados with the radicalism of Romero's final administration, orchestrated by Romero himself, only sealed their transitory political success. The misfortunes of the faction to which the dead were linked served to undermine their image as the decades passed, their memory bound to that of the radical faction, which they were locally portrayed as having died trying to reinstate. Romero, who achieved legitimacy through his politics from the marginalized eastern regions of the state as well as from lower strata of society, was ultimately hindered from making any lasting testimony to the liberal hero cult of Márquez and Gárate, due in part to his status as a non-native of the state and not being from important lineage, through which it would have been easier to have kept any lasting legacy alive.[41]

As for Márquez and Gárate's political lives as executed pronunciados, it may have been their status as leading pronunciados that hindered future commemoration. The ambivalent nature of the practice and the speculation surrounding the potential motivations that lay behind their participation in the practice (self-interest, enrichment vs. genuine interest to represent the demands of the majority) made it difficult to see these actors in unambiguous terms. Further, the failure of the 1830 pronunciamiento conveyed a reputation of leaders who had failed to whip up a mass following. Their demise in the historic memory may also have its roots in the way the actual act of the pronunciamiento has traditionally been viewed. The pronunciamiento was often disregarded by each governing authority in turn in independent Mexico as a mere military practice, a revolt, rebellion, or coup, holding few political qualities, and often as a destabilizing act detrimental to the development of the country. During the period in which Márquez carried out his plans, the pronunciamiento certainly was not viewed favorably, and with the exception of the 1829 Plan of Jalapa, it was viewed as primarily an arm

McDonald

of the *hombres de sentimientos*, the radical liberals with reformist zeal. However, that view held by the peaceful, upright and law-abiding governing elite of San Luis Potosí was only maintained as long as the pronunciamiento did not serve their purpose. The executions, then, only served to highlight the fact that, as noted by Timothy E. Anna, "rebellions and pronouncements in the name of the masses were treated differently from those that occurred in the name of creoles and their agendas."[42]

In conclusion, the political lives of these executed pronunciados saw them regarded both as criminals and as heroic martyrs at distinct moments in time, only to be largely forgotten or sidestepped. In this sense it may be said that the historic memory of the executed pronunciados is as partisan as the pronunciamiento itself.

Notes

The epigraph is from Koselleck and Jeismann (eds.), *Der politische Totenkult*, 9. The translation is my own.

1. See chapters 3 and 6 in particular. See also Fowler, "Fiestas santanistas."

2. Verdery, *Political Lives of Dead Bodies*, 33; Koselleck and Jeismann (eds.), *Der politische Totenkult*; Johnson, "Why Dead Bodies Talk: An Introduction," in Johnson (ed.), *Death, Dismemberment, and Memory*.

3. Koselleck cites this *Neuzeit* as the period post–French Revolution. Another modern historian has identified the year 1815 as the beginning of "modernity"; Paul Johnson, *The Birth of the Modern: World Society, 1815–1830* (New York: HarperCollins, 1991), cited in Van Young, "Of Tempests and Teapots," n. 10. See also Koselleck, *Practice of Conceptual History*, 291.

Koselleck, *Practice of Conceptual History*, 291.

4. Similar to the postsocialist societies of the twentieth century analyzed by Verdery in *Political Lives of Dead Bodies*.

5. Costeloe, *La primera república federal*, 262, 271.

6. Archivo Histórico del Estado de San Luis Potosí (henceforth cited as AHESLP), Secretaría del Gobierno General (SGG), 1830.47, Caja 318, anonymous author.

7. Muro, *Historia de San Luis Potosí*, 1:541–46.

8. Fontana, "Prólogo," ix. Miguel Alonso Báquer's proposal that the pronunciamiento constituted a gesture of rebellion also suggests that despite the threat and backing of a military force, the pronunciados did not actually want to engage in bloody battle. Báquer, *El modelo español.*

9. Verdery, *Political Lives of Dead Bodies*, 28–29.

10. Koselleck and Jeismann (eds.), *Der politische Totenkult*, 22.

11. Johnson, "Why Dead Bodies Talk," 23.

12. Verdery, *Political Lives of Dead Bodies*, 27.

13. AHESLP, SGG, 1830.46, Caja 317, 20 November 1846, Ramón Pastor and José Othón to Governor Manuel Sánchez, "DONATIVO voluntario que los que subscriben hacen a la valiente Guarnición de San Luis . . ."

14. Muro, *Historia de San Luis Potosí*, 541.

15. "Manuel Sánchez al ministro de relaciones" (17 November 1830), *El Sol*, 21 November 1830, 2.

16. The phrase monstrous gravity is from "Zenón Fernández al ministro de guerra y marina" (17 November 1830), *El Sol*, 21 November 1830, 3.

17. "Manuel Sánchez" (17 November 1830), *El Sol*, 21 November 1830, 2.

18. *Colección de decretos y ordenes de la Primera Legislatura Constitucional del Estado de San Luis Potosí*, 174–76.

19. Brunk and Fallaw (eds.), *Heroes and Hero Cults*, 275.

20. *Iniciativa a las cámaras de la unión de la II Legislatura de SLP, sobre el Gral. Bustamante y sus Ministros* (Mexico: Impreso por Ignacio Cumplido, Calle de Zuleta N.14, 1833), AHESLP, SGG, 1833. Vicente Guerrero was executed on 14 February 1831; his companions in arms Francisco Victoria and Juan Nepomuceno Rosains met the same fate in September of the same year, José Márquez and Joaquín Gárate in November 1830, and among the executed liberals of Morelia was Juan José Codallos, executed in May 1831. For information on these federalist pronunciamientos see Anna, *Forging Mexico*, 236–43.

21. Brunk and Fallaw (eds.), *Heroes and Hero Cults*, 17, 274.

22. Zavala, *Ensayo histórico*, 2:344.

23. Verdery, *Political Lives of Dead Bodies*, 25. "Politics help us to see political transformation as something more than a technical process—of introducing democratic procedures and methods of electioneering, of forming political parties, etc. The 'something more' includes meanings, feelings, the sacred, ideas of morality, the nonrational—all ingredients of 'legitimacy' or 'regime consolidation.'"

24. Brunk and Fallaw (eds.), *Heroes and Hero Cults*.

McDonald

25. Brunk and Fallaw (eds.), *Heroes and Hero Cults*, 267–68.

26. Sater, "Review: Heroic Myths," 154–55.

27. Zavala, *Ensayo histórico*, 345. Local historian Feliciano Velázquez also uses Zavala's recounting of events in his *Historia de San Luis Potosí*.

28. AHESLP, Impresos (IMP) 1833, "Núm. 5 El Congreso del Estado se ha servido decretar lo siguiente: . . . San Luis Potosí, Enero 31 de 1833, J. Mateo Terán, presidente, Antonio de Arce, dip. sec., José J. Barragán, dip. sec."

29. Koselleck, "The Modern Cult of Monuments," in *Practice of Conceptual History*, 291.

30. For a study of the important and broad-spanning usages of state funerals during their heyday under Porfirio Díaz's administration, see Esposito, "Death and Disorder in Mexico City," 100.

31. Verdery, *Political Lives of Dead Bodies*, 268. In her study she views this as part of the larger process of postsocialist transformation.

32. Beezley et al. (eds.), *Ritual of Rule*, xiii.

33. Koselleck, "War Memorials: Identity Formations of the Survivors," in *Practice of Conceptual History*, 285–326.

34. Koselleck, "War Memorials," 288.

35. "Decreto 95 [i.e., 99]," *Legislación Potosina o Colección completa de las disposiciones legislativas expedidas desde el 21 de abril de 1824*, vol. 1 (22 December 1832), 369. "RESUMEN: Se concede al Gobierno del Estado para conceder montepío de pensiones a las familias de milicianos ó mutilados en las acciones de guerra del Pozo, Gallinero y sitio de la Capital del Estado."

36. Koselleck, *Practice of Conceptual History*, 289.

37. Romero figured prominently in the federalist rebellion of 1837; he went on to serve alongside Ponciano Arriaga on the capital's radical ayuntamiento in 1841 and again in the restored federalist congress of 1847.

38. Koselleck, *Practice of Conceptual History*, 325.

39. Sater noted that the hero is often manipulated to serve the interests of one political faction, and therefore his popularity mirrors the political changes of the country. "Their continued acceptance may depend upon the inchoate wishes of the public or the foresight of the government. Consequently, men can cease being popular because the nation no longer considers their contribution valuable." Sater, "Review: Heroic Myths," 151–52.

40. Corbett, "Republican Hacienda and Federalist Politics," 126. "Romero was undoubtedly ruthless, ambitious, and authoritarian, and he no doubt used the office of the governor to make himself richer. Yet these characteristics in

no way distinguished him from many of his predecessors. What distinguished him was the radical content of his politics and it is there we must begin to understand the bases of his support in San Luis Potosí, along with the reason why he became known among the highland elite circle as 'the ever abhorrent and never sufficiently despised Vicente Romero.'" Only Corbett has recently suggested contextualizing his behavior in order to revise his politics and his base of support within the state as well as his hostile reception among many of the altiplano elite.

41. Corbett, "Republican Hacienda and Federalist Politics," 129. Koselleck also highlights the difficulty and effort with which any political cult of the dead can be sustained throughout the generations and suggests that to this end societal institutions are often necessary. Koselleck, *Practice of Conceptual History,* 324. Likewise, local historian Isabel Monroy notes the difference between the likes of Márquez and Romero and the traditional caudillo, such as General Luis Cortázar from Guanajuato, with important family lineage giving them natural legitimacy and thus the ability to establish and sustain networks of interest. Monroy Castillo, *Sueños, tentativas y posibilidades,* 60.

42. Anna, *Forging Mexico,* 243.

Five. Memory and Manipulation:
The Lost Cause of the Santiago Imán Pronunciamiento

> Perhaps a revolution can overthrow autocratic despotism and profi-
> teering or power-grabbing oppression, but it can never truly reform
> a manner of thinking; instead, new prejudices, just like the old ones
> they replace, will serve as a leash for the great unthinking mass.
>
> —IMMANUEL KANT

> Revolution: Political movement which encourages the hopes of many,
> disappoints even more, inconveniences almost everyone, and extraor-
> dinarily enriches a few. It enjoys definitive prestige.
>
> —ADOLFO BIOY CASARES

The Santiago Imán *pronunciamiento* of 1836–40 was the most significant and exceptional pronunciamiento in Yucatecan history. The year of 1835 had seen the demise of the federal system in both Yucatán and Mexico, with the establishment of a much more stringent and controlling centralist administration in 1836 (which came under the presidency of Anastasio Bustamante in 1837). Not only had this centralist government increased political control in all Mexican departments (formerly known as states), with centrally appointed governors replacing state-elected authorities, but centralism also resulted in increased economic and military demands from the national administration. These changes all had a severe impact on Yucatán, and the Imán pronunciamiento was the manifestation of the Yucatecans' discontent about this centralist system. This pronunciamiento was to be the epitome of the unstable relations that existed between Yucatán and Mexico during the early nineteenth century, as it was the only pronunciamiento that resulted in Yucatán's complete independence from Mexico, with Yucatán creating its own constitution; indeed, one should note that Yucatecans had temporarily seceded from Mexico in 1823 and again in 1829. Nevertheless, the pronunciamiento's initial origins would not stem from separatist desires but would arise from the discontent of the military, or more specifically the Third Active Battalion, which was stationed in towns throughout the remote east of the peninsula and was the battalion to which Imán belonged. This event thus highlighted the importance of the military's role in inspiring the pronunciamiento, a role that had been increasing throughout the 1830s.

Furthermore, the majority of those participating in Imán's pronunciamiento were lower-class military members, *campesinos* (peasants) and Mayas from the east of the peninsula, endowing it with an unmistakable element of popular pressure, which had been absent in the previous Yucatecan pronunciamientos, when the elite from the cities of Mérida and Campeche had lobbied for regional power. The elite federalists in Mérida would nevertheless be responsible for seconding Imán's pronunciamiento and thus ensuring its regionwide success, emphasizing the everlasting significance of the role of the high-class politicians in the Yucatecan pronunciamiento. These federalists did not just second Imán's movement but hijacked it and recreated it to serve their own elite purposes; this highlighted the continued and determined dominance they possessed when it came to controlling pronunciamientos and consequently political power.

The adaptation from a relatively popular movement to a selective pronunciamiento, along with the elites' disregard of the demands of the *pueblo* (the Spanish term used to describe the collective "people"), would lead to a final significant factor: the curious way in which Imán's pronunciamiento was memorialized in Yucatán. There was a determination by the federalist elite to forget the inexperienced and dangerous figure of Imán as a pronunciamiento leader, as he was a virtually unknown man from the east who had armed the Maya in his uprising. Yet simultaneously, there was a conscious elite effort to recognize and remember his pronunciamiento as the Yucatecan prototype of the perfect pronunciamiento, as one that represented the people and the voice of the *pueblo*. It was essential that they do this in order to endow their movement with the legitimacy needed to justify their overthrowing of the centralist governing administration at the time.

Before analyzing Imán's pronunciamiento, it is useful to briefly examine this unlikely pronunciamiento figure. Who was Santiago Imán and why did he feel compelled to pronounce against all odds? Born in 1800, Santiago Imán Villafaña was from a family who had achieved certain importance in the Maya-dominated east of the peninsula (a place known as the *oriente*), and more specifically in the towns of Tizimín and Espita. The Imán family was relatively wealthy, owning many properties, with investments in the dyewood industry and maintaining a trade with Havana. More important, Imán was an officer: as early as 1825, he is found in documents gathering men from Tizimín to form the then newly established Third Active Battalion, and he soon became captain of its Fifth Company.[1] He also had a penchant for pronouncing; he had seconded the pronunciamientos for the federal constitution in 1824 and again in 1832. When his time came for leading the greatest Yucatecan pronunciamiento, he already had more than a decade of military experience and was practiced in the art of seconding pronunciamientos.

Yet Imán was not a political figure, and his main reason for pronouncing was not politically related but was much more concrete. From as early as December 1835 the *sorteo* method of compulsory enlistment for Yucatecan soldiers to fight the wars against secessionist Texas had begun, targeting specifically the Third Active Battalion. Its soldiers were stationed mainly in the eastern towns of Tizimín, Espita, and Izamal and in the city of Valladolid in the east.[2] In total, it was reported by then Commander General Joaquín Rivas Zayas that more than three thousand Yucatecan troops were sent to Texas between 1835 and 1839. The sorteo solely affected the *vecino* (white) population, which constituted only one-third of the Yucatecan populace, as the Maya were not allowed to enlist in the active battalions.[3] This recruitment had several disastrous effects on eastern Yucatecan society. The members of the Yucatecan Third Active Battalion were not trained official military members; the majority of them were laborers or aged and inexperienced vecinos, simply put there to maintain the peace of the eastern towns. Industry and agriculture now suffered in these areas as thousands of workers were uprooted to be sent to Texas.[4]

How did this affect Imán more directly? Imán was heavily preoccupied about the draining of his own workforce by the forced recruitment; his employees were all members of the Third Active Battalion, targeted for enlistment to Texas. Commanding a company of 124 men, he used his position to manage a sufficient labor force, as soldiers repaid money he loaned to them by working on his cornfields.[5] With the national government ordering his men to Texas, there was no one to tend to Imán's lands, and the military authorities ignored his complaints about the "incalculable damages, because the period in which the fields should be cleared has passed."[6] Of equal significance was the fact that he was now also a captain of a regiment destined for Texas. His previously respected military position (pre-1836) now became unpopular, as he had the problematic responsibility of gathering his troops for the far-away war. When on 6 June 1836 Governor Francisco de Paula Toro demanded a further two hundred soldiers from the Third Active Battalion to go to Tamaulipas, Imán knew it was time to pronounce.[7]

The Imán pronunciamiento therefore evidently began as an elite movement; Imán himself was Hispanic and of the provincial upper class in the east, a respected figure in Tizimín society, and his main reason for pronouncing was because his workers and soldiers were being taken away from him. The call for the end of the sorteo would nevertheless not only serve the needs of the elite but would also incidentally satisfy the demands of the lower classes; the majority of those protesting against being sent to Texas were the hacienda and industry workers. A further element of popularity would be added to the pronunciamiento when, in the need for manpower in his uprising, Imán included demands in his movement that would appeal to the Maya, encouraging them to take up arms with him. The Imán pronunciamiento would thus be widened to encompass the needs of all levels of society, transforming it into a popular movement.

The centralist authorities discovered Imán's initial plans for pronouncing in June 1836, and they subsequently ordered his imprisonment; in jail, without sufficient food and shelter, Imán's resentment against his circumstances only deepened, strengthening his determination to pronounce. After he had spent two years in prison the authorities released him in the custody of a herb doctor, following his plea that his hemorrhoids condition was worsening.[8] He resumed planning to pronounce, setting up his revolutionary headquarters—named the "cuartel general del libertador del Oriente" (general barracks of the liberator of the east)—in a secret eastern location. His first attempt at a pronunciamiento was in Tizimín on 29 May 1839, as he and his followers revolted, calling for federalism and consequently relative autonomy from the center and all its decrees. His *pronunciados* made a sorry sight: some 70–80 men made up of some deserters of the Third Active Battalion, vecinos of the town, and some Haitian former slaves from the haciendas of San Fernando and from San Felipe.[9] His forces then went to Espita, where government forces roundly defeated the pronunciados in a mere two hours, the rebels fleeing.[10]

The political and military elite heavily ridiculed the pitiful and solitary attempt and the lack of prestige of the event and actors. Indeed, the elite of the main cities of Mérida and Campeche saw in Imán a nobody who was trying to play their game of pronouncing. One should note that until then, pronunciamientos in Yucatán had been mainly restricted to these larger western cities of Mérida and Campeche, as the military and civilian elite used this instrument in their bickering and battling for political power.[11] Federalist and Meridian military man Felipe de la Cámara remarked in his diary that he was shocked Imán had even dared to head a pronunciamiento: "I could not help but be extremely surprised that a military captain, dismissed from his job, without training in the art of war, known for his quiet and calm character, without convictions nor cause to give rise to them, in fact, to say it once and for all, a figure of uselessness in all respects, took upon himself the enormous weight of an event of such serious consequences . . . since then I lost faith in the success [of the pronunciamiento]."[12] Governor Pedro Marcial Guerra called Imán's first attempt to pronounce a "noisy, reckless, and insignificant pronunciamiento" and a "ridiculous call." According to him, "Santiago Imán is not an army officer by career. Without talent or training: without relations or prestige: without convictions or resources, he has acted like an outlaw: heading . . . deserters of the army and some brown idiots of the town."[13]

Imán was indeed without arms, resources, men, prestige, and connections; the things needed to make a pronunciamiento work. He himself was not the most impressive pronunciamiento leader: a mere captain from a small town in the east, he was ridiculed for the Mayan accent of his Spanish. Additionally, battle noises and gunfire gave him migraines, and horseback riding irritated his hemorrhoids.[14] As Will Fowler has pointed out, a pronunciamiento needed the element of—in Max Weber's terms—"charismatic domination," a hero-type figure who commanded respect and inspired mobilization, and a military man with experience and demonstrated success in starting and not just seconding pronunciamientos, as was Imán's case. Miguel Alonso Báquer agrees that a pronunciamiento leader had to be seen as a figure with the "necessary prestige" who would inspire others to support him and second his act, not just look on in surprise while he put on an embarrassing show.[15] In nineteenth-century Mexico, for the most part, a man only really "existed" politically and militarily if he had led a victorious and significant pronunciamiento. Imán had not done this, and consequently did not exist in this sense; the result was that "people would not know who you were, what you stood for, or how resourceful and successful you were at summoning support or effecting shifts in government policy."[16]

Throughout 1839, every time Imán regrouped and attempted to pronounce (five times in total), powerful government troops defeated him.[17] Only after successfully recruiting the Maya to take up arms with him—which he did through the promise of abolition of their religious obvention tax if his pronunciamiento triumphed—did he manage to occupy the eastern city of Valladolid and issue his pronunciamiento. The Maya numbered in the thousands. This was the turning point in the course of Imán's movement. He entered Valladolid triumphant on 12 February 1840, carried in an *inhis koché* (the Mayan term for a carriage) borne on the shoulders of his Mayan pronunciados, and issued his act.[18] It called for the national reestablishment of the 1824 federalist constitution, the voiding of all decrees of the central government, the establishment of a temporary junta in Yucatán (made up of five officials picked by Imán), and the granting to Imán of the title of General Commander of Arms of the Liberating Army, with power over the governing junta and extensive military command. It also demanded dissolution of the Third Active Battalion and abolition of the indigenous obvention tax.[19] Imán added in a manifesto on the same day the necessity of preserving Yucatán's union with Mexico, as it was important to maintain "the sacred ties" and "identify our interests with the rest of the Mexican Republic, to which we swear to belong . . . our objective is not to extract ourselves from obedience to the Supreme Government."[20]

Imán and his followers had not been the only people opposed to centralism in the peninsula. The deposed federalist authorities of 1834 had been waiting for the opportune moment to second Imán's pronunciamiento—without ever offering him assistance

Ali

or resources throughout all his struggles — and now, with his first success, they basically hijacked his plan. The Act of the Garrison of Merida that seconded Imán's on 18 February claimed to represent "an immense majority of the people" but was carried out by the federalist elite, and although they called it a *pronunciamiento de adhesión*, in reality had very little in common with Imán's act.[21] It demanded federalism, reimposition of the authorities of 1834, and invalidation of all decrees of the national centralist administration. However, it also went on to declare: "The department of Yucatán establishes itself as a free and independent state, and in so doing, reestablishes the Constitution of 1824," and that this would be the case until the national administration reinstalled the federalist constitution.[22] Imán had never wanted independence from Mexico; in fact, he had been explicit about the necessity of preserving unification. The Meridian pronunciamiento, moreover, made no mention of the dissolution of the Third Active Battalion, abolition of the obvention tax, or the empowerment of Imán — no doubt the elements closest to the hearts of Imán and his supporters and farthest from the minds of the political elite in Mérida and Campeche.

The powerful Meridians and Campecheans had consequently hijacked Imán's campesino-backed movement voicing the needs of the people and had transformed it into a traditional Yucatecan elite pronunciamiento. These same elite Yucatecans who had been trumpeting for more than a decade — and still were — that the reason for the very existence of their pronunciamientos was to serve the needs of the people, had dismissed a movement that had truly represented the voices of the lower classes, the campesinos and the Maya. No pronunciamiento in their minds had any business empowering the lower classes, or even Imán; that was too dangerous. A Yucatecan pronunciamiento was to them simply an excuse and a justification for them to gain power in the capital and implement the decrees they favored.[23]

The federalists, conscious of the clear discrepancies between their pronunciamiento and Imán's, were nevertheless careful to mask their pronunciamiento as one of "adhesión" so as to maintain the heroic appearance of Imán's act. The elite had simply used Imán and his people (after they had struggled for years) as a platform to stand on and issue their own act, which dealt with their own interests. A well-coordinated elite military apparatus carried out the adhesions to Imán's original pronunciamiento throughout the Yucatecan region. Nevertheless, even though the region seconded Imán's pronunciamiento in name, those in power knew that it was their Meridian pronunciamiento they would realize. A pronunciamiento de adhesión had consequently and intentionally become more powerful than the original act issued.

Despite the sidelining of Imán's act, and the ridiculing he had undergone and disregard he had borne in previous years, he now enjoyed for a moment the satisfaction of being a Yucatecan hero. The reestablished federalists held festivals in his honor and proclaimed 25 July as a day to celebrate "the caudillo of the Liberating Army of the East." Adornments decorated Mérida's citadel of San Benito and the government palace; guns were fired, church bells were rung. All these celebrated the Liberator and his pronunciamiento.[24] The official discourse, which had formerly denounced the "rebel Imán," rapidly changed its tune and recognized him as chief of Valladolid.[25] Newspapers such as *Los Pueblos* proclaimed the "beloved and laudable son Santiago Imán" as "Hero of freedom! Savior of the people!" — advising him and his fellow pronunciados: "Walk covered with the undefeatable successes you have gained."[26] When describing the pronunciamiento, the editors of the same newspaper proclaimed: "The simple voice of the brave caudillo of the East, of the immortal IMÁN, rose up en masse, and with a . . . noble and impressive attitude, exclaimed, 'No more suffering.'"[27] Somehow the humility of his military status was now something to be praised instead of ridiculed, with the town council of Dzibalchen exclaiming admiringly, "He is no more than a simple lieutenant, [yet] he has given us freedom and our homeland."[28] Finally, Yucatecans claimed that "there is no Yucatecan who is not thankfully giving Imán the most righteous tributes of respect and veneration, and who does not see him as the savior of his rights."[29]

Actions and words soon clashed, however, in a most ambiguous reaction. Despite the praise of Imán, it was soon made clear that no man from the east without military prestige and who was politically inexperienced deserved to mix in Meridian elite politics, despite his heroic act and his social status in Tizimín. He would not be taking any position of power, as called for in his pronunciamiento. As Juan de Dios Cosgaya reclaimed his post as governor, the federalists quickly dissolved the governing junta established by Imán's pronunciamiento, with the Congress of 1834 recommencing on 28 February.[30] The federalist elite were to exclude Imán continually; the first instance was in the battle to second the pronunciamiento in Campeche. The regular army stationed there—headed by Commander General Rivas Zayas—had issued its own pronunciamiento on 25 February, declaring its loyalty to Mexico and refusing to recognize the reinstalled authorities of 1834. Imán was not even invited to join the expedition to second the pronunciamiento in Campeche, as the Meridian elite did not want the eastern caudillo and his campesino and Maya contingent in western territory. Instead, they sent long-time pronunciado Lieutenant Colonel Sebastian López de Llergo to do the act, much to Imán's disgust. Imán arrived in Mérida with his troops on 15 March, asking the governor if he could take part in the Campechean project, only to be told that his services would be requested if needed.[31] Imán insisted, and after numerous pleas, he was allowed to go to Campeche; but the Liberator was already scrambling to retain his spotlight. After several months of negotiations and small battles, Imán and Llergo triumphed over Campeche on 16 June.[32]

The actions of exclusion of the hero nevertheless continued. The *hombres de bien* (essentially the white elite) did not fail to recognize that Imán's movement was not of "political opinion" but had, in Commander General Joaquin Rivas Zayas's words, the "character of a Caste War."[33] They wanted Imán and his armed Maya — or, as Governor Cosgaya called them, "the bizarre troops of general Imán" — back in their eastern towns where they belonged.[34] Alarm increased when a group commissioned by Imán visited the governor to complain that the Meridian pronunciamiento had not fulfilled the most important articles of Imán's act: naming Imán as chief military authority, dissolution of the Third Active Battalion, and abolition of the obvention tax.[35] To silence Imán, the federalist authorities offered him the rank of brigadier general as an honorific title, which in the opinion of Meridian Felipe de la Cámara was a move that avoided "offending the distinguished class of general officials, with a title that was clearly . . . useless."[36] With regard to the other demands, on 23 August 1840 the local government abolished the obvention tax, but they immediately replaced it with a religious contribution of 12 *reales* per year for Mayan men aged between fourteen and sixty. They declared the postponement of dissolution of the Third Active

Battalion until further notice. The federalist elite had ignored and shoved aside the east and its people.

Despite these actions, Imán remained in Campeche throughout the summer of 1840, probably still hopeful of having some kind of political career or military promotion. The press now began turning against him, frequently repeating that Imán had no intention of taking any power or reward for himself and that he only wanted to return to his lands in the east.[37] The negation of granting him any power was also manifest, as after the elections in late August 1840, Imán did not even get the role of the political representative of Tizimín, as this post was for the priest Buenaventura Pérez.[38] On 24 September the Campechean newspaper *El Anteojo* published a poem called "To the citizen Santiago Imán." Even though signed by "A Friend," the message of the poem was undoubtedly to persuade Imán to return to Tizimín. The poem presented two models for his consideration: Simón Bolívar, rejected by his own people because of his personal ambitions, and George Washington, loved by all for heading a revolution but then rejecting the title of dictator or king. The poem then urged him to choose one of the options presented.[39] Additionally, the governor declared that while all owed "an eternal gratitude . . . to the champions and other workers who have removed us from oppression and slavery," he added firmly that it was time for them to return to the east, "distinguished soldiers of our homeland: you have now finished your great act."[40]

It was time for Imán to leave. His army had been dissolved, with the majority of his campesino and Maya supporters returning to their lands to plant their fields; the traditional elite had reclaimed their positions, and he was being criticized. His inexperience in public and administrative affairs had allowed the old-time politicians to manipulate his cause easily to their advantage and subsequently to dispose of the original hero. On 15 October he published his farewell, assuring readers that he and his eighty thousand followers would always be ready to defend Yucatán against "the proud Metropolis . . . if despotism threatens us, I will appear among you to teach the traitors a lesson."[41] Perhaps this was a threat to the Mexicans, or perhaps it was his manner of reminding all what he and his force were capable of doing. He then disbanded what remained of his forces and returned to Tizimín.

Governor Cosgaya had assured the pronunciados of the east that "your memory will be passed on to future generations so that they say your names with delight and pleasure . . . your names will be eternal in the annals of the history of Yucatán."[42] This was not to be the case for Imán. He was not a model pronunciamiento figure: a Yucatecan pronunciamiento was meant to be led by a respected powerful elite political and military individual — preferably from the western city of Mérida or Campeche — whom one could remember with pride. Imán's elite status in Tizimín did not matter in the capital; Meridians simply saw him as some unknown soldier from some small pueblo in the east who had somehow been catapulted into the spotlight. In their view he had no right to pronounce for any power or causes; that was *their* territory. Imán was to them an embarrassment, and moreover a danger for arming and coopting the campesinos, slaves, and Maya into a pronunciamiento. Trawling through countless newspapers, letters, and press releases from the period after Imán's return to Tizimín in 1840 yielded *not one* reference to his name whenever the authorities mentioned the heroic pronunciamiento of 1840. This is no coincidence. While Governor Cosgaya had crowed about the "skillful and patriotic hands that have rightly known to choose 'the people' for the realization of public power," the exact opposite had happened to Imán, his followers, and his demands.[43] The elite consciously excluded him from collective memory, as he was a figure to be ashamed of, a figure to be forgotten.

Imán was not unaware of this and tried to remain in the public eye. On 22 December 1841 he pronounced in Valladolid condemning the local government for delaying the complete independence of Yucatán (independence he had initially claimed to be against; no doubt this was just an excuse to criticize the government that had shunted him aside).[44] His pronunciamiento was ignored, receiving only a small write-up in the paper. The Yucatecan administration subsequently declared Yucatán's independence anyway, until Mexico decided to return to a federalist system.[45] In response, the Antonio López de Santa Anna administration in 1842 planned the invasion of Yucatán to reclaim it. Imán once more attempted to get involved; in 1842 he wrote to the governor offering his services in the coming war, reminding him: "You and all Yucatecans are witnesses, that I was the first who, spurning the risks, outwitting the shrewdness and vigilance of our oppressors, scorning their threats and offers . . . gave in the town of Tizimín the cry of freedom in May 1839, which I maintained for a year, until the revolution happily ended with the disappearance of the monstrous and abominable administrative system from our land."[46] He then added that "I returned to my family, not to enjoy the benefits and happiness of retirement and private life, but to wait with noble concern the happy moment of leaving once more on campaign, for which we now prepare."[47] He did not enjoy being excluded; that was clear. But the government had other intentions for him; Governor Santiago Méndez replied that they would call on him if they needed his services, but the local administration did not invite him to one single battle during the year-long war against Mexico in 1842–43.

Despite the determined disregard for and blotting out of Imán and the popular demands of his revolt, his pronunciamiento of 1840 was consciously *remembered* as a movement by the pueblos. Even more ironic, not one pronunciamiento in Yucatán previous to 1838 had ever been by "the people," but as has been discovered, the iconic symbol of the pronunciamiento in celebration and in memory was one which was precisely of the *pueblos*, of the people, as they fought against the despotism and tyranny of an oligarchy. Yucatecans were thus to remember the Imán pronunciamiento as just this: in the one year anniversary of the pronunciamiento, Yucatecans celebrated the "uniform cry of the Yucatecans, with which the rapidity and sublimity of thunder echoed throughout the State."[48] In the same year the newspapers praised the pronunciamiento that had embodied what *Los Pueblos* called "irresistible moral force" and "the general will."[49] *El Siglo XIX* praised "the masses . . . the popular sectors who in one moment . . . triumphed unanimously."[50] Vice Governor Miguel Barbachano in 1842 remembered "the blood of the free that was spilled in the fields of Tizimín, Valladolid and Santa Rosa . . . the freedom and sacred rights of the people were fully reconquered."[51] Even the president of the state congress commended the "admirable revolution . . . of the people."[52]

Why ignore Imán and suppress his pronunciamiento's demands, yet memorialize the very same movement as being the prototype of pronunciamientos in nineteenth-century Yucatán, remembered as being a true popularly motivated exercise? It is because the true movement of the pueblos is what theoretically embodied the pronunciamiento; it was supposed to represent the people, their will, their desires, their needs, their rights. The actual *derecho de insurrección* (right to insurrection) against the ruling authorities was justified by the very fact that it was an expression of the *voluntad del pueblo* (the will of the people). It therefore had to be preserved and memorialized as just this in order to be legitimate in memory. The figure of Imán, however, was embarrassing when compared to the military elite who had previously headed pronunciamientos in Yucatán: figures such as Sebastian López de Llergo, José Segundo Carvajal, and Francisco de Paula Toro. Moreover, to grant Imán and his campesino followers any success was dangerous: any demonstration of the empowerment of the popular classes would only show them that perhaps *they* could pronounce from now on for their demands.

Without a doubt, the inclusion of a Maya demand in the pronunciamiento had been something more than perilous; in 1847 the Maya protest against taxes would have the suspicious beginnings of a pronunciamiento, with extensive planning and liaising occurring. When the authorities discovered the Mayas' plot and subsequently executed one of their principal leaders for crimes of conspiracy, the indigenous peoples would retaliate in a revolt that would spiral out of control, becoming the bloody Maya rebellion known as the Caste War. This war between Mayas and *criollos* (whites) would last from 1847 to 1853, provoking severe instability and destruction in the region.

Elites would thus *commemorate* the participation of the Maya and the popular aspect of the pronunciamiento, but the pronunciamiento itself should not serve the needs of the lower classes. Additionally, its leader who had incited the lower classes to practice insurrection should also be ignored in practice *and* memory. Imán not only lacked heavily in the esteem needed to be praised in pronunciamiento memory, but he was a dangerous man to be remembered as attaining success, as he had consciously encouraged the Maya to revolt. The elite would thus simultaneously remember the Imán pronunciamiento as serving the needs of the masses, to uphold its validity in memory, while they (the elite) ignored the fact that they had disregarded the demands of the lower classes. There would also be a conscious elite attempt to forget the shameful pronunciamiento leader Imán, whom they saw as an undeserving example of a pronunciamiento head.

During the following decades Yucatecans slowly forgot the figure of Imán; he disappears from newspaper and correspondence records, surfacing only in contexts of acquiring property or loans. The local government excluded him from playing any role in the Caste War of 1847–53, and records indicate that he died in 1854, of causes not yet discovered. As Terry Rugeley has pointed out, the memory and figure of Imán, rejected by the Yucatecan elite, did not even linger in his hometown of Tizimín; when the locals there were asked to choose a namesake for their town in 1878, they nominated not Imán but an unremarkable military officer by the name of Manuel Francisco Mezo. No recollections or obituaries of Imán have been found, and he has disappeared from collective Yucatecan memory.[53] Along with his pronunciamiento, he was a lost cause. For the man who had dared to change the history of a region through countless struggles and despite having all the odds stacked against him, it was indeed a sad end; and all because in the eyes of some, he was not good enough, or was too dangerous a role model, to be remembered as a hero.

Notes

My profound thanks go out to Terry Rugeley at the University of Oklahoma for providing me with information for this article as well as lending his extremely helpful input and criticism.

The epigraphs are from Kant, "An Answer to the Question," 1, and Bioy Casares, *Descanso de caminantes*, 39.

1. Rugeley, "En busca de Santiago Imán," 3.

2. The correspondence with regard to the details of the *sorteo* is extensive, and I have chosen not to go into detail here about its particulars, due to word limit constraints. For primary source information see Archivo General del Estado de Yucatán (henceforth cited as AGEY). Key documents are AGEY, Poder Ejecutivo, Correspondencia Oficial, vol. 6, exp. 9, "Correspondencia de la junta departamental de Yucatán con el gobernador," 22 April 1837; AGEY, Libro Complementario 11, "Copiador de la correspondencia del gobernador con autoridades de Tekax," 21 October 1837; AGEY, Poder Ejecutivo, Correspondencia Oficial, vol. 7, exp. 3, José María Rivas Chacón to Pedro Marcial Guerra, 11 April 1838; AGEY, Poder Ejecutivo, Correspondencia Oficial, vol. 7, exp. 4, Pedro de Baranda to Pedro Marcial Guerra, 17 April 1838; AGEY, Libro Complementario 10, "Copiador de la correspondencia del gobernador con autoridades de Izamal," 11 May 1838; AGEY, Milicia, vol. 3, exp. 24, "Filiaciones de reclutas de la compañía de cazadores del tercer batallón activo de Yucatán, 1826–1838," May 1838; AGEY, Poder Ejecutivo, Correspondencia Oficial, vol. 7, exp.4, José Patricio Iturralde and Juan J. Ramírez to Pedro Marcial Guerra, 6 November 1838.

3. As local legislation deemed it unlawful for the Maya to possess arms, only the local white population constituted the Yucatecan battalions. See Joaquín Rivas Zayas to Anastasio Bustamante, 25 August 1839, in Baqueiro, *Ensayo histórico*, 266–70.

4. Acereto, *Evolución histórica*, 70.

5. AGEY, Poder Ejecutivo, Milicia, vol. 1, exp. 13, Santiago Imán to Francisco de Paula Toro, 19 April 1836.

6. AGEY, Poder Ejecutivo, Milicia, vol. 13, exp. 11, Santiago Imán to Francisco de Paula Toro, 5 April 1836. All contemporary quotes have been translated into English.

7. Rugeley, *Rebellion Now and Forever*, 40.

8. AGEY, Poder Ejecutivo, Justicia, vol. 4, exp. 14, "Fragmento de una representación promovida por Don Santiago Imán oficial del Batallón Tercero Activo, preso por conspiración, solicitando su libertad bajo fianza por estar enfermo," 18 February 1837; AGEY, Poder Ejecutivo, Milicia, vol. 12, exp. 23, Santiago Imán to Joaquín Rivas Zayas, 7 February 1837.

9. AGEY, Poder Ejecutivo, Correspondencia Oficial, vol. 9, exp. 14, Pedro Marcial Guerra to the Escmo. Sr. Secretario de Estado y del Despacho de lo Interior, 8 June 1839.

10. AGEY, Libro Complementario 12, "Copiador de la correspondencia del

gobernador con autoridades de Mérida," 1 June 1839; Rugeley, "En busca de Santiago Imán," 6.

11. It needs to be noted here that although Imán had led *pronunciamientos de adhesión* in eastern Yucatán, he had never taken part in or headed an "original" pronunciamiento. It is thus understandable why the elite of these major pronunciamiento sites would be shocked at the audacity of Imán to pronounce without waiting on official instructions from the political and military headmen of the main cities of Mérida and Campeche, and also to form a pronunciamiento that had such grand demands.

12. Cámara y Zavala, *Memorias*, 42.

13. AGEY, Poder Ejecutivo, Correspondencia Oficial, vol. 9, exp. 14, Pedro Marcial Guerra to the Escmo. Sr. Secretario de Estado y del Despacho de lo Interior, 8 June 1839.

14. Rugeley, *Rebellion Now and Forever*, 2.

15. Baquer, *El modelo español*, 63.

16. Fowler, "'I Pronounce Thus I Exist,'" 261.

17. Baqueiro, *Ensayo histórico*, 26.

18. Baqueiro, *Ensayo histórico*, 486.

19. Baqueiro, *Ensayo histórico*, 490.

20. Centro de Apoyo a la Investigación Histórica de Yucatán, Mérida, Impresos, VIII.1840.020, Santiago Imán, Alocución de Santiago Imán, Valladolid, 12 February 1840 (Mérida: Imprenta de Lorenzo Segui).

21. Those signing the pronunciamiento were mainly the military elite of Mérida—including José Anastacio Torrens, army lieutenant colonels Clemente Trujillo and Manuel López de Llergo, Isidro Rejón, commander of the First Active Battalion Felipe de la Cámara, and José Cosgaya—along with civilian elite politicians Pedro Casares y Armas and Francisco Barbachano.

22. Baqueiro, *Ensayo histórico*, 280–83.

23. I do not mean to martyrize Imán. The point being made here is all pronunciados from the east (Imán, the Third Active Battalion, and the Maya) were undeniably being taken advantage of by the Meridian and Campechean elites. This needs to be emphasized in order to demonstrate (1) the political power of the city elites, (2) the process whereby a pronunciamiento could easily be hijacked by the powerful military and political oligarchy of Yucatán, and (3) the powerlessness of Imán and his followers to do anything about this situation.

24. Rugeley, *Yucatán's Maya Peasantry*, 122.

25. Rugeley, "En busca de Santiago Imán," 6.

26. *Los Pueblos*, 4 April 1840.

27. *Los Pueblos,* 16 May 1840.

28. *Los Pueblos,* 4 April 1840.

29. *Los Pueblos,* 30 June 1840.

30. Centro de Apoyo a la Investigación Histórica de Yucatán, Impresos, VIII.1840.002, "Alocución de Juan de Dios Cosgaya," 19 February 1840.

31. Ancona, *Historia de Yucatán,* 3:376–77.

32. Baqueiro, *Ensayo histórico,* 37.

33. Rugeley, "En busca de Santiago Imán," 7.

34. "Manifiesto que el ciudadano Juan de Dios Cosgaya, gobernador constitucional del estado libre y soberano de Yucatán, hace a sus conciudadanos, con motivo de las ultimas ocurrencias que precedieron a su entrada a esta plaza," *Los Pueblos,* 23 June 1840.

35. *Diario del Gobierno de la Republica Mejicana,* 20 February 1840.

36. Cámara y Zavala, *Memorias,* 71.

37. *Los Pueblos,* 4 August 1840.

38. *Los Pueblos,* 14 July 1840.

39. *Los Pueblos,* 1 October 1840.

40. "Recuerdo memorable para heroica Campeche, o sea el 16 de junio de 1840," *Los Pueblos,* 20 June 1840.

41. *Enciclopedia Yucatenense,* 2:203.

42. "Recuerdo Memorable," *Los Pueblos,* 20 June 1840.

43. "Exposición que hizo el E. Sr. gobernador del Estado libre y soberano de Yucatán, ciudadano Juan de Dios Cosgaya, al abrir sus sesiones el A. Congreso instalado el 20 de agosto de 1840," *Los Pueblos,* 22 August 1840.

44. *El Yucateco Libre,* 27 November 1841.

45. Reed, *Caste War of Yucatán,* 30–31.

46. *El Siglo XIX* (Yucatán), 31 August 1841.

47. *El Siglo XIX* (Yucatán), 31 August 1841.

48. *El Siglo XIX* (Yucatán), 19 February 1841.

49. *Los Pueblos,* 4 April 1840.

50. *El Siglo XIX* (Yucatán), 2 April 1841.

51. "Discurso que el Excmo. Sr. Vice-Gobernador en ejercicio del supremo poder ejecutivo, D. Miguel Barbachano, pronunció ante las augustas cámaras el día de su apertura," 1 September 1841, *El Siglo XIX* (Yucatán), 3 September 1841.

52. "Contestación del Sr. Presidente del Congreso del Estado," 21 August 1840, *Los Pueblos,* 22 August 1840.

53. Rugeley, *Rebellion Now and Forever,* 4.

Six. *Salvas, Cañonazos, y Repiques*: Celebrating the Pronunciamiento during the U.S.-Mexican War

Recent research has shed light on the ways Mexican regimes made use of public spectacles to legitimize the government and attempt to turn former Spanish colonists and ensuing generations of Mexicans into citizens of the new nation in the aftermath of independence, but historians have yet to fully explore the festivities associated with an emblematic feature of life in the early republic — the barracks uprisings and upheavals known as *pronunciamientos*.[1] While a precise model of what this practice entailed remains elusive, scholars no longer regard pronunciamientos as meaningless conflicts, a view exemplified by the preeminent nineteenth-century cartographer Antonio García Cubas. He once cynically remarked that Mexico's "perfectly established system of pronunciamientos" transformed men once praised as "saviors, regenerators, or liberators" into "arbitrary, illegal, and despotic" actors. Historians now generally agree that pronunciamientos, which became a mutable yet pervasive and effective mechanism for conducting politics between 1821 and 1876, involved a variety of historical actors and interest groups (e.g., civilian politicians, army officers, and rural municipalities) who expressed their discontent with government policies in a written text in the hope that ensuing negotiations would compel authorities to redress those perceived grievances. The hundreds of pronunciamientos that erupted in nineteenth-century Mexico thus turned into "the instrument by which the people were heard" and became as well a key component of "the process of struggle toward political identity and the creation of the nation-state."[2]

New interpretations of pronunciamientos, however, are not the only thing underscoring the need to pay greater attention to the ceremonial displays that went hand in hand with this phenomenon. One must also consider the fact that patriotic ceremony and pageantry were integral components of the political culture of pronunciamientos; the triumphant entries into Mexico City of generals Agustín de Iturbide following the 1821 Plan of Iguala, and Antonio López de Santa Anna in the aftermath of the 1832 Plan of Veracruz, clearly illustrate how such devices endeavored to validate the ideals espoused by victors in these struggles.[3]

There is yet another factor—the role of popular cultural forms like *calendarios* (almanacs) in the creation of Mexican national identity—that further highlights the importance of studying how pronunciamientos were celebrated. These inexpensive publications not only informed readers about the country's geography, architectural landmarks, and patriotic symbols but also disseminated knowledge of such uprisings in ways that helped entrench them in the collective consciousness of mid-nineteenth-century Mexicans.[4] In the section entitled "Notas cronológicas" (Chronological Notes), calendarios listed key historical events, including various pronunciamientos, as well as the amount of time that had passed between those episodes and the almanac's year of publication.[5] The chronology, according to one study of British almanacs, "served a solemn didactic function, reminding the reader of the passage of time, of the purposeful working out of providence over the years and centuries. It allowed . . . readers to place their country's recent political and religious history in a scheme of events stretching back to the creation of the world and, by implication, looking toward its end."[6] Almanacs also perpetuated recollections about pronunciamientos through lithographs and essays. The inside cover of Abraham López' 1843 calendar featured one such image of the 1841 revolt that ended General Anastasio Bustamante's second term as president, while Mariano Galván's 1848 piece, "Apuntes para la historia de los pronunciamentos en México," urged readers not to forget those upheavals. Nations needed to remember the pronunciamientos they had endured to become aware of their needs and trends and thus augment the general welfare.[7]

The present essay builds on these insights and analyzes the public celebrations associated with two uprisings that broke out during the mid-1840s, a crucial time in Mexico's history if for no other reason than that the prospect of war with the United States became a reality. To meet this threat and put an end as well to the nation's chronic political disarray, the leaders and supporters of the major rival factions in contention for power—first General Mariano Paredes y Arrillaga and the conservatives, and then *puro* (or radical) chief Valentín Gómez Farías and his adherents—staged successful rebellions and took control of the government. Having done so, the new rulers moved with determined energy to legitimize their pronunciamiento in Mexico City through rituals and ceremonies of varying intricacy and sophistication that informed residents of the capital of the rebellions' objectives. The manifold political, social, and economic problems that afflicted Mexico, however, ensured that these spectacles would fail either to cement the people's loyalty toward these nascent and ultimately ephemeral governments or to turn the pronunciamiento into a viable means of effecting political change.

Paredes's Revolt

After months of careful preparation and deliberation, on 15 December 1845 General Paredes accepted the invitation, issued one day earlier by the commandant general of San Luis Potosí, to lead a "glorious and purifying" movement that would install an "extraordinary Congress . . . with full powers to constitute the nation," so as to end the maladies brought on Mexico by José Joaquín Herrera's nefarious administration. The president and his *moderado* (moderate) cohorts enjoyed much initial goodwill because they had overthrown Santa Anna in December 1844, but the regime quickly fell into disfavor. The reasons for its precipitous decline included its unwillingness to launch the military reconquest of Texas; a failure to discard immediately the 1843 Bases Orgánicas (which many pundits associated with the excesses of Santa Anna's just-toppled government) as the nation's legal charter; and the pursuit of policies that seemed to heighten the power of the national guard (and hence the populace) while reducing the privileges and stature of the regular army.[8]

As Paredes, who commanded the Army of the Reserve, had to march roughly 220 miles from San Luis Potosí to Mexico City, and because Herrera's government took steps to put up a stiff fight before collapsing on 30 December, neither Paredes nor his allies in the capital had sufficient time to organize elaborate ceremonies to celebrate the triumph of their pronunciamiento. Therefore they marked the occasion only with a military parade on 2 January 1846, but an impressive one nonetheless, that sought to intimidate city residents as it displayed the victors' strength. Paredes entered Mexico City around noon at the head of nearly six thousand troops and twenty-one cannons, and the soldiers reached the capital's main square, the Zócalo or Plaza Mayor, some forty-five minutes later.[9] The procession lifted the spirits of Carlos María de Bustamante, one of the most astute, if biased, observers of public life in early republican Mexico. He admired "the order with which it [the army] marched, its methodical movements, and its beautiful aspect," as well as General Paredes's demeanor. Propelled by his "fiery soul" and in full-dress uniform, the victorious commander had ridden into the plaza atop a dark chestnut steed, accompanied by eight to ten aides but not by other generals or high-ranking officers.[10] Even more important, in Bustamante's opinion, the specter of social dissolution that armed resistance to the pronunciamiento might have produced never materialized; he did not detect "the slightest disorder among the populace . . . even though the city lacked a governing head."[11]

Such pomp and precision, however, belied the fact that Paredes's entry took place under less than auspicious circumstances. Despite reports that on 30 December the common people had "acclaimed" General Anastasio Bustamante because they mistook him for Paredes, popular support in Mexico City for his pronunciamiento proved nonexistent.[12] Posters went up throughout the capital on the morning of 2 January urging residents "to decorate their houses and in this way demonstrate the dictates of their patriotism," but within hours those placards had been ripped to pieces or defaced with obscenities; moreover, denizens did not hang bunting from their balconies. To avoid likely embarrassment, soldiers from Paredes's army entered the city shortly before noon to alert those who lived along the parade route to spruce up their homes. While the cue had the desired effect, nothing embellished the Zócalo aside from the "*official* decorations" in the Diputación (Municipal Palace) and the National Palace.[13] The conditions of that area further detracted from the procession's magnificence. The Zócalo resembled a cow corral because of the debris, rubbish, reeking piles of filth, and vendors who crowded the sidewalks, all of which presented "a most disagreeable aspect to one's sight and sense of smell."[14]

The limited appeal of Paredes's pronunciamiento became further evident during the 4 January *Te Deum* held at the cathedral, one day after a hastily convened junta of representatives from the various departments (as states had been called since the adoption of centralism in 1835) appointed him interim president—a decision conveyed to city residents at 10:30 p.m. via an artillery salvo and a general pealing of church bells. Archbishop Manuel Posada y Garduño greeted Paredes at the church's principal entrance, dressed with all the trappings of his office—cape, miter, and underneath a canopy—and led the general into the candle-lit sanctuary, where numerous members of the regular army were present. The cleric nevertheless bellowed the Te Deum like a cow, his atonal delivery contrasting with the ceremony's musical accompaniment. More significant, in Bustamante's opinion, the attendees' faces, including those of adherents to the new regime, expressed "sadness" as well as "*distrust* and fear of an ill-fated future."[15]

These sorts of concerns led Bustamante to suggest how Paredes should utilize patriotic and political pageantry to validate his pronunciamiento. On 7 January he urged the new chief executive to finish the "Monumento a los héroes," a shrine that Santa Anna had hoped to build in the Plaza Mayor to perpetuate the memory of Mexico's independence from Spain and to honor the heroic figures of that eleven-year struggle. Work on the column had remained at a standstill since the 16 September 1843 ceremony to lay down its first stone, so completion of the monument would complement Paredes's government as emperors Augustus and Trajan had honored Rome (Augustus transformed a city of bricks into one of marble, and Trajan built a column that was meant to become synonymous with his greatness and virtues). This achievement, furthermore, would make Mexico's foreign enemies (e.g., the United States) realize that the country intended to beautify its capital even as it prepared to resist their unjust demands.[16]

While neither Paredes nor his advisors implemented Bustamante's proposition, the regime did organize two ceremonies to legitimize the pronunciamiento of San Luis Potosí as a guarantor of social stability. First, at 2:00 p.m. on 27 January, Paredes's government published "with extraordinary solemnity" the *convocatoria* (bylaws) for elections to the new congress called for by the rebellion's plan. The regulations ensured that representatives would be "chosen exclusively on the basis of class," thus eliminating the "dangerous concepts of democracy and popular sovereignty . . . from the political landscape."[17] City residents learned of the event through the usual artillery salvoes in the Zócalo, the ringing of bells in the cathedral and the capital's other churches, and the curtains that adorned the balconies of the Diputación. But the centerpiece of the occasion was a procession of three thousand, four artillery pieces, and two howitzers along the city's main streets. Members of the Mexico City *ayuntamiento* (town council), riding in open calashes pulled by two Friesian horses, occupied the center of the column; just ahead were several macebearers on fine steeds with their respective insignias. Bustamante, who witnessed this spectacle next to Paredes from a balcony in the National Palace, remarked that "this was the first time that this corporation [the ayuntamiento] had appeared in this manner." Paredes, who himself appointed the councilmen, likely ordered them to come out and display their support for his regime.[18]

Nine days later Paredes staged the second civic ritual intended to lend credibility to the pronunciamiento of San Luis Potosí. The president needed to showcase himself as a bold and energetic commander capable of pursuing a bellicose policy against the United States that would redeem national honor; after all, the pronunciamiento had condemned Herrera for avoiding a "glorious and necessary war" that "undermined" the country's "dignity." Paredes had moved to meet such expectations within three days of taking power when he reviewed all troops under his command. He also ordered those forces to undergo daily drills, which on specified occasions he would direct.[19] These exercises culminated on 6 February with a large-scale military display or simulacrum involving approximately eight thousand soldiers in the eastern district of San Lázaro. According to Bustamante, cavalry and infantry units "executed several flashy maneuvers with uniformity and prodigious swiftness before a large crowd . . . Twelve artillery pieces of different calibers fired away along the line, and for the first time the *ambulance* corps picked up the wounded and had an effective rehearsal." He came away convinced "that these troops can stand up to enemy forces, which will not surpass their valor or discipline."[20] The editors of *La Reforma* agreed. Such a "magnificent and imposing spectacle," they wrote, had showcased the army's martial prowess, "the ability of its commander-in-chief, as well as of the brigade and corps chiefs, and even the individual instruction of subordinate officers." These journalists also targeted "previous administrations," a none-too-subtle reference to Herrera's and Santa Anna's recent regimes; those governments "had been somewhat careless in maintaining [the army's] discipline, and this had discredited the armed forces. The current president, we believe, will preserve the honor and luster of our arms."[21]

Ultimately, however, the ceremonial efforts to legitimize Paredes's pronunciamiento and showcase his ability to lead Mexico in a tumultuous time foundered amid rancorous public debate over the most appropriate form of government. In mid-1845 Paredes had entered into an alliance with Spanish minister Salvador Bermúdez de Castro and conservative politician Lucas Alamán intended to establish a monarchical regime in his homeland, but spreading reports of such endeavors enraged many of his politically conscious countrymen. Publication of the 27 January convocatoria prompted Bustamante to remark that he "was more afraid of . . . [it] than of the entire armed *leperada* [that took to the streets] on 6 December [1844]." Likewise, the appearance of *El Tiempo*, particularly its 12 February editorial that openly advocated for a monarchy, exposed Paredes to additional criticism. Subsequent measures to turn the chief executive into a more accessible figure, such as the mid-March announcement that Paredes would henceforth host one-hour public audiences every Tuesday afternoon, failed to shore up the regime.[22] Finally, the onset of war with the United States, particularly the defeat of Mexican forces early in May at Palo Alto and Resaca de la Palma, further soured the public mood. These circumstances allowed Gómez Farías to join forces with erstwhile rivals Santa Anna and the moderados in order to depose Paredes, and they struck on 4 August. The pronunciamiento of the Ciudadela (named after the building where it began, the armory in Mexico City) broke out early that morning. Two days later, cannon blasts, pealing church bells, military bands playing reveille, and multitudes shouting *vivas* to Santa Anna announced to residents of the capital that the rebels had prevailed.[23]

The Pronunciamiento of the Ciudadela

Gómez Farías and General José Mariano Salas—who spearheaded the rebellion in his capacity as commandant general of Mexico and then became provisional president—quickly moved to swing public opinion in favor of the revolt. They issued several manifestoes to publicize the merits of the pronunciamiento and endeavored to showcase the rebellion's nationwide popularity. To that end, at least eight times during the next two and a half weeks church bells rang and cannons thundered to signal that other departments, army officers, or military garrisons had backed the uprising. The public voice of Salas's regime—the *Diario del Gobierno de la República Mexicana*—also published numerous *actas de adhesión* (proclamations of support) enacted by other locales. To win the hearts and minds of Mexicans, however, the new government had to fulfill the pronunciamiento's two major aims—election of a congress that would bestow Mexico with a new constitutional structure, and the return of Santa Anna from exile in Cuba to lead the nation's armies in the war against the United States.[24]

Efforts to reconstitute the nation began on 6 August, the very day the rebels took power. The regime then decreed that the new legislature, which was scheduled to convene by year's end, would be elected according to regulations set forth in 1823 that allowed for voting on the basis of universal male suffrage. In the meantime, and at Santa Anna's and Gómez Farías's behest, the government issued a 22 August law that reestablished the 1824 federal constitution. The Mexico City ayuntamiento announced the restoration at 6:00 p.m. through a *bando* (edict), and one hour later councilmen placed a copy of the constitution in the balconies of the Diputación.[25] Word about the charter's restitution, however, had already spread throughout the capital, and the ensuing expressions of popular support indicate that the 1824 Constitution enjoyed widespread backing that imparted additional legitimacy to the pronunciamiento of the Ciudadela.

Indeed, by the time the ayuntamiento's 22 August meeting got under way at 5:30 p.m. a large crowd that wanted to speak with the councilmen had assembled outside the Diputación. "Various citizens" led the throng, the most prominent being Francisco Calapiz, who late in 1844 had joined the "Voluntarios Defensores de las Leyes," the citizen militia that then emerged to support the 6 December pronunciamiento against Santa Anna. When Calapiz addressed the councilmen he expressed his "jubilation" because the constitution of 1824 had been reestablished and beseeched the ayuntamiento, whose "patriotism was notorious," to celebrate the event. Councilman José María Godoy responded that the ayuntamiento had already resolved to carry out such a tribute, and his counterpart Juan José Baz made two additional proposals that were unanimously approved: to appoint a special committee to determine the best way to celebrate the charter's restitution, and to allot fifty pesos to "citizens Manuel Falcón and Juan Othón, two other militia chieftains, so they could purchase heavy wax candles and fireworks in order that the neighborhoods where their forces were stationed could solemnize the occasion." Another two motions passed with unanimity and received "prolonged applause"— to place the constitution that night under the main seat and canopy of the ayuntamiento's conference room, and to select a three-member commission to bring the charter there from the ayuntamiento's archives. After a brief recess to rehearse this ceremony, "the numerous part of the populace inside the building" acclaimed the constitution when it arrived and heartily applauded the ayuntamiento, Santa Anna, and Gómez Farías.[26]

By then it was approximately 7:00 p.m., but the ceremonials showed no signs of abating. Councilmen Ignacio Comonfort, Guillermo del Valle, and Baz moved to place a portrait of Gómez Farías in the ayuntamiento's conference room, and in the meantime (e.g., until one was found or painted) to inscribe his name in the corresponding place in that venue. Baz followed with an "analogous discourse" after which the people again "manifested their enthusiasm with applause." Finally, Comonfort and Baz sought to arrange for yet another commission that would thank, on the ayuntamiento's behalf, army chiefs, General Salas, the departmental governor, Gómez Farías, and the commandant general. Given the late hour, Godoy suggested that it would be wiser to discuss that motion the next morning as part of the proposal on how best to solemnize the "glorious" restoration of the federal charter. Baz agreed, and the meeting closed with another rousing speech by Calapiz. He addressed the ayuntamiento on "the behalf of the people," noted that "the tree of liberty, sprinkled so many times with the blood of its victims, will finally come back to life," and that restoration of the 1824 Constitution had filled the populace with the "purest form of enthusiasm." Calapiz then "sincerely thanked" the ayuntamiento for its role in celebrating this matter and concluded by applauding the people, the ayuntamiento, the federal constitution, the army, Santa Anna, and Gómez Farías.[27]

Publication of the bando, meanwhile, reverberated elsewhere in the capital. According to the *Diario del Gobierno* "a nearly unanimous feeling of happiness and hope then engulfed the entire city," while another eyewitness remarked that "an immense and joyous populace" ran into the streets immediately thereafter and kept up their merriment past 9:00 p.m. Residents also made their way into the cathedral and rang its bells for at least ninety minutes to fête the occasion. "What a difference—noted this observer—from the time the monarchists [e.g., Paredes's supporters] published their convocatoria! Will anyone doubt what public opinion stands for?"[28] News of the occasion spread further because shortly thereafter *El Monitor Republicano* and the *Diario del Gobierno* published the minutes of the ayuntamiento's 22 August meeting (and those of 23 August as well). By early September, moreover, the public could either peruse the 1824 Constitution in the *Diario del Gobierno* or purchase a copy of that text in various stores for two *reales*.[29]

Reports that Santa Anna had disembarked in Veracruz on 16 August provided the regime with another opportunity to consolidate the uprising's goals. Doubts about the sincerity of his latest promises of republican faith earned him a lukewarm welcome in that port city, but enthusiasm reigned in Mexico City on news of his return. Fireworks, an artillery salvo of more than 150 shots, and a heavy and continuous fusillade that rang out in the Ciudadela at 12:30 a.m. on 19 August and lasted for more than three hours marked the occasion. Crowds and bands of musicians also marched through the streets. The multitudes yelled vivas to Santa Anna and liberty, shouted *mueras* (death) to the monarchists, stoned the homes of former president Herrera and his friends, and caused "a tremendous uproar that did not let anyone sleep." The next day Federal District governor José Gómez de la Cortina informed *prefecturas* (prefectures) of Santa Anna's arrival so that they could "publicize it as much as possible," while a Te Deum at the cathedral brought the celebrations of this event to an end.[30]

But even before Santa Anna set foot on Mexican soil the leaders of the pronunciamiento of the Ciudadela and its supporters had taken steps to rehabilitate the exiled general's image. By 8

August the National Theater carried the name by which it had been known prior to December 1844—the General Santa Anna Theater.[31] Later that month an anonymous writer penned a *décima* (broadside) that called on Mexicans to forget Santa Anna's past excesses because he "had given the nation its rights and liberties" and had returned to "regenerate" his homeland.[32] Then, starting early in September, shops throughout the capital began to sell for four reales a military march dedicated to Santa Anna, to be played by a single piano.[33] But the most prominent sign of this strategy became evident on 6 September when the twelve-foot-high bronze of Santa Anna unveiled at the Plaza del Volador on 13 June 1844—which government authorities removed from its pedestal in the aftermath of the 6 December 1844 pronunciamiento to protect it from the angry mobs who roamed the capital intent on demolishing any object linked to Santa Anna—was reinstated to its original setting. Entrepreneur José Rafael Oropeza played a key role in this endeavor. He ostensibly wanted to display his patriotism and devotion to Santa Anna, and thus he financed the effort as well as requesting permission from municipal authorities on 24 August to erect the statue anew; it had lingered for eighteen months in a livery stable within the National Palace.[34]

To defuse any ill-feelings that reinstallation of the statue might evoke, the *Diario del Gobierno* put forth a novel interpretation of the circumstances surrounding its 1844 removal. It characterized that act as a "definite sign of ingratitude" because the effigy symbolized the many benefits Santa Anna had bestowed upon the country, including "the beautiful [meat and vegetable] market [at the Plaza del Volador]."[35] Despite such efforts, the statue threatened to disrupt the celebrations that sought to legitimize the pronunciamiento of the Ciudadela; it raised the specter of Santa Anna's unrestrained primacy as well as of a regime that would favor *santanista* (as Santa Anna's supporters were known) sycophants and might embezzle government funds. Oropeza's past relationship with Santa Anna contributed to this potentially nightmarish scenario. He apparently received several lucrative contracts in the early 1840s, including one to rebuild the aforesaid market, thanks to Santa Anna's free-handed use of his presidential powers. Popular perceptions about the statue added to the uneasiness. The bronze, which depicted Santa Anna extending his arm northward, meant to signify his intent to reconquer Texas, but many insinuated that his grasping hand pointed instead toward the Casa de Moneda (National Treasury).[36] On 17 September, therefore, Santa Anna asked the government to replace the statue with the Mexican coat of arms because his "dignity and patriotism" demanded the change. The general's plea delighted the moderado mouthpiece *El Republicano*, which noted that the caudillo recognized "the errors committed by those who flattered him [e.g., Oropeza]."[37] Eleven days later Governor Cortina cautiously moved to fulfill Santa Anna's request when he ordered that such an exchange take place at night to "avoid any scandal that might ensue." In the end, however, authorities took no action because of Santa Anna's renewed popularity, and the bronze remained at the Plaza del Volador until his last presidency came to an end in August 1855.[38]

The government's apparent profligacy further endangered the sense of unity and patriotism that Salas's regime attempted to construct around the 4 August pronunciamiento. Gómez Farías, at some point late in the evening of 22 August or before the ayuntamiento convened the next morning, met with those councilmen charged with determining how best to celebrate restoration of the 1824 Constitution. The government, he told them, wished to combine those festivities with observances to honor Santa Anna's entrance into Mexico City. It had the monies to do so, and the ayuntamiento should contribute what it could as long as that expense did not hinder its ability to carry out its regular duties. National authorities eventually allocated 4,000 pesos, and the ayuntamiento 200, to cover the cost of these celebrations, yet at least two key voices that opined on public affairs questioned the outlay. To pay out that much money for such a cause, argued Bustamante, was senseless; "madmen from San Hipólito [the Mexico City hospital that took care of the mentally ill] would not have done such a thing, yet we are crazier than them." He further characterized the disbursement as ill-timed, given that Mexican troops in the northern part of the country found themselves "practically naked." *El Republicano* hoped that those expenditures would not burden national finances, yet it could not find an "appropriate name to characterize this conduct, typical of Mexican governments, of spending large amounts of money on ostentatious solemnities, while public employees died of hunger and soldiers posted on the frontier lacked assistance." Because "public morality disapproved of such scandalous squandering," that periodical advised the government to apply available resources to "the nation's urgent needs" so that it could "retain the public's goodwill."[39]

To refute these charges the editors of the *Diario del Gobierno* reiterated the arguments raised in the little-known newspaper *Otro Tiempo*. They noted sarcastically, in reference to two fountains designed to spray water when Santa Anna passed Plateros (now Madero) Street on his way to the Plaza Mayor, that such "*expensive*" structures had been built thanks to the personal generosity of councilman Jacinto Pérez and one Jorge Anyslie. Next they pointed out that throughout history peoples had solemnized with pomp and magnificence the deeds of their glorious caudillos and that current circumstances did not preclude these expenses, given that Mexico City's ayuntamiento had spent more money under worse financial conditions to commemorate the *jura* (oath to the king) of Charles IV and Ferdinand VII's return to the throne after his release from a French prison in 1814. Finally, the *Diario* reminded critics that just one of the many celebrations, games, and banquets held to honor the renowned Roman citizen Cicero when he returned from exile (no specifics were given as to the circumstances and date of this event) cost more than the entire amount now spent to honor Santa Anna, our "illustrious compatriot."[40]

In the end, neither episode managed to derail the elaborate public rituals that marked restoration of the 1824 Constitution and Santa Anna's 14 September entry into the capital. On 25 August the ayuntamiento finalized plans for "two days of festivities and public rejoicing" to commemorate the occasion, and on the eve of the celebration numerous adornments in Mexico City's historic center offered bystanders striking visual reminders of the aims of the 4 August pronunciamiento.[41] In the middle of the Plaza Mayor stood a platform and podium similar to those placed in Alameda Park for the 16 September civic oration, while numerous candles illuminated the cathedral and the National Palace. Even more impressive were the "tasteful" and "exquisite" decorations that embellished the Diputación. Footlights illuminated its columns, while the building's balconies featured colored vases and lanterns and portraits of the heroes of the struggle for independence. The terraces were also interlaced with blue and white curtains (to honor the Virgin of Guadalupe) and with oval-shaped, laurel-covered tableaus engraved with the names of every Mexican state. An overhang in the main balcony displayed a tent atop a portrait of Santa Anna, a reminder of the caudillo's military exploits and of his promise to wage war on the United States. It carried the caption: "To the consolidation of Independence, [and] to the restoration of the Federal Charter by citizen Antonio López de Santa Anna, soldier of the people and founder of the Republic." A military band that played in the building's atrium completed the decorative scheme.[42]

Members of the ayuntamiento had also discussed on 25 August how to ensure popular participation in the celebrations. One way to do so, they thought, was to print invitations articulating the reasons for the revelry; *víctores* (young men who summoned neighborhood residents to attend festivities) were to distribute these throughout the capital, and the "usual means" would be employed in nearby towns. Councilmen would also encourage city residents to adorn and illuminate their homes.[43] On 8 September, in an effort to ensure the success of the ayuntamiento's call for popular involvement, the government of the Federal District issued a bando that reiterated the request for citizens to decorate their homes, invited each neighborhood to mobilize víctores to traverse the city during the festivities, and asked residents to contribute as much money as possible so that events honoring Santa Anna and the restoration of the 1824 Constitution had "a great amount of luster."[44] Although citizens surely ignored this plea for funds, the bando did help authorities hold elaborate celebrations.[45] On 13 September, according to the *Diario del Gobierno*, the mere announcement of Santa Anna's upcoming entry prompted "military bands to play reveille, the firing of rockets, and enthusiastic acclamations by an immense multitude."[46] The next day bunting adorned most city streets, the balconies of two or three well-known individuals featured Santa Anna's portrait, and víctores, some playing drums loudly, marched out to greet him and continued their cheering throughout the festivities.[47]

The early morning hours of 14 September provided residents of the capital with another eye-catching representation of what the pronunciamiento of the Ciudadela stood for. At that time a triumphal arc to honor Santa Anna—an example of ephemeral architecture, a style that had played a key role in both Aztec and Spanish ritual statecraft as means of ingraining political values among viewers—was unveiled on the corner of Plateros adjacent to the Plaza Mayor. Atop the four-story-high structure stood an eagle surrounded by military trophies. Tricolored flags and bright red liberty caps adorned its crest, and set in front of the arc, amidst a cluster of clouds, was the image of a soldier and an ordinary citizen holding the 1824 Constitution; it embodied what Gómez Farías and Salas had identified as the "fundamental basis" of the uprising, "the sincere union of the people and the army." Also on view were four inscriptions placed there on the ayuntamiento's behalf, three of which extolled Santa Anna as "the well deserving of his country," "the immortal savior of the Republic," and "the hero of Tamaulipas."[48]

Observers unanimously praised the arc's appearance. Bustamante, who had noted ten days earlier that its frame resembled a gallows, now characterized it as "beautiful and simple." Likewise, almanac editor Abraham López wrote that the arc "possessed a majestic presence," and was both "tasteful" and "very elegant," while chronicler José María Malo described it as "spectacular." The most telling comment about the arc, however, appeared in *El Republicano*. This publication also called attention to its "elegance" but, more important, emphasized the arc's "well-thought out allegorical [message]," a clear indication that its designers had made the goals of the 4 August pronunciamiento accessible to all.[49]

The splendor and magnificence of these adornments reinforced the thunderous acclaim that government officials and city residents lavished upon Santa Anna when he entered the capital on 14 September.[50] On this date, which the *Diario del Gobierno* characterized as "a long-awaited day," men, women, and children had taken to the streets since daybreak to meet him at the San Lázaro *garita* (gate) on the city's eastern edge. Given the tenor of the ayuntamiento's 25 August meeting and the 8 September bando, the *Diario* stretched the truth when it noted that they did so without "an express invitation from the government," but that assessment proved immaterial.[51] At noon a five-member ayuntamiento commission presided over by councilman Godoy joined the cheering masses at the nearby Peñón Viejo to greet Santa Anna. Godoy welcomed him as a "bold champion whose protection the country desires," and Santa Anna then made his way into the heart of the city to the sound of pealing church bells and gun salutes.[52]

Five colorful allegorical floats accompanied Santa Anna on this journey, a procession that "manifested the vigor of the symbolic practices of the baroque era" and also displayed a didactic narrative reminding spectators of their shared history and the goals of the 4 August pronunciamiento.[53] A house sat atop the first cart, and inside were two children, one dressed as a soldier and the other wearing a long coat and a tie; they stood for the union of the people and the army. The next float featured a blonde-haired girl in a white dress standing amidst a group of clouds with a red cap in her hand—she embodied Liberty. Just behind in the third coach was a ten-year-old *mestiza* dressed as an Indian, who personified the Federation. Surrounding her were twenty-three children in white pants and red liberty caps, who represented the number of Mexican states. An undetermined number of youths "bedecked with garlands and cassocks," who symbolized the country's founding fathers and Independence, traveled in the fourth cart, while the fifth transported a boy who signified Fame as well as a column behind which stood two men who constantly fired their carbines. At the rear, trailed by a squad of hussars, came the focal point of the pageant, the open stagecoach that carried Santa Anna and Gómez Farías. Dressed in "quite a democratic fashion . . . [with] a long traveling coat, white trousers and no crosses or medals on his breast," Santa Anna sat inside the cart, sunk down among the cushions, as a large banner of the 1824 Constitution with attached streamers and tricolored ribbons fluttered from a staff at his right.[54]

The messages the spectacle intended to convey, and the people's adulation of Santa Anna, continued when the procession reached the National Palace around 2:00 p.m. There Ignacio Sierra y Rosso and Anastasio Zerecero, whom the *Diario del Gobierno* identified as among his "dearest friends," met Santa Anna. The description of "dearest friend" certainly applies to Sierra y Rosso, who as a member of the caudillo's entourage since the early 1830s looked after the general's personal affairs; he also delivered a passionate eulogy at the 1842 reburial of the leg Santa Anna lost four years earlier during the so-called Pastry War with France. When it came to Zerecero, given his background as a puro sympathizer, journalist, and popular leader in Mexico City, the *Diario*'s portrayal likely stretched the truth. Nonetheless, their presence meant to reassure the public that the alliance between puros and santanistas was genuine as well as to allay fears that a popularly armed citizenry might at some point threaten the established social order

(both men had been elected as colonels in two of the city's recently reorganized national guard battalions, and Sierra y Rosso also
served as a high-ranking officer in the regular army).[55] Then, as
Santa Anna proceeded to the palace's main salon, "an immense
multitude that continuously screamed his name as the restorer of
the [federal] charter, soldier of the people, its Savior, [and] defender of their rights . . . threw itself on him . . . and wanted to
hug him, shake his hand, and at the very least get close to him."
Santa Anna reciprocated their affection and spoke to the crowd
about their freedom, their rights, and of how he hoped to defeat
the U.S. armies. He further boosted his image as a man of the
people upon reaching the salon when he refused the presidential
chair and insisted that General Salas occupy that place of honor.[56]

During the next two hours five individuals addressed Santa
Anna and the assembled multitude. The first three orators spoke
of Santa Anna and federalism in laudatory and hopeful terms.
General Salas pointed out that the monarchist plot and U.S. ter-
ritorial "usurpation" had threatened Mexico's freedom; he also
bemoaned the near extinction of the "lively and ardent enthusiasm that animated every breast when we conquered our independence." But the country's future now looked promising because "God has doubtlessly pointed to . . . [Santa Anna] as the
citizen to whom it will owe its salvation, and whose name it will
pronounce with respect and enthusism for ages to come." The
young lady who had personified the Federation in the procession
followed, and eyewitnesses commented on her discourse's verve
and power. One noted that she spoke with so much "grace, ease,
and comfort" that listeners could not help but be filled with admiration; another described the oration as "so tender that it caused
Santa Anna to shed a few tears," although the witness offered the

caveat that "perhaps his conscience was not too clean." Puro supporter and Mexico City councilman Vicente Romero spoke next. He argued that thanks to federalism, which had been in effect in 1829 when Santa Anna defeated invading Spanish forces under General Ignacio Barradas at Tampico, Mexico had demonstrated that it deserved to be free and was capable of sustaining its independence. Now that federalism was back in force, Romero added, all those who considered themselves Mexican should congratulate Santa Anna and ask that God bless him so he could protect the country's liberty.[57]

The tone and content of the next speech, however, nearly put a damper on the occasion. Popular activist and puro advocate Francisco Próspero Pérez had not been scheduled to talk, but he burst into the salon, asked for and received permission to speak, and then delivered the most critical and volatile oration of the afternoon. He rejoiced at Santa Anna's return but also encouraged him to make amends for his past errors. Próspero Pérez then called on the caudillo to embrace the populace, which would assist him as much as its capabilities allowed.[58] To defuse any ill-feelings evoked by this address (eyewitnesses did not refer to any such reaction, but the speech evidently generated some discomfort), the final speaker, jurist Andrés Quintana Roo, struck a tone of "republican moderation" when his turn came. In a speech that one publication characterized as "the day's most notable and interesting because of the concepts it espoused," he lauded Santa Anna as the "restorer of the incomparable political system to which the Supreme Court owed its legitimacy as well as the undefeated avenger of the people's sacred rights."[59]

Santa Anna took center stage when the speakers finished, and his brief response, like Quintana Roo's, was intended to downplay any animosity that Próspero Pérez's discourse might have stirred up. He thanked those in the salon for the plaudits, added that "he soon hoped to have an even more glorious day when he completely triumphed over our [foreign] enemies," and at 4:00 p.m. walked to a brightly illuminated cathedral for a solemn Te Deum. There Santa Anna provided additional evidence of his new populist persona. After being greeted by the *vicario capitular* (interim bishop), who tried to honor him as the People's Protector, he passed that mark of distinction to General Salas. Santa Anna then opted not to sit in his assigned seat and chose instead the less prominent place of a minister. Finally, Santa Anna reassured the vicario that he remained steadfast in his religious principles and beliefs and that as a Catholic, he was determined to protect the Church, its ministers, and their property and wealth.[60]

The day concluded with a wide array of activities that provided entertainment and evoked controversy as well. The populace enjoyed themselves and may even have nourished their civic conscience thanks to two wind instrument ensembles that played in the Diputación, and a "brilliant orchestra accompanied by a chorus that sang patriotic hymns" from the platform and podium that stood in the Zócalo.[61] Less successful was the gala function of French novelist Alejandro Dumas's play *La hija del regente* (The Regent's Daughter) staged at the Santa Anna Theater. The performance apparently lacked "brilliance" and was sparsely attended.[62] Most contentious was the banquet to honor Santa Anna in the National Palace. Earlier he had announced his intent to skip that feast and dine instead in the western suburb of Tacubaya with "eight or ten *intimate* friends," but at the last minute puro Minister of Foreign Relations Manuel Crescencio Rejón modified these plans. He insisted that Santa Anna surround himself with the "chiefs of the people" and invited to Tacubaya fellow puro politicians like councilmen Romero and Baz, the former's son Eligio, and Francisco Carbajal.[63] Santa Anna's behavior surely displeased those who remained skeptical of his alliance with the puros, and the *Diario del Gobierno* quickly moved to gloss over any signs of a rift. At Tacubaya, it alerted readers, Santa Anna had eaten with thirty of the "most distinguished army officers and popular leaders," while a like number of guests dined at the National Palace. Furthermore, speakers at both banquets had "delivered patriotic toasts," and "happiness and enthusiasm" had prevailed in each.

The *Diario* did not mention a drunken outburst by Baz; the councilman had "refused some pastries on the excuse that he could eat them only if seasoned with a certain kind of meat," a veiled reference either to the puros' intent to solidify their ascendancy by purging bureaucrats who did not share their political views or to Baz's own heated remarks at the 8 September public meeting that threatened the Catholic Church's privileged position. Omission of Baz's incendiary words indicated that Mexico's newfound sense of hope and unity could easily shatter.[64]

Indeed, the 14 September festivities elicited a mixed reaction among contemporary observers. The editors of the *Diario del Gobierno* considered these events harbingers of a bright future. They characterized the occasion as "the most brilliant day in the nation's history," and noted that the people celebrated because they had a premonition that "victory over [Mexico's] foreign enemies was all but certain, and so were peace, liberty, order, and all of the blessings that would surely follow. Mexico expects it all from the illustrious citizen Antonio López de Santa Anna." A more subdued, yet still positive, assessment appeared in *El Republicano*, which claimed to be deeply impressed because the "character of the solemnities had allowed the people to comprehend that their main objective was to celebrate the reestablishment of the 1824 charter, and to congratulate General Santa Anna for restoring it." Finally, almanac publisher López confidently predicted that the banner of the federal constitution Santa Anna had held during his entrance would turn into a powerful talisman that cast off evils.[65]

Others, however, viewed the ceremonies with skepticism and questioned whether such displays actually legitimized the pronunciamiento of the Ciudadela. An otherwise hopeful appraisal of the day's events in *Don Simplicio* ominously indicated that only the cathedral's bells tolled that morning; various convents, including Santo Domingo and La Profesa, had remained silent. British representative Charles Bankhead commented that although "the *cortège* was of the most simple and republican description . . . [it] did not appear to afford much satisfaction to the personage whose return it was destined to celebrate." Bustamante held the most serious reservations. Never again, he remarked, would anyone see a tableau engraved with the names of all the states like the one in the Diputación because the Californias, New Mexico, and other entities then occupied by U.S. forces could not be recovered. Bustamante also did not believe in the union of the people and the army. That combination, he wrote, "will never produce even a metaphysical chimera because they bond with each other [about] as well as grace and the sinner." Finally, Bustamante doubted Santa Anna's avowal of federalism. Having the general hold a copy of the 1824 charter was akin to having him grasp "a sack of scorpions."[66]

Unfortunately for the pronunciamiento's architects, the deep-seated political differences that gave rise to these sorts of concerns festered, and their political opponents came to believe that chaos and anarchy threatened Mexico. The ensuing tensions were further exacerbated by an 11 January 1847 decree that empowered the government, then headed by acting chief executive Gómez Farías, to mortgage or sell ecclesiastical property in order to finance the war against the United States. The decree provoked much unrest, and consequently the city's moderado-controlled newspapers began to censure Gómez Farías's administration.[67] By late February *El Trueno* had joined this campaign, and according to its editors the rebellion of the Ciudadela no longer possessed the moral authority it had garnered in its early stages. Mexico's problems, they wrote, derived from a "fatal passion" that had provoked "a revolution on that ill-fated day [4 August 1846], the horrendous effects of which the nation was feeling." Restoration of the 1824 charter, in their opinion, allowed the "demagogues" to prevail in "the tumultuous [October 1846] elections for deputies," and thus the "immense majority of the country—the sensible part—found itself in the hands of the federation's fraudsters." As the "liberticidal rabble took up Santa Anna's cause to enthrone itself, it has damaged us in as many ways as its perversity allows . . . it did not have in mind anything other than an undignified revenge, perhaps in order to derive the same pleasure that [Roman emperor] Caligula felt when he had the victims he intended to torment to death come before him."[68]

The only way to cut short such an unbearable situation, as *moderado* politicians, senior army chiefs, and high-ranking clerical leaders came to believe, was to call on the elite national guard units that had emerged in Mexico City the previous September to spearhead an uprising better known as the rebellion of the *polkos*. That pronunciamiento broke out on 27 February 1847 and submerged the capital in a bloody civil war that lasted for nearly one month. The fighting proved inconclusive because neither side obtained a decided military advantage, and consequently the fate of the revolt came to depend on who managed to court Santa Anna successfully—the embattled government or the rebels. Both factions dispatched representatives to meet with him as he retreated toward San Luis Potosí following the standoff with the U.S. army at the 22–23 February 1847 Battle of Buena Vista. Although Santa Anna's first known reaction to the revolt (dated 6 March) was to stand by Gómez Farías, by the time the general reached the capital's outskirts fifteen days later, he had decided to break with the puros. By the end of the month, after much political maneuvering, Santa Anna and his new allies had driven Gómez Farías and his cohorts from power. The pronunciamiento of the Ciudadela, and all that it represented, had met its demise.[69]

Conclusion

Ritual serves as a valuable commodity to revolutionary movements and new regimes. In the words of one scholar, it fulfills "important organizational needs, it helps provide legitimacy at the same time that it mystifies power relations, it facilitates popular solidarity even where consensus is conspicuously absent, and it leads people to conceive of their political universe in certain ways."[70] And so it was with the celebrations of the pronunciamientos of San Luis Potosí and the Ciudadela. Drawing upon past traditions and practices, these festivities represented the final act of a political drama in which the architects of these uprisings debated with the public the legitimacy and meaning of the rebellion. Having seized power by force of arms, the leaders of both pronunciamientos organized assorted ceremonies in an effort to bring Mexicans together, validate the outcome of the revolt, advocate fundamental change, and symbolically establish the authority of their regimes. Hence these commemorative spectacles constituted yet another means of political engagement by which Mexicans from all walks of life articulated their nationality, just as they did through other more formal means of political expression, namely elections.

Denizens of Mexico City took advantage of the opportunities offered by both pronunciamientos to step into the political arena and express their convictions. The muted reception afforded to Paredes's entrance into the capital may well be considered another "act of defiant respect" analogous to the silence with which residents of Veracruz greeted the new rulers of Mexico, Austrian archduke Maximilian of Hapsburg and his wife Carlota, in 1864.[71] Likewise, spectators in the upper part of the Principal Theater expressed their displeasure with *El Tiempo*'s 12 February editorial when they interrupted a performance by tossing "indecent and vulgar" leaflets critical of its pro-monarchy stance.[72] Popular participation during the pronunciamiento of the Ciudadela enjoyed a higher degree of visibility, and also represented more than elite manipulation of helpless, insolent plebeians. Recent research has shown that the popular classes in Mexico City took to the streets in support of the pronunciamientos that marked the transition to centralism in the mid-1830s; ayuntamiento members played a key role in their mobilization at that time and again ten years later during the pronunciamiento of the Ciudadela.[73] The actions and words of individuals such as councilmen Baz and Romero, as well as national guard chieftains Calapiz and Zerecero and popular activist Próspero Pérez, demonstrate that non-elites were cognizant of their power and that of their followers, and tried to channel it in ways that granted legitimacy to the Ciudadela rebellion.[74]

In the final analysis, and despite the fact that pronunciamientos left an indelible stamp in the mindset of nineteenth-century Mexicans, neither elaborate ritual and popular support nor soaring patriotic rhetoric managed to cement loyalty to the regimes that emerged from the revolts of San Luis and the Ciudadela. The words of moderado politician José María Lafragua about the pronunciamiento of the Ciudadela clearly illustrate the limitations of the rhetoric. In mid-December 1846, when Lafragua addressed Congress in his capacity as minister of foreign relations, he exalted the 22 August decree that had restored the 1824 Constitution. Lafragua characterized that piece of legislation as "without a doubt the most national and pleasing to have been sanctioned since 1834." As he put it, "that solemn act of reparation completely consolidated the government and granted to the movement of the Ciudadela a legitimacy that previous ones had sought in vain: [therefore], that movement was no longer a revolt, but a revolution."[75] Three months later, however, Lafragua concluded that it was "necessary to end that scandal [Gómez Farías's government] . . . because all of society despised it." He had no choice but to support Santa Anna's return to power in March 1847. That step "was legal, convenient, and necessary . . . I am not sorry [to have done so], and I will stand by that decision so long as I live."[76] As these comments suggest, the animosities that suffused political life in the early republic hastened the disintegration of governments like that of the Gómez Farías–Santa Anna coalition. Therefore the official ceremonies designed to celebrate and confer long-lasting legitimacy on the pronunciamiento of the Ciudadela, as well as that of Paredes, failed to be repeated with the kind of regularity that might have bolstered the authority of those regimes or allowed the intent of those rites to endure.

Notes

This essay is much improved thanks to comments that Paul Vanderwood, Daniel S. Haworth, and Mark Ocegueda made on its earlier incarnations. I am also grateful to Shannon Baker, who lent me some of her own research materials, and to Berenice Pardo for tracking down various documents in Mexico City.

1. Four examples of the growing literature on this field are Duncan, "Embracing a Suitable Past"; Baker, "Antonio López de Santa Anna's Search"; Santoni, "Where Did the Other Heroes Go?"; and Knight, "The Several Legs of Santa Anna."

2. There is, of course, much more to this brief definition of pronunciamientos. These ideas are further developed in Tenembaum, "'They Went Thataway'"; and two essays by Will Fowler, "Introduction: The Nineteenth-Century Practice of the Pronunciamiento and Its Origins," and "'I Pronounce Thus I Exist',": Redefining the Pronunciamiento in Independent Mexico, 1821–1876," both in his edited volume *Forceful Negotiations*, xv–xxxix, and 246–65. Quotes are from García Cubas's *El libro de mis recuerdos*, 615; Anna, *Forging Mexico*, 238; and Anna, "Iguala: The Prototype," 1.

3. Brief descriptions of the festivities appear in Vázquez Mantecón, "Las fiestas para el libertador, 50–52; and Warren, *Vagrants and Citizens*, 109. For an analysis of the Plan of Iguala as the archetype of nineteenth-century pronunciamientos in Mexico, see Anna, "Iguala: The Prototype."

4. Beezley, *Mexican National Identity*, 25–31.

5. For example, the *Octavo calendario de Abraham López* listed the 1828 Parián riot and the 15 July 1840, 31 August 1841, and 6 December 1844 pronunciamientos.

6. Cressy, "National Memory," 65.

7. *Quinto calendario de Abraham López*; the reference to Galván's essay appears in Herrera Serna, "La guerra entre México y Estados Unidos," 157.

8. Costeloe, *Central Republic*, 278–81; the quote is from the Plan of San Luis Potosí, San Luis Potosí, 14 December 1845, in *El Siglo XIX*, 20 December 1845.

9. DePalo, *Mexican National Army*, 94; Malo, *Diario de sucesos*, 1:292; Bustamante, *El nuevo Bernal*, 1:107; and Ramírez, *Mexico during the War*, 52–53.

10. Bustamante, "Memorándum, o sea, apuntes para escribir la historia de lo especialmente ocurrido en México," 7 January 1846. This manuscript consists of six volumes and is held at the Bancroft Library of the University of California at Berkeley. Given that Bustamante recorded on a daily basis those events he witnessed or that were referred to him, I have used the date of his entry as a reference in order to facilitate location.

11. Bustamante, "Memorándum," 2 January 1846. Members of the city council had resigned on 30 December to protest Paredes's uprising. Bustamante, *El nuevo Bernal*, 1:100.

12. *El Amigo del Pueblo*, 13 January 1846.

13. Ramírez, *Mexico during the War*, 52.

14. Bustamante, "Memorándum," 7 January 1846.

15. Bustamante, *El nuevo Bernal*, 1:108–10; and Costeloe, *Central Republic*, 276.

16. Bustamante, "Memorándum," 7 January 1846; and García Barragán, "El arquitecto Lorenzo de la Hidalga," 115. For details about the monument's design and how, with Santa Anna's help, Spanish architect Lorenzo de la Hidalga won the contest to construct it, see Tenembaum, "Streetwise History," 145–46; and Rodríguez-Moya, "Agustín de Iturbide," 227–28.

17. Costeloe, *Central Republic*, 286–87.

18. Bustamante, "Memorándum," 27 January 1846; and *El Monitor Republicano*, 10 August 1846. No information has surfaced to shed additional light on Bustamante's comment. Newspapers like *Don Simplicio*, *La Reforma*, and *El Tiempo* did not even mention the procession.

19. Plan of San Luis Potosí, San Luis Potosí, 14 December 1845, in *El Siglo XIX*, 20 December 1845; and Ramírez, *Mexico during the War*, 61.

20. Bustamante, "Memorándum," 6 February 1846.

21. *La Reforma*, 7 February 1846. The event's apparent success prompted rumors that another such exercise would soon be held and that Paredes, to defray the cost of gunpowder, intended to build an "immense stage and charge three reales (as for bullfights) so those who wished could view the spectacle in comfort." This second simulacrum was never staged. Bustamante, "Memorándum," 12 February 1846.

22. *Diario Oficial del Gobierno Mexicano*, 13 March 1846. I have not found any evidence to ascertain for how long these hearings continued or if they were held at all.

23. Malo, *Diario de sucesos*, 1:301–2; Bustamante, *El nuevo Bernal*, 2:67; *El Republicano*, 6 August 1846; and Santoni, *Mexicans at Arms*, 109–14, 117–18, and 127–28.

24. Santoni, *Mexicans at Arms*, 130–31; Malo, *Diario de sucesos*, 1:302–4; and Costeloe, *Central Republic*, 296. Three such actas—those of Texcoco, Lerma, and Santa Clara de los Cobres—are in the *Diario del Gobierno de la República Mexicana*, 24, 26, and 30 August 1846.

25. Sordo Cedeño, "El Congreso y la guerra," 49; Costeloe, *Central Republic*, 296–97; and Malo, *Diario de sucesos*, 1:304. These councilmen replaced those who had served under Paredes; they took their posts as a result of elections held on 17 August. *El Monitor Republicano*, 18 August 1846.

26. Archivo Histórico del Distrito Federal/Actas de Cabildo (hereafter cited as AHDF/AC), vol. 168-A, meeting of 22 August 1846. The units that Calapiz, Falcón, and Othón commanded emerged when residents of the capital spontaneously took up arms in support of the 4 August pronunciamiento; they subsequently received legislative sanction through an 11 September 1846 decree that revived the national guard. Santoni, *Mexicans at Arms*, 140. For government efforts to reorganize this citizen militia, and the pitfalls that derailed that process, see Santoni, "Failure of Mobilization"; and Amador Zamora, "El manejo del fusil y la espada."

27. AHDF/AC, vol. 168-A, meeting of 22 August 1846.

28. *Diario del Gobierno de la República Mexicana*, 23 August 1846; and Manuel Echeverría to Manuel Doblado, Mexico City, 22 August 1846, in García (ed.), *Documentos inéditos*, 26:15.

29. AHDF/AC, vol. 168-A, meeting of 23 August 1846; Cástulo Barreda to the editors of *El Monitor Republicano*, Mexico City, 27 August 1846, in *El Monitor Republicano*, 29 August 1846; and *Diario del Gobierno de la República Mexicana*, 27 and 31 August, 1 and 2 September 1846.

30. Santoni, *Mexicans at Arms*, 133; *Diario del Gobierno de la República Mexicana*, 19 August 1846; *El Monitor Republicano*, 18 and 20 August 1846; Bustamante, "Memorándum," 18 August 1846; and José Gómez de la Cortina to the Ministry of Foreign Relations, Mexico City, 20 August 1846, in the *Diario del Gobierno de la República Mexicana*, 26 August 1846. Quotes are from the latter two sources. A feature of centralist governance under the constitution of 1836, prefecturas were administrative districts subject to the executive authority of a prefect who served in an intermediary capacity between local (e.g., the ayuntamiento) and regional (e.g., the department) government. Costeloe, *Central Republic*, 103. Cortina's use of the term reflects the fact that federalism had not been restored as of 20 August.

31. Bustamante, "Memorándum," 8 August 1846.

32. For the full text of this popular verse, entitled "Entrada del General Santa Anna," see Avitia Hernández, *Corridos de la capital*, 40–41.

33. *El Monitor Republicano*, 4 September 1846. This ad appeared intermittently for the next thirty days or so.

34. Bustamante, *Apuntes para la historia del gobierno*, 265–66, 364; Zárate Toscano, "Héroes y fiestas," 143; González y Obregón, *Las calles de México*, 1:177; Bustamante, "Memorándum," 6 and 7 September 1846; and "Oropeza, Don Rafael, solicita colocar en el centro del Mercado Principal la estatua del Gral. Santa Anna," Mexico City, 24 August 1846, Archivo Histórico del Distrito Federal/Historia—Monumentos (henceforth cited as AHDF/H — M), vol. 2276, exp. 6, doc. 1. The only reference I have found about the rites related to this event merely notes that denizens "found the statue in a storage vault and triumphantly carried it to its former place." Reyes de la Maza, *Cien años de teatro*, 36.

35. *Diario del Gobierno de la República Mexicana*, 6 September 1846.

36. Lorenzo, "Negociaciones para la modernización, 92, n. 18, 93–94; and Bustamante, *Apuntes para la historia*, 266.

37. Antonio López de Santa Anna to the minister of [Foreign] Relations, Tacubaya, 17 September 1846, in *Diario del Gobierno de la República Mexicana*, 19 September 1846; and *El Republicano*, 19 September 1846. In a similar vein, the caudillo had earlier warned the owner of the Santa Anna Theater of his intent to administer the death penalty on any sign of "*vile adulation.*" *El Monitor Republicano*, 10 August 1846.

38. Manuel Crescencio Rejón to Santa Anna, Mexico City, 18 September 1846, in *Diario del Gobierno de la República Mexicana*, 19 September 1846; "Oropeza, Don Rafael, solicita . . . Santa Anna," Mexico City, 24 August 1846, AHDF/H — M, vol. 2276, exp. 6, doc. 5; and Bustamante, *El nuevo Bernal*, 2:100. For the statue's ultimate fate, see Zárate, "Héroes y fiestas," 145–46; and Baker, "Antonio López de Santa Anna's Search," 77.

39. AHDF/AC, vol. 168-A, meeting of 23 August 1846; Bustamante, "Memorándum," 4 September 1846; and *El Republicano*, 4 September 1846. Quotes are from the latter two.

40. *Diario del Gobierno de la República Mexicana*, 14 September 1846. Bustamante, *El nuevo Bernal*, 2:93, describes the fountains' appearance.

41. AHDF/AC, vol. 168-A, meeting of 25 August 1846.

42. Bustamante, "Memorándum," 14 September 1846; and Bustamante, *El nuevo Bernal*, 2:93–94. Quotes taken from Malo, *Diario de sucesos*, 1:306, and AHDF/AC, vol. 168-A, meeting of 25 August 1846.

43. AHDF/AC, vol. 168-A, meeting of 25 August 1846.

44. "Invitación a los vecinos de la ciudad de México a participar en los festejos," Mexico City, 8 September 1846, Biblioteca Nacional de México, Colección José María Lafragua, vol. 422, exp. 5.

45. I come to this conclusion about donations because of the lack of information about such contributions (the *Diario del Gobierno*, for instance, never publicized any donations), the financial hardship that the war imposed on Mexico, and the inability of Mexico City's Junta Patriótica since its establishment in 1825 to develop a steady source of income to finance Independence Day celebrations. Costeloe, "Junta Patriótica," 21, 36.

46. *Diario del Gobierno de la República Mexicana*, 13 September 1846.

47. *Diario del Gobierno de la República Mexicana*, 14 September 1846; *Don Simplicio*, 16 September 1846; and *El Monitor Republicano*, 15 September 1846.

48. Information on ephemeral architecture comes from Vázquez Mantecón, "Las fiestas para el libertador," 47–48; and Curcio-Nagy, *Great Festivals of Mexico City*, 22, 44–46, 71, 104–5, 118, 146, 163, n. 32, and 173, n. 19. Details about the arc are in *Noveno calendario de Abraham López*, 57; and Bustamante, *El nuevo Bernal*, 2:93. The first quote is in "Proclama de Valentín Gómez Farías y José Mariano Salas," Mexico City, 4 August 1846, in *El Republicano*, 6 August 1846. For the inscriptions, see Callcott, *Santa Anna*, 242. The lithograph was sketched by Hesiquio Iriarte, a well-known caricaturist, illustrator, and printmaker. Esparza Liberal, "Abraham López," 23.

49. Bustamante, "Memorándum," 4 September 1846; Bustamante, *El nuevo Bernal*, 2:93–94; *Noveno calendario de Abraham López*, 57; Malo, *Diario de sucesos*, 1:306; and *El Republicano*, 15 September 1846.

50. Ten days earlier Jalapa's councilmen had greeted Santa Anna with many rituals later employed in Mexico City, including triumphal arcs, and the public display of the 1824 charter. They also engaged in a *besamanos* (a hand-kissing ceremony). Santa Anna then passed through Puebla on 11 September, where another ceremonial arc in his honor graced that city's main street. Fowler, "Fiestas santanistas," 431; and *El Regenerador* (Puebla), 12 September 1846, in *Diario del Gobierno de la República Mexicana*, 17 September 1846.

51. *Diario del Gobierno de la República Mexicana*, 14 September 1846.

52. *Noveno calendario de Abraham López*, 54; *El Espectador*, 16 September 1846; Malo, *Diario de sucesos*, 1:306; Bustamante, "Memorándum," 14 September 1846; and "Orden general de la plaza del 13 al 14 de Septiembre de 1846," in *Diario del Gobierno de la República Mexicana*, 15 September 1846. The quote from Godoy's speech appears in *El Monitor Republicano*, 15 September 1846. For the remaining members of the ayuntamiento commission, see AHDF/AC, vol. 168-A, meeting of 28 August 1846.

53. The quote is from Granados, "Pequeños patricios," 29; also see Esparza Liberal, "Abraham López," 23.

54. This portrayal draws on those sources that described the carts and the procession—AHDF/AC, vol. 168-A, meeting of 25 August 1846; *Diario del Gobierno de la República Mexicana*, 15 September 1846; *El Monitor Republicano*, 15 September 1846; *Don Simplicio*, 16 September 1846; *El Republicano*, 15 September 1846; *Noveno calendario de Abraham López*, 54–55; and Bustamante, "Memorándum," 14 September 1846. The quote is from Ramírez, *Mexico during the War*, 77.

55. Details about Sierra y Rosso and Zerecero come from Costeloe, *Central Republic*, 48–49; Baker, "Antonio López de Santa Anna's Search," 68–69; Amador Zamora, "El manejo del fusil," 61–62; Santoni, *Mexicans at Arms*, 112, 140, 167; and *Diario del Gobierno de la República Mexicana*, 22 August 1846.

56. *Diario del Gobierno de la República Mexicana*, 15 September 1846.

57. Quotes from Salas's speech and the first reaction to the girl's oration are in the *Diario del Gobierno de la República Mexicana*, 15 September 1846. For the other quote about the girl's address and Romero's talk, see *Noveno calendario de Abraham López*, 55–56.

58. *Noveno calendario de Abraham López*, 56; and *El Monitor Republicano*, 15 September 1846.

59. Quotes are in Granados, "Pequeños patricios," 30; *El Monitor Republicano*, 16 September 1846; and *Noveno calendario de Abraham López*, 56.

60. The quote is from *Noveno calendario de Abraham López*, 57; and Bustamante, "Memorándum," 14 September 1846. For government efforts to persuade the Church to help fund the war effort, see Costeloe, "Church-State Financial Negotiations."

61. *Diario del Gobierno de la República Mexicana*, 15 September 1846.

62. Olavarría y Ferrari, *Reseña histórica*, 1:451; and Maza, *Cien años de teatro*, 36–37.

63. Fowler, *Santa Anna of Mexico*, 214; Bustamante, *El nuevo Bernal*, 2:96; and Santoni, *Mexicans at Arms*, 142. The first quote appears in Ramírez, *Mexico during the War*, 77–78; and the second is from Riva Palacio (ed.), *México a través de los siglos*, 4:578–79.

64. Quotes are in the *Diario del Gobierno de la República Mexicana*, 15 September 1846; and Ramírez, *Mexico during the War*, 78. To contextualize the events to which Baz alluded, see Santoni, *Mexicans at Arms*, 137–40; his comments at the assembly are in Prieto, *Memorias de mis tiempos*, 252.

65. *Diario del Gobierno de la República Mexicana*, 15 September 1846; *El Republicano*, 15 September 1846; and *Noveno calendario de Abraham López*, 54.

66. *Don Simplicio*, 16 September 1846; *Noveno calendario de Abraham López*, 54; and Charles Bankhead to Lord Palmerston, Mexico City, 29 September 1846, in Public Record Office, Foreign Office, Series 50, Mexico, vol. 199, 254. Bustamante's quotes are taken from "Memorándum," 14 September 1846, and *El nuevo Bernal*, 2:95.

67. For an analysis of how Mexico's political situation unraveled after the 14 September festivities, see Santoni, *Mexicans at Arms*, 143–82.

68. *El Trueno*, 23 February 1847. Recent scholarship belies the charge concerning electoral results. Moderado deputies enjoyed a slight majority over puro congressmen, 55 to 44; there were also 11 lawmakers who were considered neutral, and 4 whose political affiliation could not be determined. Sordo Cedeño, "El Congreso y la guerra," 55–56.

69. Costeloe, "The Mexican Church"; and Santoni, *Mexicans at Arms*, 182–97.

70. Kertzer, *Rituals, Politics, and Power*, 153.

71. Beezley, *Mexican National Identity*, 13.

72. *El Monitor Republicano*, 15 February 1846.

73. Pérez Toledo, "Mobilización social," 343–58. Other works that highlight the involvement of the urban masses in political affairs during the early republic include Warren, *Vagrants and Citizens*; Di Tella, *National Popular Politics*; and Santoni, "Lucas Balderas."

A regionally focused study that explains how rural political actors participated in pronunciamientos is Michael T. Ducey's "Municipalities, Prefects, and Pronunciamientos." For additional evidence concerning the issue of whether pronunciamientos actually represented popular elements—such as the adherence of common people locally, regionally, and/or nationally to such occurrences—see Jaime E. Rodríguez O.'s "Origins of the 1832 Rebellion" and Josefina Zoraida Vázquez's "Los pronunciamientos de 1832: Aspirantismo político e ideología," both in Rodríguez O. (ed.), *Patterns of Contention*, and see Fowler's "Joseph Welsh." The three essays indicate that in this particular instance popular support for the pronunciamiento did exist.

74. These developments call into question an unsubstantiated assertion made by a prominent historian nearly seven decades ago—that the enthusiasm shown in mid-1846 by crowds in Mexico City upon learning of Santa Anna's

return might have been prompted by the "judicious distribution of cash so the rabble could indulge in pulque." Callcott, *Santa Anna*, 242.

75. Lafragua, *Memoria de la primera secretaría*, 55.

76. Lafragua, *Miscelánea de política*, 46. For details about Lafragua's actions, see Santoni, *Mexicans at Arms*, 194–96.

MELISSA BOYD

Seven. Contemporary Verdicts on the Pronunciamiento during the Early National Period

I n his 1851 book *Porvenir de México*, Luis G. Cuevas, a lawyer who was foreign minister six times as well as minister for Mexican affairs in both the United States and Great Britain, declared: "There is almost no discussion, private talk or article in the press that does not concern the causes of our ills, the remedies that need to be applied to them and the danger that threatens our nationality."[1] From the 1820s onward, analyzing the state of the nation and the historical events that shaped it became a constant concern for politicians and intellectuals in Mexico. The problem of the *pronunciamiento*, and its associated revolts and revolutions, formed one of the most recurrent threads running through the writings of the early national period. In view of the extensive coverage of revolutions and pronunciamientos in the available writings, I have chosen to concentrate specifically on (1) how a sample of representative nineteenth-century Mexican intellectuals highlighted and analyzed the role played by the military in most pronunciamientos; (2) how they understood the legitimacy of one pronunciamiento versus the illegitimacy of the next; (3) how factional disputes were perceived to inform the recurrence of this practice; and (4) the reasons they gave to explain occurrence of pronunciamientos and the recommendations they made to avoid these in the future.

Luis Gongaza Cuevas, José María Luis Mora, Mariano Otero, Lorenzo de Zavala, Manuel Crescencio Rejón, Melchor Ocampo, Valentín Gómez Farías, Manuel Gómez Pedraza, José María Lafragua, and José María Gutiérrez de Estrada all reflected on the phenomenon of the pronunciamiento, and whether they criticized or approved it, the importance they gave it was unanimous.[2] Their analyses and constant references to the pronunciamientos were designed to clarify the events that had led up to the revolts in an earnest attempt to find solutions to Mexico's continual upheavals. However, these analyses were also their vehicle for justifying those in which the authors themselves had actually taken part. In their favor it must be said that it was also their intention to keep these events alive in the memory of the nation, so that Mexicans could learn from the past and avoid making the same mistakes in future.

Before launching into an analysis of their attitudes toward the pronunciamientos, it should be pointed out that although they were all politicians, ideologues, and writers, these Mexican intellectuals all had very different motivations, and their opinions were affected by different events. Cuevas (1800–67), for example, a lawyer, politician and diplomat, was interested in using a historical study to explain the nation's situation in 1850. When it was published he had recently left the Ministry of Foreign and Internal Affairs. One of his main tasks had been to enforce the 2 February 1848 Guadalupe Hidalgo Treaty, ratification of which brought the Mexican-American 1846–48 War to an end. The questions Cuevas raised in *Porvenir de México* reflected the bitterness he felt at the losses sustained in the war. Why was the nation in such a state, so weak and so divided? What had led to its losing huge swathes of its territory? His conclusion was that the instability, the degradation, the appalling state of the country could be blamed to a great extent on the pronunciamientos that had weakened national unity, leaving Mexico defenseless in the face of the invading forces.

He was not the only one to reach this conclusion. Mariano Otero (1817–50), a shrewd politician, the ideological standard bearer of the *moderados* and a staunch federalist, was facing the same quandary when he wrote his *Ensayo sobre el verdadero estado de la cuestión social y política que se agita en la República Mexicana*. In it he ascertained the origins of the problems facing Mexico in 1842 and, on the basis of his findings, suggested those reforms he thought would save the nation. In Otero's case, however, this was not the only reason he was writing. Whereas Cuevas was driven by the experiences and outcomes of the recent conflict with the United States, Otero was propelled by his defense of the 1841 Revolución de Jalisco. The opening of the Constituent Congress in June 1842 meant that all of Otero's writings and conclusions were geared to one end—buttressing his attempts to introduce a new constitution for the nation—and the opinions expressed in the *Ensayo* were echoed in his speeches and the motions he raised in Congress.

Lorenzo de Zavala (1788–1836), on the other hand, was a radical Yucatecan politician. He had participated in the 1824 Constituent Congress, and backed Vicente Guerrero's presidential candidacy during the 1828 Acordada Rebellion, but was forced into exile in May 1830 following the conservative victory that resulted from the Jalapa pronunciamiento of 4 December 1829. His *Ensayo histórico de las revoluciones de México*, written barely a decade after independence, sketched the history of independent Mexico as he looked for the root to the ills affecting the nation in the early 1830s. Once again, however, this was not his prime reason for writing. A member of Guerrero's ousted government, exiled in Paris when the first volume was published and in New York for the second, Zavala was intent upon getting his views across by explaining his actions and proving that his participation in recent events had been in the best interest of the nation.

These writers, and they were not the only ones, upheld their different views on pronunciamientos, on the right to revolt, and on the necessity for revolutions at specific points in time. As a result, the works they left behind present ambivalent, not to say contradictory, stances. In their writings, newspaper articles, or speeches, the men under scrutiny here were interested not only in publicizing their version of recent events but also in bolstering a party position or justifying a current viewpoint. If commentators often remarked that the participants in the events of the early national period were inconsistent and conflicting in their political stances, the same can be said of their views on pronunciamientos. Similarly, many of these views were determined by the specific external episodes shaping individual opinion, so that each one painted a picture of pronunciamientos not, perhaps, as they were, or even as they were seen, but as each individual wanted them to be seen, to justify his particular stance to his contemporaries as well as to future generations. However varied their stances might be, there emerges one common thread. The role of the military in the rebellions, revolts, and revolutions usually began with a pronunciamiento.

The Military

A significant number of Mexico's intellectuals, while disputing other contributions to the country's ills, were united on one main

point—the army was to blame for the phenomenon of the pronunciamiento that had plagued Mexico in the years following
independence. As far as they were concerned, the army not only
participated in but actively planned and carried out pronunciamientos across the country. The military strength provided by
army backing led to the practice becoming an accepted form of
airing one's grievances. It became a focal point of many of their
writings, and the role of the army was openly abhorred by most.
At the same time however, it has to be said, some saw it as a means
of achieving their own goals.

Beginning with the revolution with which Mexico attained its
independence, Zavala looked back on the disturbances and revolts that had affected the nation up until 1830.[3] He presented the
movement for independence as an essential revolution, as the only
likely outcome after three hundred years of Spanish rule.[4] With
the consummation of Independence, however, Zavala became
concerned with the direction the nation was taking. Although he
admitted that as a newborn nation it was only to be expected that
much would be based on trial and error, he also pointed out that
the revolts and pronunciamientos following independence could
have been avoided from the very beginning.[5] In hindsight, he argued, one of the first errors was not forcing the army to adopt its
proper position as defender of the nation by banning its involvement in politics. It was this involvement that produced the disasters overwhelming the nation and led to the "empire by bayonets."[6] This view was shared by Melchor Ocampo (1814–61), a
liberal politician who exerted great influence as the governor of
Michoacán but also on the national stage with the mid-centu-
ry Reform Laws and the signing of the McLane-Ocampo Treaty
with the United States between 1859 and 1860. While discussing

constitutional regulations as a deputy in the 1842 Constituent Congress, and under the shadow of an impending military-led dissolution of the said Congress, he stressed that the army was one of the main problems facing Mexico at that time.[7] He argued that there could be no such thing as a free, independent nation while a permanent army existed within it. He believed that no equilibrium would ever be maintained when the military forces were so clearly oblivious to the fact that they were also citizens.

In line with the radical liberal ideology Zavala fervently upheld, of separating church and army from the affairs of the state, an emphasis on the removal of the armed forces from any active participation in the political sphere was to become a recurring theme in all his writings. He argued that armed interference meant there was no way of knowing what the nation and its people wanted, and that the military not only intervened but actively ruled over a country so accustomed to its subservient role that it was unable, or unwilling, to challenge this status quo.[8] Indeed Zavala went so far as to state that as long as the armed forces were involved in the machinations of the political factions, it was impossible for these to succeed, no matter what other support they could muster.[9] Logically, therefore, in Zavala's mind, any intervention by the military in the political issues of the day was to be viewed as a direct attack on national sovereignty. Rightful authority was being usurped. Ocampo, again, agreed, finding the situation had not changed much by the early 1840s. Ocampo stressed that in advanced nations the army was nothing more than a servant of the nation, a mere tool at the disposal of the political bodies.[10] He made the point that this was not the case in Mexico in 1842, where by taking advantage of the lack of any strong legal or constitutional binding, the army had forged a position for itself within the very heart of state affairs. Once the army had been allowed to express support for a cause or an opinion through force, there could be no other outcome to events.[11] Therefore the military needed to be controlled and constrained to ensure that it was unable to pronounce, regardless of which sector of opinion it supported or which faction it backed, and forced to submit to national sovereignty embodied in a strong constitution. Once this had been accomplished, the army, stripped of all power, would have become a tool for peace, a means of protecting the country against foreign invasion, and it would remain isolated from political involvement.

Even so, Zavala was capable of praising the army, albeit in passing. He argued that the troops were not always the instrument of the oppressors, as they often split their support between the various factions.[12] However, he felt that whenever they pronounced for liberalism, federation, and republicanism, a cause Zavala himself supported, the adherence of these troops could not be sincere, as the ultimate goals of this liberal faction were the abolition of the privileges and the *fueros* the military enjoyed; something it obviously could not and would not tolerate.[13] Zavala even went so far as to set a specific point in time when military intervention signaled the end of hope for the nation. Prior to the 1828 elections to replace Guadalupe Victoria as president, and the subsequent Acordada Rebellion, in the main the country was peaceful, and he attributed this to the fact that the "military might had not yet profaned the sanctity of the law."[14] This changed. Elections, which should have been purely political processes, degenerated into wars between factions, factions that included members of the army. This immediately meant elections were no longer political but military affairs.[15] As such, the troops slowly took over, and ever after, few of these military men accepted their salaries

Boyd

as sufficient recompense for the work they did. Governorships, local government positions, or even the presidency were considered to be theirs by right, and in order retain these privileges, they needed to maintain their stranglehold on the political process.[16] So much so that at the time of publication in 1831, Zavala feared there was no power in Mexico other than that of the "bayonets"—no rules, no regulations, no conscience, no sense of duty, no constitution or legislation or laws that were respected by the military. Nothing could be achieved without its support. The army, on the other hand, could achieve anything it wanted, by raising its voice and issuing a pronunciamiento.

Decades later José María Luis Mora (1794–1850), a radical politician who had lived in exile in Europe since 1834, acknowledged in letters to the Mexican minister of foreign and internal affairs, dated 1848, that José Joaquín de Herrera's government's main task was to bring peace to the nation—not only following the war with the United States but also after the incessant rebellions that had torn the country apart and left it on the brink of a precipice, so weak as to be unable to offer any resistance to an invading force.[17] In order for the administration to accomplish this task, Mora strongly urged the minister to reform the army, as it was the principal threat to the government. He went on to state that the military was famous for fabricating any pretext to revolt or pronounce, and that the point was being reached where it would soon start to do so without any reason at all. The only way the country could survive and begin to reconstruct itself in the face of the overwhelming defeat of 1847 would be when the military was completely overhauled, and the officers who had maintained power for so long were forced to resign, enabling the government to establish civic militias and regain control.[18]

Unlike Mora, Manuel Gómez Pedraza (1789–1851), a high-ranking officer who was a moderate politician and head of this faction in Mexico City, argued that it was not the army that had begun the constant revolts and pronunciamientos. Like Zavala, Gómez Pedraza pinpointed a specific moment, at the very beginning of the national period, when one could identify the initial revolutions that corrupted the army.[19] Where Zavala had highlighted the late 1820s, for Gómez Pedraza 1822 and 1823 were the critical points in time when the army, which had been called on to support different political stances, became corrupt and lost all respect for the duly constituted authorities. Luis Gonzaga Cuevas backed Gómez Pedraza's view. Where the movement for independence had been supported by the army, it did so without any personal motives. Like Zavala, Cuevas saw the army's participation in the struggle for independence as justified. However, once the military's participation had been cemented by the success of the movement, corruption began, and pronunciamientos and revolts ensued. With its victory, Cuevas argued, the military saw a new route to rewards and prizes, achievable much more quickly by revolution than by any lawful path. From this moment the military ensured that no government would be able to rule without its support. The military chiefs of the independence period — and more surprisingly, Cuevas remarked, those who succeeded them — were to use the freedom they helped to acquire as a badge of authority, which meant they owed no obedience to any government, law, or institution, thereby seriously undermining the legally elected authority.[20]

These are but a few of the opinions expressed by some of the foremost intellectuals of the early national period that associated the practice of the pronunciamiento with the political role the army acquired following independence. On closer inspection, however, it remains the case that they were capable of portraying the military, and the pronunciamientos in which the army took part, as forces of either tyranny or liberation, either for the greater good or for evil and chaos, depending on whether they supported or opposed a given pronunciamiento cycle or not. Zavala, to mention but one of them, regardless of his condemnation of the army's propensity to disobey and challenge the civil authorities, actively supported, participated in, and benefited from the pronunciamiento of the Acordada barracks in November 1828.

The Will of the People

Stemming from the ambivalence of pronunciamientos, most Mexican politicians found themselves not only reflecting on the practice as an arguable praetorian tradition but also pondering more abstract issues, such as the will of the people or the good of the country, issues that were part of the justification of most pronunciamientos. The will of the people was a major concern for nineteenth-century Mexicans. With their independence all Mexicans, and particularly those engaged in politics, were faced with the issues and questions of representation. Legitimacy was one such concept, and its construction was at the forefront of the preoccupations of those men involved in the transition from colony to independent nation and who, in the years that followed, wrote and reformed constitutions, participated in congresses, and addressed the concerns of the embryonic nation in other ways. Only a legitimate government would be able to give Mexico the necessary stability, and without it, the nation could not flourish. Included in this was the need for the actions and reactions of the political classes to represent and respond to the will of the nation, to address the concerns of "the people." Not surprisingly, this was also a concern for the pronunciados, who often took up the banner of the will of the nation in a bid to legitimize their counter-constitutional actions.

Zavala was one who could not attribute all the ills of the nation to military involvement in politics. He argued that political factions should also be blamed for the instability of the governments. Elections were not a powerful enough tool, as they were dismissed and pronounced against, sometimes even before a result had been officially announced. The outcome of such pronunciamientos would be a successful faction that, having taken over the capital, would immediately proclaim its victory, citing its obedience to the will of the people, only to be contradicted equally quickly by the opposing faction making a similar claim, and each side adamant that the people's voice had been silenced by the other side's tyrannical forces, in power illegitimately.[21] Indeed, other accounts coincide with Zavala's.

Manuel Crescencio Rejón (1799–1849), a radical politician, active in his home state of Yucatán as well as in national politics as a writer, legislator, and politician, argued that in Puebla he and his colleagues had been forced to adhere to what in his opinion was a legitimate uprising in support of public opinion and against injustice, oppression, and tyranny.[22] Mariano Otero, who was strongly against revolution and pronunciamientos, came out in favor of the 1841 Revolución de Jalisco, arguing that it was a movement that should not be confused with "a mutiny and one that profoundly shook the foundations of society producing a general movement that excited the interest and action of all men and all parties" — except, of course, those who were being violently deposed from power.[23] In Otero's opinion this pronunciamiento was different from the rest, as its intention was only to unite the country, invoking the will of the people as its justification. Otero ignored the fact that the revolution had moved against a legitimately established government and had replaced existing powers and laws with those promulgated by the revolt. Barely a year later, however, he grumbled in his personal correspondence that the very people with whom he had sided in 1841, and now opposed to his call for the reestablishment of federalism, were purporting to represent the will of the nation, "which is to say, that of the garrisons."[24] His double standard was evident: the will of the nation was only truly the will of the nation when invoked to suit his purpose.

This was a view shared by José María Lafragua (1813–75), a liberal politician and man of letters, native of Puebla but heavily involved in central politics as a legislator and journalist until his death in 1875. Reflecting on the general events of the U.S.-Mexican War, and more specifically on the Polkos pronunciamiento, he too referred to the will of the people and distinguished between the conjectural and the published motives of the Polko rebellion and the real causes that brought it into existence. Although publicly the pronunciamiento sought to repeal the law on the sale of church property, it was in fact the downfall of the government, specifically the removal of Valentín Gómez Farías, that was the pronunciados' ultimate goal. He went so far as to admit, in the interest of honesty, that while public opinion was on their side, they did not have the necessary money or soldiers, essential ingredients for success. As a result, and in order to be able to assure the triumph of the national will, they were forced to ally themselves with the church, which provided the funds, and to involve certain regiments, which provided the military force, before they could accomplish their real goal of bringing down Gómez Farías and recalling Santa Anna.[25] Thus what had originally been "the will of the nation" had been transformed into a pronunciamiento financed by the church and therefore representing its will instead.

For some individuals, when under attack, the will of the people, used as a tool by so many, became nothing more than an excuse. Facing criticism of his position and with a pronunciamiento brewing against him, Valentín Gómez Farías (1781–1858), radical politician and interim Mexican president on several occasions, argued that his enemies were trying to pass off something that was nothing more than resentment and envy as the voice of the people, backed by no more than a handful of people, seduced or bought by his enemies.[26] However, when his position shifted and he found himself on the side of the opposition, his discourse also shifted. In 1838 he asked himself if those who had armed themselves were right to have done so and immediately responded that they were. They were merely representing the national will; having sought change peacefully through the press and by filing complaints with the government, they had been ignored, forcing them to take justice into their own hands.[27] He went so far as to prod General José Urrea to continue his plan to establish a federation, as this would show that the pronunciados were in touch with the voice of the people. To achieve this, he accepted the adhesion of the military as a support tool for carrying out the wishes of the immense majority of the nation.[28] In his quest for power and the reestablishment of the federal constitution Gómez Farías argued that "revolution is evil, but a necessary evil."[29] However, when in 1847 his acting presidency was under threat, the man who had led the 15 July 1840 pronunciamiento against President Anastasio Bustamante now struck out against the Polko rebellion, arguing that its perpetrators did not, and could not, represent the will of the people and that any revolt was unacceptable with the U.S. troops on the doorstep. On this occasion he asked rhetorically who it was that allowed the rebellious forces to believe they had the power to set themselves up as regulators of the country.[30]

Manuel Gómez Pedraza, writing in 1827 in reaction to the pronunciamiento of José María Gallardo, emphasized that anyone who broke the law by assuming the faculties of a duly constituted government, or who disturbed the national order, should be considered a criminal. In addition he argued that nobody had the right to lead the people against the established government under any pretext, as the country would descend into anarchy, and it could only lead to disaster. This was why he considered the pronunciamiento headed by Gallardo as criminal. However, he felt the troops involved in it were merely acting from misguided patriotism and not from any more sinister motive.[31] The image that he was portraying was that of a lone individual, whose resistance to the established order was merely the consequence of his own misguided motives and not the will of the nation. Gómez Pedraza wanted to ensure that he would be remembered not for his crushing the pronunciamiento but for ending the lunacy of one man, so that the incident would not be seen as opposing the national will. A few years later he described pronunciamientos as the political fevers of the nation and stated that they could be useful or pernicious, depending on how they developed.[32] At this point, in 1832, when a revolution was being orchestrated to bring him back from exile to complete his term as president, the portrayal he offered shifted. He argued that revolutions could either compromise and degrade the good of the nation or advance and improve it. They were indeed dangerous and could result in anarchy, disorder, and woe, but if well managed they could be used for the good of the nation. This applied particularly to this latter revolution, which would be used specifically to restore the legitimately elected executive, consolidate peace within the nation, and stabilize the country, which in turn would close the door on any future revolts.[33] All this, of course, could be accomplished only with Gómez Pedraza as president.

Factional Disputes

From what has been noted so far it becomes evident that the way individuals behaved politically governed their view and remembrance of the pronunciamientos. In order to reinforce their political and ideological positions, they were more than willing to present two nearly identical situations as being complete opposites: one right, the other wrong, one legitimate, the other illegitimate, depending on their own memories and those they wished to transmit to the nation.

These men represented specific ideological views at specific times and were usually associated, some loosely, others more closely, with different factions and political standpoints. How these factions were seen by those involved, by those on the sideline of the national political scene, and by their bitter rivals also sheds light on how pronunciamientos were viewed as a tool of these opposing groups. For Zavala, these political factions were warring over ranks, positions, and control of the nation. To achieve their aims they rode roughshod over constitutional procedures and laws and regulations debarring them from pursuing these ends on the battlefield. They moved away from political maneuvering and plotting, reasonable debate, and purely political intrigue to garner from military factions the support that they were unable or unwilling to find in lawful procedures.[34] Pronunciamientos often unfurled a banner of freedom, liberty, or justice that in reality became nothing more than a struggle for advancement, a means of obtaining power or of addressing personal grievances.[35] Zavala maintained that revolts and rebellions were often nothing more than a tool used by separate factions to defeat rivals driven by ambition or vengeance. This in turn led to constant upheavals being planned and executed, with first one side then the other emerging victorious. The losing faction would never acknowledge the winner's triumph, generally on the grounds that it had been achieved illegally, and the victors abused their position and behaved tyrannically, thus widening the breach. Victory would make some daring and others resentful, a situation ensuring that altercations began almost immediately, thus perpetuating the struggle for power and the need for pronunciamientos as a means of achieving said power.[36] Gómez Pedraza added that each time one faction won, it would ensure that every position of political power—locally and nationally, in the military and the church, special emissaries and governors—would be occupied by those who had pronounced. When the tables turned, positions were reversed.[37] These constant shifts and reshuffles meant that the country was not in a position to prosper or even to establish a stable authority, let alone a durable constitution, and so pronunciamientos prospered as the easiest way to achieve the goals of all factions, perpetuating a vicious circle, which in Zavala's view meant nothing would ever be achieved. Lafragua agreed with him, arguing that each time a revolt or revolution succeeded, the winning party treated the losing factions with scorn, leading to the original victor being scorned in turn by the people, creating instability and uncertainty.[38]

Valentín Gómez Farías also highlighted the dissention between political parties, and the revenge each hoped to inflict upon the other, as one of the main causes of pronunciamientos. He argued that the country was so divided that there were factions willing to support peace only when they themselves were in power and who, when unable to achieve the political position they coveted, would scheme and plot.[39]

Sometimes pronunciamientos brought radically different factions together; but Otero argued that they did so only insofar as factions shared a common enemy or goal. However, once the enemy had been defeated, once the goal had been achieved, any adhesion between the groups vanished; they separated and immediately began a new fight against each other in a bid to gain power and position.[40] Zavala—speaking of the downfall of Iturbide, a pronunciamiento that was classed as an insurrection designed only to bring down the despotic emperor—argued that it was only supported in the capital as a means of ensuring that the disturbance ended promptly. He also admitted that in this, and in many of the pronunciamientos that followed, those involved were unable to contain them. As the pronunciamientos and *actas de adhesión* spread, each geographical area and interest group would add its own specific articles dealing with local or personal concerns, and this meant the final results often had nothing in common with the intent of the original pronunciamiento.[41]

The Solutions

Because revolutions, revolts, pronunciamientos, uprisings, and rebellions were seen by many writers of the time as one of the defining factors in the early national period, these events are a recurring theme in their writings. We have seen their opinions on military involvement in pronunciamientos, on the voice of the nation in pronunciamientos, and on the perpetuation of the practice due to factional disputes. However, these writers were not content merely to analyze and discuss the phenomenon; they also put forward tentative solutions.

Zavala strongly believed that pronunciamientos were caused by the friction between the factions, and once one had revolted and achieved victory through violence, the precedent was set. This could have been avoided, and an end made to pronunciamientos, if from the very start there had been a properly constituted authority with the competency to examine the actions of each faction and judge each accordingly. In addition, as mentioned previously, he maintained that the role of the military had a great deal to do with the spread of pronunciamientos across the nation, and better regulation of the army would quickly have reduced the number of revolts. Yet he also felt there were more deep-seated causes, which if resolved, would have put an end to the tumult and division experienced by the country.

The treasury stood empty, and the demands made upon it grew each day. Mexico having lost trade with Spain, commerce was slow to gain ground after independence, and the constant revolts meant that the new nation was unable to flourish as expected, being seriously affected by the length of time taken to establish new trade deals with foreign countries. The lack of revenue meant that the military, public employees, and many key figures were not being paid and were more likely to join a revolt that promised them a quick recompense. No government was in a position to repel any violent attempt against it.[42] Given the attention they deserved, many of the underlying issues used as excuses by rebels would disappear, leaving those wishing to pronounce with no supportive base to assist them in their goals. The pretext of "the will of the nation" should also be removed as, without it, no group could claim to represent it. Justice or injustice should not be judged by governments or individuals but by laws and courts.[43]

Although Zavala did not specify how these issues should be addressed, he did open up the debate. He asked himself: "Up to what point must the people suffer oppression in order to have the right to rise against their government; when one faction is compelled to comply when it is not in its best interests without offering any resistance; when one party can legitimately call itself national, and this august denomination, so frequently usurped, bestows the right to shed the blood of the inhabitants, by revolutionary tribunals, by military court or even without any legal body."[44] He also raised other points he felt should be addressed. One was the necessity for a strong legislature and the establishment of specific regulations dictating what was acceptable and what was not. Break them and punishment should be immediate. It was essential to establish that Congress, and only Congress, was the true representative of the will of the people, and the only institution with the legal status to hear and resolve conflicts and complaints and answer grievances of the sort usually shrouded in pronunciamientos. Guaranteed a fair hearing and a prompt decision, those with grievances would have no reason to pronounce, and the need for pronunciamientos would gradually disappear.[45] He called on the deputies to discard all old-fashioned legislation incompatible with a newly independent nation and demanded that "timid policies, petty artfulness, the mysterious conduct of the previous government be replaced by noble frankness, good faith and energy in its decisions."[46]

Manuel Crescencio Rejón went further, specifically stating that what the country needed the most was a code or constitution powerful enough to ensure that laws and legislation were unchallengeable, as without an immutable rule, the country would only erupt in further revolts. Decisions by Congress should be sacrosanct, thereby gaining respectability and support for national representation.[47] He even went so far as to argue that Congress should be given the power to judge and punish not only those involved in suspending Congress in 1844 and 1845 but also any political, civil, military, or clerical entity or any individual who had contributed to the dissolution of any congress since independence.[48] His argument formed part of his justification for his political stance between 1841 and 1844, and his preoccupation with being remembered as a fine upstanding citizen who had supported the just movements of 1841 and had turned his back on the evil and tyrannical movements of 1844 and 1845 that led to his exile.

José María Gutiérrez Estrada (1800–67), who had worked tirelessly for Spanish recognition of Mexican independence, and who eventually supported a constitutional monarchy for the nation, also argued in 1840 that the ills of the nation were caused by the lack of an established constitution. The pronunciados who stormed the National Palace and took President Bustamante prisoner in July 1840 were able to do so, he thought, only because the majority of the nation was against the 1836 Constitution.[49] With such readily available excuses, the revolts and revolutions that affected the nation would never cease. He too argued for a constitutional solution, but he pointed out that it would be impossible to use either the 1824 Constitution or the 1836 Constitution as a template, as each had both fervent supporters and enemies and, irrespective of which one was chosen, revolts would occur automatically as each faction fought against what they saw as an inadequate solution.

Only by drafting a new constitution addressing the needs and requirements of the separate factions would remove all the excuses used to date to start and support pronunciamientos.[50]

Pronunciamientos were a way of life in the early national period. Anyone closely connected to the events of the time would have been involved in a pronunciamiento, proclaimed a pronunciamiento, or suffered the consequences of a pronunciamiento. Zavala, Otero, Cuevas, and their contemporaries, when writing their accounts of these occurrences, were therefore spurred by the necessity of justifying their participation in one or several of these actions. In semiautobiographical glosses, they exculpated protagonists from charges of private gain and vindicated their own actions as being in the best interest of the budding nation, while castigating their opponents for doing exactly the opposite. All these men were unanimous in their condemnation of pronunciamientos, but regrettably, when it suited their purpose or benefited them, they were quite happy to look the other way and even to instigate the actions. Personal advantages or political jockeying for power frequently outweighed such considerations as the good of the nation. After achieving high political office on the back of a pronunciamiento, they complained loudly at any attempt to unseat them by the same modus operandi, even when couched as the voice of the people. Toppling a president was acceptable until it was their own presidency that was being toppled. Equally, when it was not in their best interest or that of their political faction, they were vehement in their condemnation of a practice that lacked legality. In short, they considered it a highly questionable activity — until it suited their personal agenda. They were, however, united in their opinion that military interference in affairs of state, supporting one or other of the warring political factions, was the main cause of pronunciamientos being seen as a solution to right the ills affecting Mexico or as an easy route to personal or political advancement by their opponents. In their defense it must be said that they frequently put forward suggestions that they hoped would abolish these practices and see them confined to the past. The apparent contradictions emerging from the ambivalent accounts of the early national period in Mexico highlight one key point — the importance of seeing the events and the practices of this period through the eyes of the men who lived through them. The manner in which these individuals remembered and presented the events of the decades following independence shaped the generations to come, and even now their views are reflected in the current commemoration of independence and the construction of Mexican national identity.

Notes

1. Cuevas, *Porvenir de México* (1992), 1:43.
2. I have drawn their views from their works: Cuevas, *Porvenir de México* (1992); Briceño Senosiáin et al. (eds.), *Mora: Obras Completas*, vol. 8; Reyes Heroles (coord.), *Mariano Otero: Obras*; Zavala, *Ensayo histórico*; Rejón, *Pensamiento político*; Ocampo, *Textos políticos*; Briceño Senosiáin et al. (eds.), *Valentín Gómez Farías*; Solares Robles, *La obra política de Manuel Gómez Pedraza*; Galeana de Valdés (ed.), *José María Lafragua*; Gutiérrez de Estrada, "La monarquía como posibilidad."
3. Zavala, *Ensayo histórico*.
4. Zavala, *Ensayo histórico*, 1:24–31.
5. Zavala, *Ensayo histórico*, 1:121–22.
6. Zavala, *Ensayo histórico*, 1:124.
7. Ocampo, *Textos políticos*, 1:24–27.
8. Ocampo, *Textos políticos*, 1:137.
9. Ocampo, *Textos políticos*, 1:152.
10. Ocampo, *Textos políticos*, 1:25–26.
11. Ocampo, *Textos políticos*, 1:27.

12. Ocampo, *Textos políticos*, 1:153.

13. Ocampo, *Textos políticos*, 1:153.

14. Ocampo, *Textos políticos*, 1:225.

15. Ocampo, *Textos políticos*, 1:226–27, 252.

16. Ocampo, *Textos políticos*, 1:259–60.

17. Briceño Senosiáin et al. (eds.), *Mora: Obras Completas*, Miscelánea, 8:256.

18. Briceño Senosiáin et al. (eds.), *Mora: Obras Completas*, Miscelánea, 8:256

19. Solares Robles, *La obra política de Manuel Gómez Pedraza*, 1:126.

20. Cuevas, *Porvenir de México* (1992), 2:66.

21. Zavala, *Ensayo histórico*, 1:152–53, 184, 217, 252; 2:10, 27–29, 34, 38, 50, 66, 102–3, 133, 142, 176.

22. Rejón, *Pensamiento político*, 3.

23. Reyes Heroles (coord.), *Mariano Otero: Obras*, 10.

24. Reyes Heroles (coord.), *Mariano Otero: Obras*, 115.

25. Galeana de Valdés (ed.), *José María Lafragua*, 62–64.

26. Briceño Senosiáin et al. (eds.), *Valentín Gómez Farías*, 325–26.

27. Briceño Senosiáin et al. (eds.), *Valentín Gómez Farías*, 331.

28. Briceño Senosiáin et al. (eds.), *Valentín Gómez Farías*, 336–37.

29. Briceño Senosiáin et al. (eds.), *Valentín Gómez Farías*, 358.

30. Briceño Senosiáin et al. (eds.), *Valentín Gómez Farías*, 384.

31. Solares Robles, *La obra política de Manuel Gómez Pedraza*, 1:158.

32. Solares Robles, *La obra política de Manuel Gómez Pedraza*, 1:183.

33. Solares Robles, *La obra política de Manuel Gómez Pedraza*, 1:263–267.

34. Zavala, *Ensayo histórico*, 1:225–26; 2:10, 142.

35. Zavala, *Ensayo histórico*, 2:50.

36. Zavala, *Ensayo histórico*, 2:66.

37. Zavala, *Ensayo histórico*, 2:133; Solares Robles, *La obra política de Manuel Gómez Pedraza*, 1:269–70.

38. Galeana de Valdés (ed.), *José María Lafragua*, 130.

39. Briceño Senosiáin et al. (eds.), *Valentín Gómez Farías*, 312.

40. Reyes Heroles, *Mariano Otero: Obras*, 44.

41. Zavala, *Ensayo histórico*, 1:184.

42. Zavala, *Ensayo histórico*, 2:126–31, 261.

43. Zavala, *Ensayo histórico*, 2:79.

44. Zavala, *Ensayo histórico*, 2:105.

45. Zavala, *Ensayo histórico*, 2:110–19.

46. Zavala, *Ensayo histórico*, 2:119.

47. Rejón, *Pensamiento político*, 3.

48. Rejón, *Pensamiento político*, 82–83.

49. Gutiérrez de Estrada, "La monarquía como posibilidad," 276–77.

50. Gutiérrez de Estrada, "La monarquía como posibilidad," 279–81.

ANTONIA PI-SUÑER LLORENS

Eight. The Crumbling of a "Hero":
Ignacio Comonfort from Ayutla to Tacubaya

I n *El Libro Rojo*, published between 1870 and 1871, Manuel Payno addressed the figure of Ignacio Comonfort, pointing out
that it was not his intention to write a biography but only "the
familiar memories of some of the most striking features of a man
who, in any case, would have to be taken into account in our contemporary history."[1] The subtitle of the book was "Bonfires, gallows, scaffolds, martyrdoms, suicides, gloomy and strange events
that happened in Mexico during the civil and foreign wars," since
its purpose was to remember those individuals who had been sacrificed for the country. Comonfort was at that time considered
a martyr of Mexican history—at least by the editors of *El Libro Rojo*. A year later, in 1872, Manuel Rivera Cambas included
in his *Gobernantes de México* a biography showing great respect
for Comonfort. According to Rivera, Comonfort had "a great
soul" and his acts were always sound until "he took a false step,"
the coup d'état of December 1857. Nevertheless, Comonfort had
atoned for his errors by his self-exile, with the Foreign Intervention having offered him "an honorable vindication." Although he
had been courting death since the siege of Puebla in 1863, he unfortunately did not die in particularly heroic circumstances until several months later.[2]

When these biographical sketches were written, the Juárez

administration was, in its turn, vindicating Comonfort. In February 1868 his remains were transferred from San Miguel de Allende to the cemetery of San Fernando in Mexico City and were honored with "solemn funeral rites" in Congress. The ceremony was attended by all the secretaries of state, congressmen, and "many other public servants," with president Juárez at the top of the list.[3] A possible reason for the presence of the latter and his staff—among whom were Sebastián Lerdo de Tejada and José María Iglesias, former friends and collaborators of Comonfort—could have been that they also believed the late president "had expiated his fault" dying for the Republic. But there is also room for the conjecture that there was another more pragmatic reason: Comonfort was not so greatly mistaken in his appreciation of how difficult it was to govern with the 1857 Constitution.

Payno's statement that "in any case" Comonfort would have a place in Mexican history was probably founded in his belief that as time went by, the judgment of History (with a capital H) would not be as harsh toward Comonfort as that of the Liberal Radicals after what they called the coup d'état of December 1857. Payno's view would prove mistaken. Given that the 1857 Constitution became the liberal banner of the wars of the Reforma (1858–60) and French Intervention (1862–67), and moreover that it was triumphant in both conflicts, emerging as the national symbol of radical liberalism, the image of Comonfort as the president who had disowned it in December 1857 resulted in his losing the heroic dimension that two historical works had given him. These were *Historia de la revolución de México en contra de la dictadura del general Santa Anna: 1853–1855* and *México en 1856 y 1857: Gobierno del general Comonfort*, both written by the Spaniard Anselmo de la Portilla, the first in 1856 and the second two years later, in New York, where the exiled president was living at the time.

In spite of their epic and flattering discourse—it is interesting to remember that José María Mata ironically called the one written in New York "la Comonforteida" (the Comonfortiad, in reference to Virgil's *Aeneid*)—these two books became the main sources for all the successive historians who undertook the task of reconstructing the events that took place between the *pronunciamientos* of Ayutla and Tacubaya. They followed these two works closely—sometimes copying them without qualms—albeit diverging from them as to the perception of Comonfort and his acts. In this essay I aim to show the coincidences and disagreements between these first books and those published between 1860 and 1901, all of them written in very different circumstances and with diverse intentions.

Considering these works in chronological order, I have reviewed the *Memoria sobre la revolución de 1857 y enero de 1858* that Manuel Payno wrote to explain his participation in the coup d'état and defend himself from the accusation of treason. From this same author I have also used the Comonfort biographical sketch in *El Libro Rojo* mentioned at the beginning of this essay. My third source is the Comonfort biography Rivera Cambas included in his *Gobernantes de México*, to which I have already referred. These last two texts arose out of the concern of the Restored Republic's intellectual elite to construct a historical discourse that would lead the nation to conciliation and integration. It was believed that this necessary step could be accomplished by putting forward the lives of the most relevant figures of national history, an act that paved the way for the construction of a monumental history. Years later and in more peaceful times, the historical discourse would not be restricted to biographical sketches but would undertake the task of reconstructing all the political events from pre-Hispanic times to the victory of the Republic over Maximilian's empire (1864–67). This was the trend followed by the first general histories, of which the *Historia de Méjico* by Niceto de Zamacois, published in Barcelona between 1876 and 1882, was the most ambitious. Of this *Historia*, I have reviewed volumes 13 and 14, which cover the events of interest here. It is self-evident that this work, written in Spain by a conservative Spaniard who was a devout Catholic, could not be adopted by a nation that prided itself on being liberal and secular. Hence the triumphant liberals undertook the writing of a history that eventually became the official version of the Mexican historical process. Of this discourse I first analyzed the *Lecciones de historia patria*, written as a high-school text by Guillermo Prieto and published in 1886, and then the relevant chapters of *México independiente* by Enrique Olavarría y Ferrari and of *La Reforma* by José María Vigil, both volumes belonging to the grand *México a través de los siglos*, which appeared in the 1880s. In these same years Rivera Cambas wrote an important work on Mexico's foreign history, *Historia de la intervención europea y norteamericana en México y del Imperio de Maximiliano de Habsburgo*, which I have also consulted. The last of my sources is Justo Sierra's historical review for *Mexico: Su evolución social*, published in 1900–1901.

I have divided this essay into five parts according to the questions posed concerning the different historians' interpretations of Comonfort and his actions in the pronunciamientos of Ayutla and Tacubaya as well as during his presidential terms. The answers indicate how different the approaches and versions of the facts were.

The Pronunciamiento of Ayutla: Its Origin and Authorship

Anselmo de la Portilla presented Comonfort as the main promoter of what he called "the revolution" of Ayutla (1854–55), a term that was used by all subsequent authors as an equivalent for pronunciamiento. According to Portilla, although generals Juan Álvarez and Florencio Villarreal had been plotting an insurrection against Antonio López de Santa Anna's dictatorship since January 1854, it was Comonfort who forced the two generals to act without further delay. When "the elderly General" Álvarez saw in "Comonfort's resolute spirit" the likelihood of success, he gave the promise that he would immediately bring together his followers and grant the pronunciamiento "his name's prestige and his person's weight in the region."[4] The idea of formulating a plan that would bring together all the forces opposing the dictatorship and could be accepted by all who took part, by means of producing an assertive statement of the causes and purposes of the action, was also attributed to Comonfort. Without this "solemn" document, which would become "the law of the revolution," Comonfort would never have dared to enter the political battlefield.[5]

Manuel Payno did not follow this reconstruction of the events in his *Memoria* on the coup d'état of December 1857. According to Payno, after being removed by Santa Anna from his post as customs officer in Acapulco, Comonfort had no other option than to join Álvarez and become one of the leaders and supporters of the Plan of Ayutla.[6] Nevertheless, Payno himself changed his opinion when he wrote the biographical sketch of his former superior and friend and presented him as the "true promoter and author of the Plan of Ayutla."[7]

Thirty years later the liberal historiography gave another version of the authorship of that "revolution," with a clear political inflection. The first to follow this approach was Guillermo Prieto in his *Lecciones de historia patria*, in which he asserted that the Plan of Ayutla had been "the brainchild of the Radical Liberal Party" and that Comonfort had modified it in Acapulco in order to make room for the Moderate Party.[8] This perception was shared by Olavarría y Ferrari, for whom Álvarez had been "the soul of the saving outcry." His "patriotic recklessness" had won him Tomás Moreno and Florencio Villarreal's admiration and devotion and attracted Comonfort's cooperation. Comonfort, "a man of less extreme democratic ideas," had modified the plan in Acapulco and introduced "minor changes," as he considered convenient the inclusion of "partisans of middle ground ideas, who were still very numerous."[9] Moreover, Olavarría was faced with Portilla's statement that History had neither the "necessity nor the obligation" to ascertain who the original plan author was.[10] Olavarría insisted that the rights of a leader of a grand revolution and "the glory of having prepared and started it" were not "a trivial matter."[11] For his part, the liberal-conservative Justo Sierra considered that Comonfort was the instigator of the revolution.[12]

The Pronunciamiento of Ayutla: Its Purpose and Meaning
According to Portilla, the purpose of the pronunciamiento was to overthrow Santa Anna's tyrannical regime and establish a new one that would combine liberty and order. In his opinion, when the dictator left Mexico in August 1855, the plan appeared to have won the day. Nevertheless, things turned out not to be so simple, and Comonfort had to face a series of problems with which only he, "such a gifted politician, cautious negotiator as well as fearless soldier and brave general," could deal. When he had succeeded in this intent, "the liberator" was regarded as "the people's idol,

applauded as a hero, shrouded in the shining aura of victory and praised by all the social classes and political parties."[13]

Olavarría did not share this point of view. To him, the pronunciamiento of Ayutla, as any other before it in Mexico, had been a truly popular uprising, starting without any leader or direction. Its success was due, in his analysis, to the fact that people knew it was supported by Álvarez, "the last of the insurgents." In fact, Olavarría was even harsher in his judgment and stated that Comonfort, with his moderate tendencies, had brought the revolution to the brink of total disaster, a blemish that could never be washed away.[14] Guillermo Prieto, as I have already mentioned, argued that two different tendencies could be detected from the beginning of the pronunciamiento: one that strove for "a compromise with the past and its vices," represented by Comonfort, and the other "uncompromising and assertive," headed by Álvarez.[15] For Justo Sierra, the plan of Ayutla itself had been similar to all the previous pronunciamientos and therefore "had not offered anything new to sensible people." Following Portilla's opinion—but without this author's usual epic tone—he granted Comonfort the merit of having succeeded in "humanizing the civil war" and organizing "the formless" armies of the revolution, achievements that had won him an enormous popularity.[16]

All these considerations show how the perceptions of the purpose and sense of the pronunciamiento of Ayutla changed with time. Already Portilla had insisted that possibly Comonfort's only error had been "to follow strictly and to the letter the conditions of a revolutionary plan the spirit of which had not been fully understood by its most ardent supporters."[17] But what did he mean by "spirit"? Apparently, to convene an extraordinary Congress that, with "the people's sovereign will," would give the country a constitution. All the subsequent historians agreed with Portilla on this issue but added a second one: to accomplish "the reform." It is interesting to note that this term was mentioned only in the third article of the Plan of Acapulco, which asserted the right of the *ad interim* president to reform all the branches of public administration.[18] It is therefore pertinent to ask how it came about that this term became strongly linked to the pronunciamiento of Ayutla.

In his *Historia de la revolución* Portilla argued that Comonfort, "the hero of Ayutla and Acapulco," on becoming president on 11 December 1855, was seen as "the man of liberty, reform and progress, but free from political exaggerations and revolutionary passions."[19] To be a man of "the reform," for Portilla, meant to accept that the present was linked to the past as it would be tied to the future; that society's progress had to be spontaneous but not violent, and that the rule of liberty could not be established without due respect for the creeds and traditions of the people.[20] The road pointed out by the reform obeyed "the spirit of the time," and Comonfort had followed it, seeking improvement of the moral and material conditions of the Republic through the creation of schools, organization of public administration, and reorganization of the army. In his second book, on Comonfort's presidency, Portilla asserted that it had never been the president's intention to attack the Church.[21] He then accused the reactionaries of having turned into a religious issue all the political and social measures adopted by the government and spread the idea that Comonfort was an enemy of religion and persecutor of the Church, when in truth he knew "how to be a liberal, a reformer and a man of progress without being irreligious and anarchical."[22]

In fact, by 1858 the term *reform*, understood as a movement directed against the power of the ecclesiastical institution, was already indissolubly linked to the Plan of Ayutla, when paradoxically, in neither of its two versions was there a single allusion to the clergy. The word *reform*, which had repeatedly been used by the conservatives Lucas Alamán and Luis G. Cuevas in reference to the need to put an end to "the evils of the nation," was now given to the laws enacted during the administrations of Álvarez and Comonfort, as it would later be applied to those imposed by Benito Juárez in 1859 and 1860.[23] Still more interesting is that the term came to be used to designate an entire historical period, albeit changing "the spirit" — or the meaning — of the original plan. Manuel Payno was the first to point out in his *Memoria* on the coup d'état that Mexico was going through a revolutionary period that he called "the Reform." According to Payno, the majority of nations, if not all, had experienced in the course of their history three great "convulsions": Conquest, Independence, and Reform. The first was bloody and selfish; the second was enduring and full of glory, and the third was violent and destructive. He argued that with more or less speed, ideas reached the farthest parts of the earth, "causing the clash of bodies against bodies, institutions against institutions and masses against masses." Mexico, where Conquest and Independence had already taken place, was now living through the Reform. The country was therefore going through a period of transition from the old ideas to the unavoidable progress and transformation that all nations had to endure.[24] Payno thought all this might be an unavoidable scheme of Providence, which allowed all these things "to happen on the face of the earth," and that men partook "in greater or lesser degree in this grand plan."[25] With such a line of thought — which he developed in his defense before the Grand Jury of Congress in May 1861, Payno seemed to say that he, as well as Comonfort,

Pi-Suñer Llorens

had been no more than mere instruments of Providence. With this assumption, what did the coup matter if sooner or later the reform would impose itself?

I have considered it pertinent to go into this digression on Payno's proposal because his division of Mexico's historical process was the one accepted by the ensuing liberal historiography. "The Reform" was the title that Vigil gave to the fifth volume of *México a través de los siglos*, and it covered the years between 1855 and 1867; that is, from the triumph of the pronunciamiento of Ayutla to that over Maximilian's empire. From a very radical point of view, thirty years later and with hindsight of the result of the process initiated in Ayutla, Vigil followed Payno's hypothesis, although without mentioning it, that "the substance, the soul, the real and positive revolution" had been the confrontation in Mexico of "the two principles represented by the head of the State and the head of the Church."[26] Justo Sierra gave the name "The Reform" to the years between 1848 and 1867, considering that the disastrous end of the war with the United States had been a turning point and the beginning of a new era.

Comonfort: His Commitment to the Reform

As we have already seen, Portilla presented Comonfort in his first book as "a man of the reform," "a man of the future," and "a friend of freedom" but opposed to "demagogy in politics." In his second book, Portilla insisted again in highlighting Comonfort's decision to push forward the reform and stated that proof of this was the decree by which public servants had to take an oath swearing their allegiance to the constitution and the enactment of the Iglesias law. According to Portilla it had been the liberal radicals who had constructed a negative image of the president, spreading the idea that he was a reactionary who had not allowed the revolution of Ayutla to follow its course. For him, Comonfort had forestalled the social revolution of the nineteenth century with "cautious and appropriate reforms" in order "to sooth its fury and prevent its havoc." He had proven his sensibility by not opposing the changes made to old institutions while alleging that they had to be respected and should remain in the same state they had been "in other ages." To be more precise, he resorted to the comparison of the owner of an old building who refused to repair it because he did not wish "to lose the slightest part of its ancient shape."[27]

Payno also pointed out that Comonfort was in favor of the reform but wanted it to proceed "step by step, in a philosophical way and without violence and bloodshed."[28] For Rivera Cambas the president had had the "the happy and lucky idea" of promoting the reform.[29] In contrast, Niceto de Zamacois, from his standpoint of extreme Catholicism, judged Comonfort as too engaged with the reform. Zamacois claimed that the obligation to take an oath on the constitution had been a strategy for increasing the ranks of the reformists, since the government intended to carry out other "innovations regarding the Church and needed to prepare the ground."[30] José María Vigil considered that Comonfort had proved himself to be "a man of the reform" from the moment he enacted the intervention of the property of the Church in Puebla in March 1856. As he went on writing about the presidency, Vigil argued that "although Comonfort did not keep stride with the radicals, he did not hold back on the way to the reform."[31] Vigil therefore disavowed those who accused the president of being a supporter of "it is not yet time." Nevertheless, when he arrived at the point where he had to write about Comonfort's revocation of the Puebla decree, Vigil had to change his discourse and presented him as being completely opposed to the reform.[32] From this moment on, the president showed "a total lack of that kind of spirit, of that faith that spurs on the reformists who are fully committed to the task at hand."[33]

Justo Sierra was the only author to point out that there was not a single reference to the reform in the Plan of Ayutla.[34] When he referred to the Álvarez administration, Sierra did note that it had behind him "the bulk of the Reformist Party" and that Comonfort was forced to take his side because of the uprising in Puebla.[35] This was the moment when he enacted the decree to expropriate the Church property in that diocese. This act was the definitive declaration of war between the secular state and the Church. Sierra considered that the reform was a necessity of fate, "the necessary consequence of our entire history" — in which assertion he agreed with Payno and Vigil.[36] On the other hand, Comonfort, with his "highly conciliatory agenda," had hoped to force the country to swallow the reform little by little.[37] Although Sierra is the only one among my sources to record "the exceptional standing" that the Organic Statute, enacted by Comonfort's administration in May 1856, had given the clergy "within the body of citizens forbidding it to vote and be voted," he refused to accept that the president was at that time a true reformist.[38] By 1901 the judgment of the liberal historiography on Comonfort was already past. For Sierra, "he was not the leader needed by the Reformist Party, he was not a moderator but a moderate, unable to enact the ultimate measures demanded by the circumstances."[39]

The Constitution of 1857: Consistent with Mexican Society?

For Anselmo de la Portilla the constitution was the only enemy that Comonfort could not defeat. Before it, "his thoughtfulness, his dedication, his fortitude were of no avail to him; . . . his star darkened and fortune, which so often had been on his side, deserted him."[40] Congressmen, he stated, while enacting new legislation that would alarm and arouse new enemies of political freedom, put under chains the power that had to defend this freedom; that is, the executive.[41] To reinforce his argument Portilla surmised that Miguel Lerdo de Tejada, as a candidate to the presidency, had declined to present his political program because he believed it would be impossible to implement given "the restrictions that the Constitution imposed on the executive power." If any of the branches of government needed a free hand, Portilla insisted, it was precisely the one that, having to impose an innovative program, would have to overcome the most powerful opposition.[42] Justo Sierra agreed with Portilla. He considered that the constitution did not give the executive power sufficient maneuvering room to and that it put a straitjacket on the president.[43]

The second objection Portilla addressed to the constitution was that it included ideas too "democratic" for the Mexican circumstances and thus did not respond to the national will.[44] Nobody had faith in it, neither the congressmen who had drafted it nor the government that had to enact it, and least of all the common folk "who awaited it as the talisman that would put an end to their ills."[45] Zamacois supported these arguments, stating that "the Constitution was in contradiction to the ideas, the feelings, the intimate beliefs of the society," and therefore it had been "an error of judgment" to enact it.[46] For Vigil, on the contrary, Mexican society had undergone a profound change through the thirty years in which it had struggled to free itself from the power of the Church and was, therefore, ready to support the reform.[47] Rivera Cambas argued that if the constitution had withstood so many assaults it was because the people understood "how necessary was such a link to achieve peace and even to preserve the idea of nationality."[48] Such concepts were very much in vogue at the time when Cambas wrote his history on the foreign interventions in Mexico. For Prieto, the constitution was received with joy and enthusiasm by the Liberal Party, who hoisted it from then on as a symbol.[49] Sierra was more in agreement with Portilla and Zamacois, as he pointed out that the ideas of innovation did not spring from "the spirit of the common people." The reform was the agent that would change society, would open the road to progress, and would allow the great principles of the new constitution to become a reality.[50] Following Prieto's text almost to the letter in his appraisal of the constitution, Sierra repeated that it had been the result of "idealistic views and was largely still so," although it was a necessity "to preserve the Reform . . . that it embodied."[51]

The Oath on the Constitution

The obligation to take an oath on the constitution gave rise to different interpretations. Portilla sustained that Comonfort, even though he did not fully agree with the *Carta Magna*, had taken the oath himself and forced the public servants to do the same because he wanted to comply with the legality of the Plan of Ayutla. In his eagerness to avert the blame from the president, this author asserted that it had been an error of the secretary for internal affairs, Ignacio de la Llave. This obligation had given rise to the idea that the administration was against religion when Comonfort did not have any prejudice against the clergy.[52] Zamacois was the historian who devoted more attention to the obligation of taking the oath. For him, it had been "an unwise act" and a contradiction to force people to take an oath on a document that asserted liberty of conscience.[53] He thought it to be so since from his extremely Catholic point of view, the fact that the constitution did not establish the Catholic faith as the state religion implied that religious freedom had become the law.[54] He thought it had been this obligation to take the oath, which for Comonfort was "a transcendental measure," that had led to the confrontation between the government and society and started a political-religious war that would be impossible to stop. Zamacois took care in adducing a great number of examples, presented in a very dramatic way, to show how the public servants had been forced to choose between their conscience and their jobs and how the majority had refused to take the oath. This was "a mark of honor for the Mexican people."[55] According to this author, the only way the Mexicans would have accepted the reformist legislation would have been through a decree from the Pope.[56]

Rivera Cambas argued that Comonfort had taken the oath on a constitution he did not like because he preferred a legal order, even a bad one, to a pronunciamiento. As for the enforcement of the oath, he thought it to have been "the origin of the scandal," the major cause of "complaints and lamentations" among the people. It had given the "Reactionary Party" a pretext for sedition and for accusing the government of being tyrannical. It is interesting to examine what Rivera Cambas thought about the reaction of the church. For him, the true cause of the clergy's aversion to the constitution was not fear that it would lessen religious feeling but a sense of exclusion from the official oath — resenting this as a blow to Church influence and a deprivation "of the very earthly fruitions offered by money."[57] Vigil argued that the obligation to take the oath had not been an error: it was the president's duty to enforce it since this had been customary up to this moment. Moreover, since this was in agreement with the reforming ideals of the pronunciamiento of Ayutla, to take the oath on the constitution was an obligation.[58]

Tacubaya: "Error," "Moral Suicide," or "Vulgar Conspiracy"?
Portilla took great pains to justify Comonfort's decision to accept, eventually, the Plan of Tacubaya. He insisted that in accordance with the legality of the Plan of Ayutla, he had enacted some measures demanded by public opinion but had been "roughly" attacked because of them. Later on he had enacted the constitution, also to accomplish the promises of that plan. Nevertheless, the *Carta Magna* turned out to be a powerful weapon in his enemies' hands, which forced him to accept a military pronunciamiento that would disavow it.[59] Several factors assisted him. In the first place, the constitution did not respond to the national will, and its enactment had caused a worsening of the already existing state of war. Second, the *Carta* was not being obeyed in a great number of states. Third, Comonfort's recent electoral victory as constitutional president had led him to believe that public opinion saw in him a token of assurance for the cause of liberty and progress.[60] The fourth reason was that with the pronunciamiento having already been decided upon, he feared that if he did not join it, the Reactionary Party would take control of the new situation. Portilla considered that the Plan of Tacubaya was "liberal in the hands of liberals and reactionary in the hands of the reactionaries: with that Plan one could either take the road to freedom or to despotism."[61] While Comonfort was part of it, the spirit of the plan would be of conciliation and progress, since the president had proved himself to be a man of liberty, and the people knew this, as evidenced in the way they had given him

the electoral victory. In spite of all that, Comonfort had found himself alone on this road while those who pushed in the opposite direction appeared to be "countless."[62] For Portilla it had not been a coup d'état, although "it had carried all the heinous connotations associated with this term." There had not been any previous agreement, Comonfort did not take any preparatory step, the armed forces started the pronunciamiento almost against his will, and for two days he doubted before finally accepting the plan, apparently under the threat of the bayonets. A coup would have implied previous machinations with Comonfort assuring the help of his friends, distributing and placing his forces in a convenient way, and declaring resolutely: "Down with this Constitution which compromises the cause of liberty and reform and leads us to anarchy and later to despotism."[63]

Payno gave a different version of the facts when he set forth the details of the pronunciamiento of December 1857. His account shows that indeed there was previous organization: that Comonfort, in front of Felix Zuloaga, Juan José Baz, General De la Parra and Payno himself, had spoken of a revolution and prepared a list of the states and governors "in order to explore the opinion of the nation," distributing the task of carrying out these steps. Payno agreed with Portilla when he pointed out that the Plan of Tacubaya had not represented an act of treason against the Liberal Party, just a change of policy.[64] For him, Comonfort had governed with an extraordinary sense of equilibrium "until he awoke the lion"; that is, the power of the Church. It was not the president's intention to hand over the government to the reactionaries, but neither did he intend going on with the reforms that had encountered so much opposition from the clergy and the conscience of the faithful. He then considered that he had to make some concessions but with the consent of "the influential members of the Liberal Party." Such had been the meaning of the "so-called coup d'état," which sprung from the wishes of a man who refused to be "the butcher and oppressor" of the same citizens who had brought him to power.[65]

In Payno's opinion, the outcome of the revolution had been diametrically opposed to the initial expectations, basically because the Radical Party of Mexico City broke with Comonfort the day after the pronunciamiento, when, as a matter of fact, all those who had conspired were liberals, and not a single person of the opposing party had taken part in the movement. It was then that the hope that there would be a general reconciliation after a common effort to help the president faded away. Comonfort's ever-vacillating attitude and his political isolation caused the death of the revolution.[66] Payno denied that the term *traitor* could be applied to them since this word was used to refer, among other things, to "the most vile and despicable persons of mankind," which they were not.[67]

Rivera Cambas sought to explain the coup through Comonfort's character. According to him, Comonfort's life had gone through a constant dithering between the Moderate and the Radical parties, it "having been his undeniable hope to achieve the union of the liberals and of all of those who professed republican principles." Opting to back the coup d'état had been "a moral suicide," since his administration had its origin in the principles of the reform, even if at the time of his inauguration as constitutional president he looked tired and lacking in the necessary strength to carry out the reforms.[68] His weariness had brought distrust, but when the rumor spread that he supported the pronunciamiento, it was impossible to imagine "so much lack of judgment." According to

Rivera, the unstoppable chain of events that took place after the coup proved, once more, that errors are not the exclusive preserve of a certain class of people or of individuals with a particular education. In spite of having insisted in his biographical sketch of Comonfort that Mexico was living in a state of civil war, Rivera argued in this new text that the president's unforgivable sin had been "to drown his country in blood" with the Plan of Tacubaya.[69]

For his part, Niceto de Zamacois never used the term *coup d'état*. For him it had been a new "revolution" triggered by two events: on the one hand, the forced oath on the constitution, and on the other, the fact that Comonfort had told Congress he knew the *Carta* did not agree with the will of the country and contained the seeds of disorder and disunion. For Zamacois this was the harshest statement that could be made on the new constitution and justified those who stood up against it.[70] It was inconceivable that the president could have asked for extraordinary powers to impose what he himself considered was against the will of the nation.[71] It was at this juncture that Comonfort had accepted Félix Zuloaga's and Payno's invitation to uphold a plan that would reconcile the interests of the liberals with those of the Catholics. Such a wish, Zamacois argued, even though noble and patriotic, was unfeasible, since ambiguous positions in critical circumstances can only result in one outcome: the ruin of those who adopt them. This is the only value judgment pronounced by this author regarding the coup d'état.[72]

Guillermo Prieto referred to the coup concisely but vehemently, trying to arouse his students' feelings. He presented Comonfort as being demoralized by "his old mother's grief" in the face of the reformist policy, which had brought about his estrangement from the Liberal Party and driven him into "scandal." It had been Payno who, with "utmost skill had prepared the fateful coup" by which the president, destroying his legitimacy, had put the revolutionary movement in the hands of the army that was assertively supported by the clergy. A few days later Comonfort became aware of the abyss into which he had fallen, and tried to defend himself, but did not succeed. He felt the void around him and began dithering, tripping and losing his track. The notorious loss of the popularity he had won through "his honorable and kind character" demoralized him completely and prompted him to leave the capital on the last day of January 1858.[73]

For Vigil, the coup d'état "implied the victory of the reaction as an unavoidable necessity." The most staggering fact was that the idea of the pronunciamiento seemed to be shared by an administration that "with so much fortune" had laid the groundwork for the reform, defeating in so many battles its fiercest enemies.[74] When deciding to support the coup, the chief of state — "who had climbed to that highest position hailed by public opinion and carrying with him the holy receptacle of the votes and hopes of the nation" — pushed along by a dark destiny, was heading toward the border of the abyss into which he fell unavoidably as a vulgar conspirator, after shredding the lawful titles that placed him at the head of the Republic.[75] It is interesting to point out that Vigil followed the leaflet that Juan José Baz had published in 1859 to defend himself from the imputation of having supported the coup d'état, the tenor of which was very radical, as was its author himself.[76] Thus Vigil argued that Comonfort had disagreed with the spirit of the Radical Party captured in the constitution and that, in such a state of mind, he magnified the difficulties he was facing. "The uproar of the Conservative Party, the fuss about the oath and the Iglesias Law, the attempts behind the conspiracies, the bands of *pronunciados* everywhere in the country, took in the president's eyes colossal proportions, largely exaggerating the reality."[77] In making this statement, Vigil contradicted himself, since throughout his version of the events he had insisted on the chaotic nature of the situation Comonfort had to confront. For him the president had not been able "to fathom the juncture," it being his greatest error to forge a revolution without a clear definition of its goal and without reckoning with the necessary elements for its success.[78]

Sierra, who followed Vigil's text, nevertheless disagreed with him regarding the state of civil war that prevailed in the country before the coup d'état. In his usual bombastic style, Sierra argued that from the very beginning of the reform program "there had not been a single day without a pronunciamiento, a sedition, a mutiny, an uprising; there was a continuous trepidation as if an eruption was about to happen; the situation was like sitting on a hidden volcano." Bringing peace to the country was such a complex enterprise that its undertaking required "a truly heroic disposition." Comonfort, fully aware that this state of affairs was untenable, showed "a kind of terror" in departing from the road of legality and dithered, as was his habit. Eventually the president judged it necessary to put an end to this situation, and in one hour he retraced the road he had so far followed, bringing the republic back to the same condition that prevailed the day after the revolution of Ayutla. Out of this terrible error, "this disgrace that could not be atoned for," "this intelligence without flight," according to Sierra's categorical judgment, had been born the most blatant case of political suicide recorded in Mexican history.[79]

Final Comments

Comparison of the texts reviewed allows me to confirm, once more, that the construction of a historical discourse depends on the time and the political circumstances in which it was written, the author's ideological persuasion, and the purpose of the work. As we have seen, for all the historians who wrote after the pronunciamiento of Tacubaya, Comonfort was not, not even for a single moment, the hero or the man of destiny who figured in Anselmo de la Portilla's early accounts. Zamacois was the only one who viewed him as having been completely devoted to the reform and who acknowledged him as sincere in his pursuit of progress. This image was destroyed by the historiography of the victorious liberals, for whom the Constitution of 1857, which had been "the result of the heroic efforts of the Congress of 1856," became the real heroine. The *Carta Magna* was enshrined together with a new hero, Benito Juárez, whose determination and "truly revolutionary spirit" had guided Mexico through the difficult times of the Reform. For this historiographical trend, what the country needed at that juncture was not a man with a great heart but one with great strength of character: not a Comonfort but a Juárez. Justo Sierra pronounced the harshest judgment on the first of the two: even if the Republic had forgiven the patriot the error of the statesman, History, if it had the right to judge and not mere analyze and synthesize, would cast a negative vote on him. As is well-known, this view prevailed during the entire twentieth century.

Comonfort's greatest mistake, which became the tragedy of his life, was to abandon the road of legality—of which he had been the staunchest supporter—by accepting the Plan of Tacubaya, an act that in itself was not so unusual at the time. What he could not foresee was that the Constitution of 1857 would become, from then on, the liberal banner of the wars of Reforma and Intervención and that Juárez, who upheld it, would become the hailed hero. What must be taken into account is that Don

Benito himself did not have to enact the *Carta* due to the state of civil war that prevailed during those ten years and that when he had to do so in August 1867, he put forward the need to reform it. Since his proposal was not accepted by those who brandished the constitution—calling themselves *constitucionalistas* and supporting Porfirio Díaz—he had to rule resorting to extraordinary powers. Even more paradoxical is the fact that it was this political group, also known as the *tuxtepecanos*, who eventually wrote what would become the official version of the history of Mexico, which undermined Comonfort's image for having disowned the 1857 Constitution. By then Díaz had been in government for more than ten years, purporting to rule with this constitution but in fact acting as a dictator.

Notes

1. Payno, "Comonfort," 513.
2. Rivera Cambas, "D. Ignacio Comonfort," 3, 283.
3. Rivera, *Anales mexicanos*, 156.
4. Portilla, *Historia*, 50.
5. Portilla, *Historia*, 52.
6. Payno, *Memoria*, 46.
7. Payno, *Memoria*, 46.
8. Prieto, *Lecciones*, 373.
9. Olavarría y Ferrari, *México independiente*, 395–97.
10. Portilla, *Historia*, 52
11. Olavarría y Ferrari, *México independiente*, 397–98.
12. Sierra, *Evolución*, 270.
13. Portilla, *Historia*, 243–47.
14. Olavarría y Ferrari, *México independiente*, 420–23.
15. Prieto, *Lecciones*, 374.
16. Sierra, *Evolución*, 268.
17. Portilla, *México en 1856 y 1857*, 275.
18. "Plan de Ayutla reformado en Acapulco," in Matute, *Antología*, 287–95.
19. Portilla, *Historia*, 255.

20. Portilla, *Historia*, 332–33.

21. Portilla, *Historia*, 34, 36.

22. Portilla, *Historia*, 361.

23. Alamán, *Historia de Méjico*, 5:861–66, 927–52. Cuevas, *Porvenir de México* (1852), vol. 2.

24. Payno, *Memoria*, 90–96.

25. Payno, "Defensa que hace el ciudadano," 112.

26. Payno, *Memoria*, 49.

27. Portilla, *México en 1856 y 1857*, 350–51.

28. Payno, "Comonfort," 518.

29. Rivera Cambas, "D. Ignacio Comonfort," 311.

30. Zamacois, *Historia de Méjico*, 14:528.

31. Vigil, *La Reforma*, 9, 149.

32. Vigil, *La Reforma*, 261.

33. Vigil, *La Reforma*, 257.

34. Sierra, *Evolución*, 266.

35. Sierra, *Evolución*, 274.

36. Sierra, *Evolución*, 277.

37. Sierra, *Evolución*, 273.

38. Sierra, *Evolución*, 276.

39. Sierra, *Evolución*, 278.

40. Portilla, *México en 1856 y 1857*, 183.

41. Portilla, *México en 1856 y 1857*, 188–89.

42. Portilla, *México en 1856 y 1857*, 252–53.

43. Sierra, *Evolución*, 286–87.

44. Portilla, *México en 1856 y 1857*, 188–89.

45. Portilla, *México en 1856 y 1857*, 183.

46. Zamacois, *Historia de Méjico*, 14:452–511.

47. This is Vigil's hypothesis throughout his account.

48. Rivera Cambas, *Historia de la intervención*, 1:217.

49. Prieto, *Lecciones*, 379.

50. Sierra, *Evolución*, 283–87.

51. Sierra, *Evolución*, 286.

52. Portilla, *México en 1856 y 1857*, 192.

53. Zamacois, *Historia de Méjico*, 14:484.

54. Zamacois, *Historia de Méjico*, 14:484.

55. Zamacois, *Historia de Méjico*, 14:511–44.

56. Zamacois, *Historia de Méjico*, 14:556–60.

57. Rivera Cambas, "D. Ignacio Comonfort," 314.

58. Vigil, *La Reforma*, 228.

59. Portilla, *México en 1856 y 1857*, iv.

60. Portilla, *México en 1856 y 1857*, 289.

61. Portilla, *México en 1856 y 1857*, 294.

62. Portilla, *México en 1856 y 1857*, 294.

63. Portilla, *México en 1856 y 1857*, 296.

64. Payno, *Memoria*, 40–45.

65. Payno, *Memoria*, 50–55.

66. Payno, *Memoria*, 69–77.

67. Payno, *Memoria*, 61.

68. Rivera Cambas, *Historia de la intervención*, 1:220.

69. Rivera Cambas, "D. Ignacio Comonfort," 314–26.

70. Zamacois, *Historia de Méjico*, 651. This historian is the only one who notes that when Comonfort asked Congress to give him extraordinary powers, he let them know what he thought about the constitution.

71. Zamacois, *Historia de Méjico*, 664.

72. Zamacois, *Historia de Méjico*, 693–98.

73. Prieto, *Lecciones*, 377–80, 466–67.

74. Vigil, *La Reforma*, 252.

75. Vigil, *La Reforma*, 265.

76. Baz, *Manifiesto*.

77. Vigil, *La Reforma*, 271.

78. Vigil, *La Reforma*, 272–76.

79. Sierra, *Evolución*, 281.

Nine. Porfirio Díaz and the Representations of the Second of April

On 9 March 1867 Porfirio Díaz rebelled against Maximilian of Habsburg and placed the city of Puebla under siege. On hearing that Leonardo Márquez and his imperial troops were approaching to free the besieged city, Díaz decided to attack, and Puebla surrendered to him on 2 April.

This event was not a *pronunciamiento* as such, or at least it was not a pronunciamiento in the sense that historians have come to define this practice in recent years, even though it was a military rebellion and it did result in the government having to change its policy.[1] Díaz did not present any written demands either, but instead made a stand by taking up arms against the government's injustice. There was no space for negotiation other than to expel the enemy. The goal was to reestablish order through a military action. The leader of this military action, Porfirio Díaz, would later orchestrate two veritable pronunciamiento cycles—La Noria (9 November 1871) and Tuxtepec (10 January 1876). Although the Plan of La Noria would fail to achieve its aims, the Plan of Tuxtepec would bring the Mexican era of the pronunciamiento to an end, enabling Díaz to sit comfortably in the presidential chair for several decades. However, unlike for some of the pronunciamientos studied in this volume, commemorating the date of the Plan of Tuxtepec proved difficult because of the changed political situation toward the end of the century. As a result the commemorative efforts of Díaz's government turned toward a less controversial date, which also had greater symbolic value, because it stood for Díaz's defense of national sovereignty against the French Intervention and imposition of an Austrian prince on the Mexican throne (1862–67). While the essays in this book have shown how the celebration of given pronunciamientos sacralized or legitimized their instigators' role in Mexican history, here we have a case where a serial *pronunciado*—the pronunciado of La Noria and Tuxtepec—was celebrated through the commemoration of what might have been seen as a less divisive action; that is, what amounted to a patriotic military victory against a foreign aggressor, as opposed to a pronunciamiento that was launched to gain control of the national government.

From the very beginning 2 April 1867 was linked to the strongman from Oaxaca. Nine days later, in the city where Díaz was born, we find the first commemoration of this military action. By December of that year a grateful Benito Juárez issued a collection of commemorative medals from the presidential chair to which he had been restored.[2] Thereafter a long list of ceremonies, speeches, images, and publications can be found commemorating the event, stretching from 1867 until 1914. Although these celebrations were not all equally intense, they all had the purpose of turning Porfirio Díaz into a hero and turning 2 April into an important civic festival, given that the action contributed to the defeat of the intruding emperor.

In this chapter I explore how commemorations were employed as a means of consolidation by the ruling groups, including men who rose to power through pronunciamientos, to understand the mechanisms they used to succeed in this task. This particular

Zárate Toscano

case is interesting because its date was associated with someone who survived in power for a very long time, and thus unlike heroes who obtain such notoriety when they die, Díaz earned his place at the Olympus of immortals during his lifetime. Such an achievement, if we can deem it this, was shared in his own time by Antonio López de Santa Anna.[3] Agustín de Iturbide made similar efforts to use civic festivals to consolidate his hold on power.[4] However, their long presence in positions of power or their closeness to the powerful were not enough to guarantee the durability of the very recognition they were hoping to forge as unquestionable and timeless national heroes, in spite of the enormous efforts that were invested in achieving this. Yet although 2 April, 11 September, and 27 September are not celebrated today because all three pronunciados (Díaz, Santa Anna, and Iturbide) were defeated by history, in their own time they caught the attention and imagination of the Mexican people and thus contributed to the formation of an emergent national imaginary.

The Date in the Civic Calendar

Festivities were used to contribute to the conformation of historical memory and to justify leadership. To commemorate means to evoke publicly a person or an event, to remember, to bring historical memory to the present. This revival is as selective as the state wishes it to be and as recent or distant as is convenient.

In the war against France (1862–67), it all began and ended in Puebla, the backdrop for two meaningful battles in which the Mexican Army defeated the imperial troops. Ignacio Zaragoza inflicted the first major victory upon the most powerful army in the world on 5 May 1862, and although Mexico lost the war and had a foreign emperor imposed upon the country, that date entered very soon into the annals of national history and the civic calendar. Five years later, the Ejército de Oriente defeated the imperial troops again, thus opening the gates to a definitive victory and the restoration of the nation's sovereignty. Other actions from this war could be included in the civic calendar. Starting in 1897, the recapture of Querétaro (15 May 1867) and Mexico City (21 June 1867) were also intended to become part of the official festivities but were never as important as 5 May or 2 April.

With 2 April we find the same conflicts of interest that surrounded the commemoration of independence (see chapter 2), over the question of which date should be remembered, the beginning or the end, 16 or 27 September. Nowadays 5 May is firmly ingrained in our collective memory and is still useful to the powerful, reliving the battle with parades and public speeches, upholding it as a "national festival" but not a "bank holiday." On the other hand, 2 April is of less importance. However, since 2001 the *Diario Oficial* does publish a resume of what happened on 2 April and has registered this as a solemn date to be marked with the hoisting of the flag. Evidently this does not compare with the amazing commemorations that were arranged in Porfirian times.

This date had a peculiar transformation in 1887 when the municipality of Guadalupe Hidalgo in the Federal District declared it was to be a "Day of trees" and invited all neighbors to contribute to its splendor.[5] By 1907 the council asked the Ministry of Development (Secretaría de Fomento) to give them some plants to organize the celebration along with the fortieth anniversary of 2 April.[6] Even in 1914, with Porfirio Díaz enjoying his exile in Paris, this type of commemoration was still very much in vogue in public gardens, with the planting of trees taking place in the streets.[7]

Due to the religious calendar, the celebration of 2 April was complicated because often it coincided with Holy Week, and in Mexico, in spite of the separation between church and state, those days were very important and official activities came to a halt. In the newspapers of the period we can read the comments of those who opposed the commemoration, and although the critics were against the interruption of sacred rituals, in the end they were also against the worshipped hero and the celebration of a military action.

There were other years when the festivity took place the day after the opening session of Congress, and the two events were linked to highlight the importance of President Díaz, who rendered a report on his activities and received all kinds of tributes. During the forty-three years in which the celebration took place while Conqueror Díaz was living in Mexico, some elements remained and others changed as the festivity underwent all the transformations needed to adapt to particular political moments. In the beginning, we can have no doubt that the fiesta was very much intended to present Díaz in a good light so that he would be considered a worthy presidential candidate.[8] Once he occupied the presidential chair he profited from the celebration in consolidating his power, and there were even some years when it took place during presidential campaigns. The commemoration of 1910 was a prelude for what would be Díaz's last reelection.[9] And precisely because of that powerful bond between the figure and the date, between the hero and the event, the commemoration would fall with the dictator.

Festive Structure

To analyze a civic fiesta we have to pay attention to different aspects: the participants, the space in which it was held, the timing or historical context, and the financing of the celebration. The participants in commemorations range from the organizers to the members of the audience. During the first half of the century a Junta Patriótica was established to deal with all these tasks and responsibilities.[10] This celebration likely followed the patterns established for other commemorations, involving bureaucrats in charge of resources, transportation, licenses, materials, etc. The difference was the participation of certain political associations, like the Amigos del Presidente, or the Asociación Patriótica, which organized the celebration of 1888.[11] The Comité Central Porfirista and the Círculo Porfirista took over in 1892 and 1903 respectively.[12]

Other important groups participating in the celebration were composed of war veterans who had taken part in the assault on the city of Puebla, and who attended the ceremony as special guests and recipients of public recognition, although clearly some received more attention than others. The cover of *El Mundo Ilustrado* in 1904 shows a photo with an explanation: "General Díaz receives in Anzures felicitations from a former old subordinate."[13] Years earlier, in 1892, a similar encounter took place and the press reported: "Among the people who congratulated General Díaz on Saturday, there was a poor invalid from the 2nd of April and in embracing him, the Sr. Presidente filled his hand with bank notes."[14]

Worth mentioning also is Carlos Pacheco, who lost an arm and a leg during the siege of Puebla and was compensated fourteen years later with an appointment to brigadier general: "general de brigada efectivo del ejército."[15] There were other attempts to compensate the veterans, like the one issued by Puebla's government in 1869.[16] During the 1895 commemorations there were awards for generals Porfirio Díaz and Mariano Escobedo, and for other officials and soldiers who had participated in the action in Puebla, and also for those involved in the siege of Querétaro.[17] The festivities included theatrical staging of an awards ceremony filled with adaptable symbolism and part of the political machine, in which Mariano Escobedo, as president of Congress, honored President Díaz, who in turn did the same for the general who had ended Maximilian's empire.[18] From then on Díaz would wear his insignia on his gala uniform, especially during the mock battle.[19] It is clear that with these acts of benevolence toward his former comrades in arms, Díaz was building for himself an image as benefactor, a godfather for his contemporaries, many of whom he outlived.

Besides Díaz's starring role, often criticized in the press, there were other actors involved in the battle who survived in the collective memory because they were included in reviews of the war and because while they were alive, they attended the official ceremonies of commemoration, melding with the rest of the audience.

We must remember that space conditions the quantity and quality of the audience. In closed spaces, access is limited, while in the open air there is a chance for bigger crowds. The list of guests who attended the banquet held during the inauguration of Puebla's penitentiary in April 1891 was limited to 250 people.[20] On the other hand, the mock battle of 1900 had an attendance of around 3,500 people.[21] The outdoor space was divided to include a VIP zone with grandstands. In 1888 the newspapers reported that there were around 2,000 people in the stands and a crowd of 10,000 people.[22] Similar accounts of other military displays use comparable figures and describe how the viewers arrived at the distant "battle fields" in carriages, by train, or on foot, depending on their means. Such reports indicate great variety in the audience and that people were willing to travel some distance to witness the great display of resources and participants moved by the dictator's followers to worship him.

As for the segments of the celebration, we can distinguish preparatory, central, and complementary stages. Preparatory activities involved all the details concerning organization of the event, and there was usually a commission in charge of it. The central festivities were those that attracted the people's attention and were intended to fulfill the goal of exalting a heroic figure or a certain date in the official calendar. They included speeches, music, fireworks, and parades. Finally, the complementary stage added importance to the celebration through shows and recreational moments but also made sure that this special occasion was kept alive in the nation's collective memory through the construction of new buildings, monuments, urban services, etc.

The financial aspect of the commemoration is not easy to trace because of a lack of economic detail similar to what has been found for other celebrations.[23] Newspaper articles do note, however, that the organization of mock battles was quite expensive. In 1890 a report informed readers that it would not be possible for the authorities to carry out the expected military exercise because it would be too expensive to transport the troops.[24] Some critics considered this was a waste of money, although others considered it a good investment, showing the strength of the regime. This kind of celebration entailed more than having the city council pay for the illumination or the fireworks, or having the neighbors contribute to the decoration of their facades; instead it involved installation of camps, feeding the troops, and paying for the gunpowder. Perhaps there was a hidden reason for not holding the reenactment or simulacrum, since all efforts and attention that year were focused on the decree that would allow the indefinite reelection of President Díaz.

Regional Variants

It is worth remembering that the commemoration of 2 April took place not only in Mexico City as the center of power but elsewhere as well. Even inside the Federal District there were different commemorative scenarios, including in Colonia Guerrero in 1886, Guadalupe Hidalgo in 1882 and 1887, Azcapotzalco 1888, Coyoacán 1889, and Tacubaya 1892. An extensive festive geography all over the country emerges from press reports and the private letters received by Porfirio Díaz around that particular date. José María Cortés provides an account from Oaxaca in 1867.[25] Other commemoratives took place in Mérida in 1868, Cuautitlán 1878, Querétaro 1883, Campeche 1887 and 1900, San Juan Bautista (Tabasco) 1900, Morelia 1902, Chilpancingo 1903, San Luis Potosí 1903, Tepic and Tampico 1905, Durango 1907, Guadalajara 1909, and Pachuca 1910.[26]

A peculiar celebration took place in 1868 in Mérida, Yucatán.[27] The reason was that General Ignacio Alatorre, costar in the battle, was commissioned in that city. He could combine the honors for Díaz with attracting attention to himself. A detailed review of the celebration was published, with a cover that does not include the names of Díaz or Alatorre but instead mentions Zaragoza and De la Llave, offering a tribute to these heroes. The review includes an image of the main square decorated for the festivity.[28] Speeches and honors celebrating the heroes of 2 April already incorporated unlimited praise for the participants even though only one year had passed since the event. Fresh memories were used as a means to exalt the importance of Díaz after the failure of his attempt to become president and his forced retirement to the Hacienda de la Noria, a reward he received for his actions.

As a site of memory and the scenario of the clash of arms, Puebla became the center of attention and of the commemoration from the first moment and remains so today. Several articles from the newspapers in Mexico City describe the commemorations in Puebla in several years.[29] But these celebrations became more prominent when Díaz himself attended them in 1891. The important newspaper *El Monitor Republicano* sent Enrique Chavarri Juvenal as a reporter. He wrote a long and detailed description with his customary keen style.[30] He emphasized the resonance of the inauguration of the penitentiary, where Manuel María de Zamacona gave a speech "that served as an apotheosis of the culture of that time."[31] In the evening Díaz attended a bullfight, and later Governor Rosendo Márquez offered a reception where champagne ran freely. Juvenal praised the extent to which electric light now shone throughout the city.

Another place of importance was the city of Monterrey, Nuevo León. Governor Bernardo Reyes organized a great commemoration there and invited Díaz, but he could not go there until December 1898. However, although he missed the festivity of 2 April, it was like having April in December.[32] There was a mock battle and a monument was unveiled. Reyes's strategy was to attract his friend-enemy to his territory and put on a show of local strength. As time went by, the competition between Reyes and Díaz would intensify until Reyes left the country when he lost the possibility of occupying the presidential chair. The 1898 Monterrey festivity was significant not only to praise the hero but also to promote the ambitions of the organizer.[33] Throughout the country similar actions were taken to celebrate the uprising or Porfirio Díaz and, in so doing, to reaffirm the people's bonds and loyalty to the regime and its leader.

Zárate Toscano

The Images

Historical events are transmitted from generation to generation through different channels, which range from oral histories to visual records. In order to have a greater impact on the population and to contribute to a nationalistic pedagogy, they are also spread through the written word in newspapers, reviews, and books. With Mexico's elevated rate of illiteracy, images had—and still have—a bigger impact, offering through their circulation additional possibilities of interpretation and understanding. The characteristics and nature of a given text necessarily conditions the number of recipients who may be open to its message. Evidently by including a visual element this message became accessible to far more people. As a result poets, writers, musicians, and painters were soon accompanied by sculptors, engravers, and later photographers and filmmakers to record the event and register its commemoration.

In the case of Porfirio Díaz and 2 April we have a wealth of records and resources in different media, including visual media. We not only have historic paintings but also photographs in the press and drawings made in the heat of the festivity to supplement witnesses' accounts.

Historical painting in the nineteenth century, in terms of its scale and importance, almost fades into insignificance when compared to the works that were produced during the golden age of muralism that flourished after the Mexican Revolution as part of José Vasconcelos's educational program. Furthermore, large-format paintings were not as common in Mexico as they were in France and Spain. Yet we do have some examples of gigantic paintings that were inspired by the star of a given historical event. Francisco de P. Mendoza produced a painting of the 2 April battle that measures 5 by 8.30 meters.[34] It appeared in the press in the year of its production.[35] Photographs show the moment when it was unveiled, hanging on one of the walls high above the main staircase at the Castle of Chapultepec, occupied at the time by the Colegio Militar, the military academy.[36] However, it was later taken down and is now kept rolled up in one of the storage rooms of the National Museum of History. Catalogued by the authorities in 1905, it is described as a military painting, although in fact it shows the moment of Porfirio Díaz entering the city of Puebla after victory in battle.[37] This was one reason for critique of the painting: it does not show the tension of the battle.[38]

Inspired by Mendoza's painting, at the Museum of No Intervention at the Fort of Loreto in Puebla is a low relief made of copper and dedicated to "General Porfirio Díaz, hero of this day."[39] The same work of art inspired an anonymous piece with an explanatory inscription indicating that it represented the "Triumphant entrance of General Díaz in Puebla following the glorious battle of 2 April," showing "General Díaz on his dashing horse."[40]

From an aesthetic point of view, we can recognize the use of classical iconography, following the typical models of war representations. Several paintings repeat the same angles to emphasize important architectural structures, such as the cathedral on the left and the government palace on the right. Other versions are from the opposite standpoint, like the one painted by Manuel Prieto.[41] However, the city center of Puebla is always shown as the nucleus of the battle and the site that is the heart of power. Another representation is from the perspective of the government palace.[42] Yet another provides more slight variations.[43] This lithograph appeared in a brochure-like publication titled *2 April*.[44] The brochure also contained images of generals Díaz, Alatorre,

Zárate Toscano

Carlos Pacheco, Manuel González, Luis Figueroa, Rafael Cravioto, Juan de la Luz Enríquez, and Luis Mier y Terán.[45]

Some of the images devoted to the action in Puebla are quite unusual. In their *Porfirio: La guerra (1854–1867)* Enrique Krauze and Fausto Zerón-Medina highlight the lithograph *2 de April*, taken from *Apuntes históricos de la carrera militar del señor general Porfirio Díaz, presidente de la República Mexicana*, published by Ignacio M. Escudero in 1889.[46] This representation depicts a particularly intense moment of the battle in the barricades, including fist fighting. It is quite different from the image included in *México a través de los siglos*, entitled "Puebla, the temple of San Agustín after the assault," where there is no sign of war except for an unmanned barricade.[47] Presumably this author or editor was looking for a conciliatory view and so minimized the horrors of war through using this image.

In the *Mundo Ilustrado* of 2 April 1905 is an almost unknown image illustrating an article titled "A military painting," where we learn that another huge painting by Francisco de P. Mendoza was placed at the Colegio Militar. This astonishing painting shows the hero sometime between 4:00 and 6:00 p.m. on 1 April, the eve of the battle, planning his strategy.[48]

One could criticize these paintings for having a purely decorative purpose, but the fact is that the artists did not have the exposure or experience to capture real war scenes. That is why their works are so different from the oil painting by the Catalan José Cusachs, *Batalla del 2 de abril*, where we can recognize a hand better trained in this matter.[49]

Such paintings and monuments are common in other places in Latin America where there has been an attempt to pay tribute to the past, political stability permitting. Let us not forget that memory supports itself on the visibility of images and monuments.[50] Finally we should note that these "modern" paintings were officially commissioned between 1902 and 1905, while the lithographs belong to the last decades of the nineteenth century.

Other Support Material for the Historical Imaginary

We must now pay attention to the depiction of heroes in stone or marble, a representation more commonly known as "bronze history." Díaz had a firm understanding of the role monuments had as part of a civic pedagogy and supported the project of turning the Paseo de la Reforma in Mexico City into an open history book.[51] As part of this program each state proposed two important individuals for recognition, and their monuments were inaugurated during official civic dates. Hence on 2 April 1890 the unveiling of the statues from the state of Yucatán took place: Andrés Quintana Roo and Manuel Zepeda y Peraza, sculpted by Epitacio Calvo.[52]

However, Don Porfirio was much more careful when it came to turning his own heroism into marble and did not order any monument of himself, at least not publicly. His long-lasting period of rule did not allow him to die and have a monument erected in his memory, like the other heroes. However, in 1900 the Italian Adamo Boari, responsible for the Palace of Fine Arts, planned a monument to Porfirio Díaz with traces of indigenous architecture.[53] The project never came into being, but it is representative of the cultural ideas in vogue in the latter half of the nineteenth century, with a desire to meld the roots of Indian origin with the newly acquired modernity, ignoring the period that unfolded in between (i.e., the three centuries of Spanish dominion). This link between the distant past and the present can be found in the artistic program from the Porfiriato, and a monument to its leader would be no exception. It seems he did know what history could be used for praising the past and also the present.

Another monumental project that did come into being was apparently not an initiative of Díaz himself but of Governor Bernardo Reyes, who invited the president to Monterrey in 1898 for its unveiling, as earlier mentioned. The monument was situated on Avenida Oriente at Alameda Porfirio Díaz, named in honor of our hero. The personification of Winged Victory appeared holding a banner in one hand bearing the words "2 de abril de 67," and in the other hand a picture of Díaz showing him at the age he must have been at the time of the battle. The pedestal was inscribed: "The State of Nuevo León to Porfirio Díaz, glorious caudillo in times of war, eminent statesman in times of peace."[54] It would appear that the sculpture of this Winged Victory was subsequently recycled in another monument at Monterrey.[55]

In 1875 Puebla would see yet another commemorative monument "on the anniversary of the glorious day of the assault on Puebla of 2 April 1867," inaugurated by Colonel Carlos Borda, former governor and military commander in Chiapas.[56] According to interviews conducted in Puebla, the obelisk was still standing a few decades ago outside a school named "Dos de abril," but it was removed in the course of some urban redevelopment.[57]

Another source used to fix memory is music written specifically for commemorative events. Such is the case of the "Himno sinfónico" composed by Gustavo Campa for the inauguration of the National Library on 2 April 1884.[58] Although in that year the president was not Porfirio Díaz but Manuel González, the intention in selecting that date for the inauguration was no less representative: the two had fought side by side in the siege of Puebla.

From Don Porfirio's letters we know that in 1886 Mariano Ruiz sent him a military march titled "2 April," composed by "the music director of my corps and dedicated to your person."[59] The letter accompanying the composition specified that although it was not a piece of great merit, it was sent as a souvenir from a dedicated subordinate. Díaz answered asking him to thank "señor Pineda" for the music.[60] The composition by Miguel Lerdo de Tejada entitled "El Gran Presidente" can also be included in this series of commemorative music.[61]

The most important musical composition related to 2 April is the opera *Anita*, written by Melesio Morales and dedicated to Porfirio Díaz. Morales had had international success with *Ildegonda*, becoming the first Mexican to have an opera performed in Italy (although with an entirely European and medieval subject). Morales then got caught up in the commemorative mood around Díaz and wrote an opera that takes place at the time of the siege of Puebla, presenting a love story between a Mexican lady and a French soldier. The opera was not staged during the author's life, and it was not until recently that it had its operatic debut.[62]

We should also note the play by Eduardo Gómez Haro with music by Carlos Samaniego, composed in 1905, its action likewise taking place in Puebla on 2 April 1867. Gómez Haro himself described it in a catalogue of his works as a *zarzuela* (Hispanic operetta), but the copy I have seen does not include the sheet music. However it can be considered part of the musical scene of that time and was well accepted by the audience.[63]

Finally, we must emphasize that historical memory is also present in official nomenclature, as a way to highlight facts, names, and dates. Towns, streets, schools, markets, parks, etc. named 2 April or Porfirio Díaz are no longer common in Mexico, as opposed to the highly popular names of other people or dates related to the

French Intervention, such as Mariano Escobedo or 5 May, which serve as important reminders of this historical event.

Voices and Words

In this commemorative history the use of words by those specifically invited to participate in the celebrations through speeches, poems, and hymns contributes to the formation and consolidation of the nation's images. In the events held around 2 April we find the usual civic speeches, but unfortunately not many have survived and very few have been published. As years went by the euphoria expressed through these speeches faded away, although contemporary opinions were still printed in newspapers. Writers articulated their thoughts and described the characteristics of the commemorations, but the press also became the forum where polemics took place around them.

These public texts where the battle and its main star are celebrated find a complement in other sources with much more limited circulation, such as Díaz's correspondence held at the Universidad Iberoamericana. Looking for letters related to this subject yielded several written to congratulate the president on the anniversary of battle. As if it were a birthday and not a war memory, he received congratulations such as the following one: "I will not cease to serve you as a companion and loyal subordinate, in congratulating you for the splendid triumph attained by our national arms in Puebla twenty-four years ago, against the traitors," signed by R. León in 1891.[64] But there were also demands and petitions for help, as if Díaz were a cacique. And, of course, the letters were sometimes accompanied by presents, including a horse named "2 April," a box of cognac, and a barrel of wine.[65]

As early as 1868 we find evidence of use of the telegraph to send congratulations to the general, and he too was very aware of its purpose and used it as part of his effort to unite the country through communications and transportation.

Well-known authors such as Ignacio Manuel Altamirano and Guillermo Prieto also wrote about the heroic action of 2 April 1867. The former regretted that in 1880 all the champions who fought together under one flag were divided.[66] The latter pointed out that Puebla was situated in a symbolic circle beginning with the victory of 5 May and ending on 2 April.[67]

Díaz himself felt the need to give his own version of the events. His *Memorias* were prepared in 1892 by Matías Romero, and one hundred copies were printed.[68] Besides the war report, he included chapters relating to the preparations (chapter 80) and the assault itself. Díaz wrote:

> This account would become excessively long were I to detain myself relating all the acts of valor and commitment that my subordinates showed in the assault of 2 April. All I will say is that I consider this engagement to have been one of the most important I took part in during the War of the Intervention.[69]

Porfirio Díaz has generated a vast historiographical production with titles that have induced intense polemics, including *México a través de los siglos*, and works by historians such as Francisco Bulnes, Daniel Cosío Villegas, Enrique Krauze, and Paul Garner.[70] A thorough analysis of this subject continues to require further research. Suffice it here to note the fact that the Porfiriato is studied and evaluated more and more, and that notwithstanding this renewed interest in Díaz, it is still difficult to find books that exalt the heroic characteristics of a man who was in charge of the government for more than three decades.

Zárate Toscano

Military Exaltation

There is another element in this commemoration that deserves a wider analysis: the military element expressed in the form of mock battles, taking place year after year to bring back to life the emotion and effectiveness of certain military actions. It can be understood as a mechanism to show off the strength of the regime, both inside and outside the country, not only as a military exercise but also as a show in itself. A mock battle is something that imitates reality, taking into consideration only appearances. The concept of a simulacrum is one that entails the figured representation of something, whether it is an image, portrait, statue, or even a mannequin.[71] And all those elements were present during the military commemorations of 2 April.

Recalling all the documentation, we find several of these exercises:

1888 at Molino del Rey
1894 at San Lázaro
1895 at Peralvillo
1899 at San Lázaro and Peralvillo
1899 at San Lázaro and Peralvillo
1900 at Mexico City
1901 at Mexico City
1904 at Mexico City
1904 at Oaxaca
1905 at Mexico City[72]

Space does not permit outlining what each of these events entailed, but the focus here is on the importance of the images used to publicize them. Reviewing images used over a long span of time shows that the illustrations drawn for the early simulacrums were later replaced by photographs taken in situ.[73] The images not only show General Díaz but also include views of the general headquarters or a map of the place used in the mock battle.[74]

Marking their locations on a map would reveal that these "powder spectacles" took place in the surroundings of Mexico City, not within its urban center, which meant that the spectators had to travel several miles to witness them. They left a deep impression on people because of the demonstration of military might, but reports in the press also criticized the lack of experience of some soldiers and recommended that they train a little more in future. It is worth noting that these mock battles were staged not only to commemorate the victory of 2 April but also took place in memory of 5 May, although in a different setting, the fields of La Vaquita, Ixtapalapa.[75]

As part of the show of strength in Mexico's military tradition, in 1895 an emotional ceremony was held where former war veterans paraded holding Mexican flags that had been used or were related to the most glorious events of the nation's history.[76] The following year the ceremony was repeated, and the press emphasized:

> The old yet glorious flags that, in Puebla and Querétaro, floated victorious in the wind, punctured by bullets, stained with the smoke from the gunpowder, torn by time, were taken by two army veterans, and alongside them marched the heroes of Querétaro and Puebla, generals Escobedo and Díaz, sword in hand, escorting them.[77]

Final Thoughts

The 2 April commemoration was used not only to praise but also to criticize. With the press serving as a battlefield in its own right, opposing factions and their spokespersons argued around the pertinence of the festivities, the fact that Díaz became the center of attention, the character of official festivities, the involvement of the military class, and more.

According to Roger Chartier, a commemoration can be placed at the crossroads of two cultural dynamics. On the one hand, there is the invention and expression of traditional culture shared by a majority, and on the other, the pedagogic project of a dominant culture.[78] In this sense the commemoration involves participation and education. We can conclude that throughout the nineteenth century the dominant class was really interested in promoting these kind of festivities. These were not merely political events but also a way to increase the country's historical conscience, built upon all those elements of local and national identity.

We may wonder whether it was politically correct to commemorate insurrection and to give the leaders of such movements — including pronunciamientos — the aura of heroes. But in this particular case, it is worth remembering that this military action proved extremely important because it put an end to a foreign invasion. Even after Díaz was overthrown and living in exile, it was still possible to organize a fiesta pointing out that "it was not the anniversary of a man's victory but the anniversary of an [entire] country's victory."[79] These lines were published in 1912, when in spite of having his enemy Francisco I. Madero as president, a group of Diaz's loyal followers pressed Congress to obtain an important victory: 2 April was raised to the category of National Commemoration.[80] It is not surprising that after Madero himself was supplanted by Victoriano Huerta, one of Díaz's trusted generals, the commemoration of 2 April continued, and it involved more honors for the former president, giving him the newly created title of General del Cuerpo del Ejército.[81] Commemoration during the Mexican Revolution continued, at least until 1914, with more involvement of "*felixista* and *reyista* clubs, *mutualista* societies, [and] political club delegations," with the government's tolerance and complicity.[82]

However, in his birthplace, Oaxaca, the remembering of Díaz induced confrontation between his followers and the authorities. When in 1912 a group of distinguished ladies, merchants, foreigners, workers, and students approached the obelisk in honor of Díaz, they were received by armed policemen "with orders to take away and throw to the ground the floral offering that was there to be placed." Verbal confrontations erupted, and hostile actions were taken by the demonstrators against the houses of the political leaders.[83] This repression of a spontaneous recognition of Díaz's act of heroism was the beginning of the end of the commemoration. In spite of it being probably the country's most important military action, public memory of it was threatened because it was associated with a leader who stayed in power for too long.

The military action of 2 April included some elements of a pronunciamiento, but it is precisely its military character that stands out throughout the commemorations. Almost all civic dates in Mexico's official calendar are related to war, with the exception of the commemoration of the 1917 Constitution on 5 February. The difference may be that this action was made by a formal army, instead of the chaotic followers of Miguel Hidalgo. And the survivors became sacred icons on which it was possible to build a country.

In 2010 Puebla was the setting for such commemorations, which made Sealtiel Alatriste write:

> With time, power went to Porfirio Díaz's head and he became a dictator, whose longevity in power gave rise to the [1910] Revolution.

A century has gone by since then and yet 47 years before that he was declared a national hero. Should we celebrate him for this rather than condemn him? It is just a question.[84]

Notes

1. Fowler, "El pronunciamiento mexicano," 12. Definition taken from Enciclopedia Microsoft Encarta Online 2007. For more recent definitions of the pronunciamiento see Fowler (ed.), *Forceful Negotiations*, and *Malcontents, Rebels, and Pronunciados*.

2. They had the inscription "Vencieron a los defensores de Puebla, dos de abril de 1867." Meza, "Pedro Silva Meneses."

3. Zárate Toscano, "Héroes y fiestas."

4. Zárate Toscano, "Agustín de Iturbide," and "Las pervivencias."

5. Archivo Histórico del Distrito Federal (henceforth cited as ADHF), Guadalupe Hidalgo, Festividades, inv. 95, exp. 2, 1887.

6. ADHF, Guadalupe Hidalgo, Festividades, inv. 96, exp. 22, 1907.

7. ADHF, Guadalupe Hidalgo, Festividades, inv. 96, exp. 64, 1914. It would be interesting to study this new meaning and find out if it was related to the use of trees as symbols of freedom after the French Revolution. See *Les arbres de la liberté*.

8. This research is based mainly on the Porfirian press although we could also profit from some documents issued by the municipalities and the Distrito Federal and also from the graphic materials. I want to thank Gabriela Guerrero, César Hernández y Rodrigo Moreno for their help in this matter.

9. Abrassart, "El pueblo en orden."

10. Costeloe, "The Junta Patriótica."

11. "El simulacro del 2 de abril," *El Diario del Hogar*, 1 April 1888; *El Monitor Republicano* (Mexico City), no. 81, 4 April 1888.

12. Casasola, *Seis siglos de historia gráfica*, vol. 3. The Círculo Porfirista organized a demonstration where workers and mutualistic societies took part in honor of General Porfirio Díaz to commemorate the battle of 2 April in 1903. Casasola, *Biografía ilustrada*, 91.

13. "Los miembros del Ejército Nacional felicitan al general Porfirio Díaz en su aniversario de la batalla del 2 de abril, 1903," *El Mundo Ilustrado*, 10 April 1914.

14. *El Monitor Republicano* (Mexico City), no. 83, 6 April 1892.

15. *El Monitor Republicano* (Mexico City), no. 81, 5 April 1881.

16. *Decreto núm. 117 [para la premiación de los ciudadanos].*

17. "Condecoraciones para los generales Porfirio Díaz, Mariano Escobedo, oficiales y soldados que tomaron parte en el asalto y toma de Puebla, así como a los del sitio de Querétaro". Gustavo Casasola, *Biografía*, 69.

18. "El presidente del Congreso de la Unión, general Mariano Escobedo, condecora al general Porfirio Díaz, al celebrarse el aniversario de la toma de Puebla, 1895." Casasola, *Biografía ilustrada*, 69.

19. "Miembros del ejército recibiendo condecoraciones por el general Porfirio Díaz en la ceremonia del 2 de abril de 1900," in Casasola, *Biografía ilustrada*, 80.

20. "Las fiestas de Puebla," *El Monitor Republicano*, 4 April 1891.

21. *El Imparcial*, 3 April 1900.

22. "El simulacro de ayer," *El Diario del Hogar*, 11 April 1888.

23. Zárate Toscano, "Septiembre."

24. *El Monitor Republicano*, 1 April 1890.

25. Cortés, *Discurso pronunciado*, 14.

26. We have press reports for 1869 and 1904, but fully establishing the festive geography would require checking the local press and official documents of the town councils from places outside Mexico City.

27. Guzmán (ed.), *Corona cívica.*

28. "Plaza de armas de Mérida adornada para las fiestas del 2 de abril de 1868," in Guzmán, *Corona cívica.*

29. We have information for the years 1869, 1875, 1891, 1901, 1909, and 1910.

30. "Las fiestas de Puebla," *El Monitor Republicano*, 4 April 1891.

31. Zamacona, *Discurso pronunciado.*

32. *La visita del señor presidente.*

33. Years later, however, Reyes would publish a biography of Díaz: Reyes, *El general Porfirio Díaz.*

34. Francisco de P. Mendoza, *Episodio de la Batalla de Puebla del 2 de abril de 1867*, siglo XIX, Museo Nacional de Historia, Instituto Nacional de Antropología e Historia (henceforth cited as INAH). In Casasola, *Biografía ilustrada*, 42, it is captioned: "Entrada triunfal del general Porfirio Díaz a la ciudad de Puebla la mañana del 2 de abril de 1867."

35. "Dos de Abril. Entrada del General Díaz seguido de su Estado Mayor a la Plaza de Armas de Puebla, al acabar de dar el famoso asalto. (Este cuadro fue pintado por el señor Francisco de P. Mendoza teniendo en cuenta detalles de testigos)," *El Imparcial*, 5 April 1903.

36. I want to thank Salvador Rueda Smithers, director of the museum, for

the information and the images. The caption he provided reads: "Revelación de la pintura de Mendoza en el Castillo de Chapultepec cuando era Colegio Militar: De la pintura de Mendoza en el Castillo de Chapultepec cuando era Colegio Militar."

37. Báez, *La pintura militar.*

38. Báez Macías, "Pintura militar."

39. W. H. Mullins Company, "*Al señor general Porfirio Díaz, héroe de esta jornada,*" bajorrelieve en cobre, Museo de la No Intervención, Fuerte de Loreto, INAH. Image from Báez, *La pintura militar*, 165.

40. Anonymous, *Entrada triunfal del general Díaza la Plaza de Puebla en la gloriosa bataya [sic] del 2 de abril donde el general Díazen su brioso caballo . . . a los cadetes,* (1925?), óleo sobre tela, Museo Regional de Puebla, INAH. Image from Báez, *La pintura militar*, 165.

41. Prieto, *Episodio de la Batalla de Puebla, 2 de abril de 1867*, siglo XIX, óleo sobre tela, Museo Nacional de Historia, INAH. Image from Báez, *La pintura militar*, 162.

42. "Se encontraban sitiando la ciudad de Puebla las tropas del Ejército de Oriente, cuando se supo que el general Leonardo Márquez iba a reforzar la plaza, entonces el general Porfirio Díaz decidió romper el fuego y tomó por asalto la ciudad, el 2 de abril de 1867. *2 de abril,* litografía." Image from Krauze and Zerón-Medina, *Porfirio* 2:63: "Asalto y toma de la plaza de Puebla por el ejército republicano al mando del ilustre general Porfirio Díaz," litografía, Hesiquio Hiriarte, reprinted from the magazine *El Álbum de la Mujer* (1883–88).

43. Casasola, *Biografía ilustrada*, 42: "Se encontraban sitiando la ciudad de Puebla las tropas del Ejército de Oriente, cuando se supo que el general Leonardo Márquez iba a reforzar la plaza, entonces el general Porfirio Díaz decidió romper el fuego y tomó por asalto la ciudad, el 2 de abril de 1867. Pintura a partir de litografía de 'Asalto y toma de la plaza de Puebla por el ejército republicano al mando del ilustre general Porfirio Díaz,' litografía, Hesiquio Hiriarte,

44. Litografía basada en la de Hesiquio Iriarte. En *2 [dos] de abril: periódico ilustrado*, ed. González Pérez.

45. These comments were published in *El Monitor Republicano*, 4 April 1893.

46. *2 de abril,* litografía Ignacio M. Escudero. *Apuntes históricos de la carrera militar del señor general Porfirio Díaz, presidente de la República Mexicana* (Mexico City, 1889), Colección Eduardo Rincón Gallardo. Image from Krauze and Zerón-Medina, *Porfirio*, 63.

47. "Puebla, el templo de San Agustín después del asalto del 2 de abril de

1867 dado por las tropas republicanas al mando del general Porfirio Díaz," in Riva Palacio (ed.), *México a través de los siglos, vol. 5.*

48. Frente a Puebla, movimiento estratégico del 1 de abril de 1867 (Cuadro de F. de P. Mendoza). *El Mundo Ilustrado,* 2 April 1905.

49. José Cusachs, *Batalla del 2 de abril,* óleo sobre tela, 1902, Museo Nacional de Historia, INAH. Image from Báez, *La pintura militar,* 137. According to Krauze and Zerón-Medina, *Porfirio,* it is called "Batalla del 2 de abril. Díaz da instrucciones a sus tropas."

50. For European perspectives see Nora (ed.), *Realms of Memory.*

51. I have analyzed this monumental plan in Zárate Toscano, "El papel de la escultura conmemorativa," and in "El Paseo de la Reforma."

52. "Inauguración: Estatuas," *El Monitor Republicano,* 2 April 1890.

53. Fernández, *El arte del siglo XIX,* 179.

54. Monumento conmemorativo del 2 de abril de 1867 en la Avenida Oriente de la Alameda Porfirio Díaz en Monterrey. See *La visita del señor presidente.*

55. This is noted in electronic comments on *La visita del señor presidente.* See www.google.com/books?id=HoFDAAAAYAAJ&hl=es&source.

56. *El Eco de ambos mundos,* 31 March 1875.

57. Testimonios de Fernando Osorio y de Luis Gerardo Morales, located on the street named 5 de mayo, between 10th and 14 west, 2010.

58. Campa, *Himno sinfónico,* "Ejecutado a grande orquesta el 2 de abril de 1884 en la Biblioteca Nacional de México, para cuya solemne inauguración fue escrito."

59. Colección Porfirio Díaz (henceforth cited as CPD), Universidad Iberoamericana, Mariano Ruiz to Porfirio Díaz, L. 11, C. 09, doc. 004148, Guanajuato, 13 April 1886.

60. CPD, L. 11, C. 09, doc. 004149, 26 April 1886.

61. Lerdo de Tejada, *Marcha Polka al gran presidente.*

62. This opera has been played several times as a concert but finally on 24 June 2010 it had its worldwide debut at the Conservatorio de la Música in México. It was composed in 1903 as a lyric drama in one act and fourteen scenes, with a libretto in Italian by Enrico Golisciani and music by Melesio Morales.

63. Gómez Haro, *El héroe del 2 de abril.*

64. CPD, L. 16, C. 08, doc. 003917, 2 April 1891.

65. CPD, L. 14, C. 07, doc. 003264, "2 de Abril de 1889."

66. *La República,* 2 April 1880, in Giron (ed.), *Ignacio Manuel Altamirano,* 74–76.

67. *El Monitor Republicano,* 3 April 1886.

68. Díaz, *Memorias del gral. Porfirio Díaz*.

69. Díaz, *Memorias del gral. Porfirio Díaz*, http://www.antorcha.net/
biblioteca_virtual/historia/porforio/presentacion.html, accessed 28 May 2010.

70. Riva Palacio (ed.), *México a través de los siglos*; Bulnes, *El verdadero Díaz*;
Cosío Villegas, *Historia moderna de México*; Krauze and Zerón-Medina, *Porfirio*;
Krauze, *Místico de la autoridad* (Biografía del poder, vol. 1); Garner, *Porfirio Díaz*.

71. *Diccionario Manual de la Lengua Española Vox*, Larousse Editorial, 2007.

72. For San Lazaro in 1894 see "El general Porfirio Díaz observando los efec-
tos de la metralla en el blanco. Simulacro de 1894 en San Lázaro," in Casasola,
Biografía ilustrada, 68: "Las baterías de artillería, antes de iniciar sus tiros de
precisión. Simulacro en San Lázaro, 1894"; for Peralvillo in 1895 see *El Monitor Republicano*, 2 April 1895. For Mexico City in 1900 see Casasola, *Historia
gráfica*, 12, and "Maniobras militares," 2 April 1900; in 1904 *El Mundo Ilustrado*, 10 April 1904, image with the Castillo de Chapultepec in the background;
and in 1905 *El Mundo Ilustrado*, 9 April 1905.

73. *El Imparcial*, 4 April 1899. Also "El Gral. Díaz en traje de campaña (de
apuntes tomados en el simulacro de Peralvillo). Recordamos a nuestros lecto-
res que en los dibujos que tomados de apuntes publican los diarios, es imposi-
ble exigir retratos completos," *El Imparcial*, 4 April 1899.

74. "Plano de la situación de los cuerpos y servicios del ejército de la guarnición en la revista de hoy, 4 abril 1899. El cuartel general," *El Imparcial*, 4 and
5 April 1899.

75. On the simulacrum of 1900 and 1901 see Casasola, *Biografía ilustrada*, 86, 89.

76. See *Reseña de las fiestas del 2 y 3 de abril*, and *Monitor Republicano*, 2
April 1895.

77. *El Siglo XIX*, 3 April 1896. "Durante las fiestas del 2 de abril de 1895, el
general Porfirio Díaz y altos jefes del ejército escoltaron a las históricas ban-
deras," Casasola, *Biografía ilustrada*, 69.

78. Chartier, *Sociedad y escritura*, 20.

79. *El Imparcial*, 2 April 1912.

80. Several reports were published in *El Imparcial* between 2 and 7 April.

81. *El Imparcial*, 4 April 1914. Huerta himself sent Díaz a telegram to Paris to give him the good news.

82. *El Imparcial*, 3 April 1913.

83. *El Imparcial*, 6 April 1912.

84. Alatriste, DE MEMORIA, "El héroe en cuestión."

Ten. Juan Bustamante's Pronunciamiento and
the Civic Speeches That Condemned It:
San Luis Potosí, 1868–1869

I n the 1860s social groups in Mexico coexisted in the midst of
intense disputes to control the political sphere. Divisions and
fighting arose from the hub of the various political parties as
members and followers sought to define the kind of government
they believed the nation should adopt. The conservatives and the
monarchists insisted on finding a prince from one of the European sovereign houses who, in addition to leading a country incapable of "governing itself," could boast the kind of profile that
would prove ideal to serve their particular interests. The liberals,
on the other hand, both radical and moderate, were convinced
that they could not go back on the reforms they had led in Mexico's institutional life. From these obstinate stances, the Mexicans
began the second half of nineteenth century.

The political groups of San Luis Potosí witnessed in the 1860s
an escalation in the disputes to take control over their local institutions such as the city councils and the state congress. These
disputes took place as much on the battlefield as in the political
and intellectual arenas. Army officers, merchants, landowners,
and politicians supported different political ideologies, such as
conservative, pro-monarchist, liberal, and republican. They sub-
scribed to or undermined the diverse political plans that emerged
at that time; their support relied on the extent to which each plan

could benefit their group and personal interests. One of the means that allowed these groups to implement their plans was the *pronunciamiento*, which was a combination of military, intellectual, and political strategies "to force changes in government policies" or to attain government positions.[1] These pronunciamientos were sometimes successful. In the case of the Mexican state of San Luis Potosí, experts in the analysis of the pronunciamiento claim that from the 1820s onward, a significant number of pronunciamientos took place as part of attempts to access positions of power or to pressure the government into modifying its policies.[2]

In this chapter I analyze the 1869 pronunciamiento of Juan Bustamante. Bustamante was elected governor in 1867 and a year later was demoted by the state congress because he no longer represented the interests of the local political class. Bustamante was forced to ask for a leave of absence, and several months later he and his supporters started a pronunciamiento to reclaim the governorship. As soon as the pronunciamiento began, his opponents redoubled their efforts to destroy his reputation and persecute him until they secured his definitive removal from local politics in 1869.[3] Bustamante's adversaries were numerous and had enough clout to turn the decisions and actions of other social actors against him. The majority of members of the state congress—the Second Constitutional Legislature of San Luis Potosí (1867–69)—joined to form a compact group of *anti-bustamantistas*. They used the debates that took place during the state congress sessions as a venue to hurl accusations against Bustamante and discredit him politically.[4]

One of the strategies used by Carlos Tovar, Bustamante's substitute governor, was to take control of the 1869 Independence Day celebrations.[5] The members of the Junta Patriótica, organizers of the event, offered him their support, as did the anti-bustaman-tista intellectuals. Their first task was to appease those of Busta-mante's supporters who sought his restitution as the "legitimate" governor of San Luis Potosí. The Junta Patriótica organized a se-ries of activities for 15 and 16 September that included a harangue consisting of two speeches. Members of the junta, following Gov-ernor Tovar's instructions, chose two speakers to address the pub-lic with messages that touted the unity of Tovar's government and discredited Bustamante's pronunciamiento.[6] Junta members chose the speakers carefully, because these men had the difficult task of persuading the audience that the pronunciamiento was unaccept-able. The speakers were required to convince the listeners that the pronunciamiento and its political plan contradicted in every way the principles of democracy and freedom that "our parents" had fought for in their own way.[7] In other words, the governor and the organizers of the civic celebrations took control of the festiv-ities and turned these into their own political platform.

In my analysis the civic speeches help us to understand just how the authors — who ironically had been vehement support-ers of Juan Bustamante and Benito Juárez only a few years earli-er — idealized the figure of Miguel Hidalgo y Costilla, "providen-tial patriarch of Mexico," and used his image to inveigh against Bustamante, "tyrant, antidemocrat and representative of disor-der." Bustamante became the antithesis of the Hidalgo idealized in the authors' speeches.

The chapter is divided into three sections: first I provide the view of Juan Bustamante from the historiography of his time as well as a description of some of the aspects involved in his rise and fall from politics. In the second section I examine how the fall of Governor Juan Bustamante was plotted from the state legislature,

Salazar Mendoza

and I also describe the beginning and the outcome of his pronunciamiento. In the last section I analyze the civic speeches written and delivered in the September celebrations by Fortunato Nava and Benigno Arriaga, who took upon themselves the task of convincing the "troublemakers" that the pronunciamiento was undemocratic and therefore an act of aggression against the institutional life of the state.[8]

Perspectives on Juan Bustamante

Juan Bustamante García was born in the town of Valle de San Francisco, today known as Villa de Reyes, San Luis Potosí, in 1818. His parents were Manuel Bustamante and Marcelina García. He attended the primary school there and several years later moved to the capital city of the state of San Luis Potosí. At the age of twenty-eight he was interested in strengthening his links with the army, initially as purveyor selling goods to the Mexican Army in the mid-1840s, and later as an active participant in the famous battle of Palo Alto (8–9 May 1846). In 1847 he fought in the battle Angostura–Buena Vista (22–23 February). I was not able to find information on the merchandise Bustamante provided the Mexican Army; however, it is well known that before he began his political career he was engaged in mercantile activities that allowed him to accumulate the kind of capital later enabling him to purchase during the 1850s and 1860s several properties in the cities of San Luis and Guadalajara.[9]

According to the Potosino historian Nereo Rodríguez Barragán (an enthusiastic panegyrist of Juan Bustamante), Bustamante was forced into exile as a result of his liberal ideas, just before the Reforma War started in 1858. During the time he was in exile Bustamante worked on establishing close relationships with members of the liberal militias, such as Santiago Vidaurri, Santos Degollado, and Ignacio Comonfort. These generals respected Bustamante because of his patriotic actions and promoted him in rank during the late 1850s; he became a colonel of the National Guard and later a general. However, Bustamante rejected the titles he was offered. He even declined the rank of cavalry colonel that President Manuel González offered him in 1882.[10]

According to Nereo Rodríguez Barragán, Bustamante played an important role in local politics, his actions motivated solely by his interest in serving the *patria*. I consider, however, that Bustamante was not such a disinterested politician. The sources I have consulted demonstrate that he acted in order to preserve his control over the institutions of the government of San Luis Potosí. For example, he decided which taxes were levied, determined the kind of education offered in schools, and established restrictions regarding the participation of the Catholic Church in public events. Other kind of evidence demonstrates that Bustamante was also interested in modernizing the state institutions. In March 1867 he reopened the Instituto Científico y Literario and asked the *jefes políticos* each to choose from among the population of their towns two distinguished students who would become part of the academic programs of the instituto; the chosen students were to receive a fellowship for their studies. He also promoted the establishment of a small meteorological observatory and furthered the creation of a museum of natural history. Finally, he renamed several streets in the city center, changing religious names to secular ones. The Calle de la Concepción thus became that of Ignacio Zaragoza, and similarly the Calle de la Cruz turned into that of the Cinco de Mayo, thanks to him. He ordered the establishment of Civil Registry offices in each of the principal municipal

Salazar Mendoza

towns as well.[11] Undoubtedly, Juan Bustamante was a controversial figure in his time. While some of his actions and views affected the interests of certain groups that did not agree with his form of governing, others gladly welcomed the benefits he provided. The local historiography is divided in its consideration and treatment of Bustamante, as revealed in the official newspaper *La Sombra de Zaragoza*, in which the publishers praised the patriotic actions he undertook when the Supreme Government resided for a second time in San Luis Potosí in 1867.[12] During the pronunciamiento of 1869 the once supportive editors took a different view and turned openly hostile toward him. They took up the cause of the substitute governor Carlos Tovar and even wrote an editorial that read in part: "Let the blood that has been spilled fall on D. Juan Bustamante and his supporters! The government shall work energetically to repress in its cradle the insolent progress of this ambitious despot, who with his actions has denied his ridiculous proclamations, in which he asserted that he did not conspire against the state's peace."[13] According to the editors, reason stood with Tovar and had abandoned Bustamante.

The withdrawal of support for Bustamante by the official newspaper was not the only setback for him. Another politician and liberal intellectual, Manuel Muro, who tried to refrain from openly criticizing Bustamante personally or professionally, was unable to conceal a certain animosity toward him in the pages he wrote about Bustamante in his *Historia de San Luis Potosí*. In the year of the pronunciamiento Muro was a deputy for the state congress, where he reiterated his opposing views.[14]

The attacks launched by the anti-bustamantista politicians against Juan Bustamante did not stop even after the failure of the pronunciamiento; years later historian Primo Feliciano Velázquez in his own *Historia de San Luis Potosí* questioned without trepidation the political role of the republican; he pointed out emphatically Bustamante's anticlericalism and intolerance toward Catholics and maintained that such radical stances only served to unite old enemies who did everything to prevent his return to power.[15]

In short, the public crusade to change opinion about Bustamante was effective; the political capital he had gathered since 1864 was exhausted. His patriotic image was quickly tarnished and he became a figure overlooked.[16]

The Legislative Branch against Bustamante

Juan Bustamante surfaced on the political scene of San Luis Potosí in the first half of 1864 when Benito Juárez appointed him governor and military commander.[17] At that time and until the fall of the Second Empire, Bustamante dedicated himself to supporting the republican army, focusing his efforts on raising funds and others types of resources.[18] The principal moneylenders were local and foreign landowners and retailers, whom he persuaded eloquently or through force to contribute to the cause of the war. His government offered written guarantees stating that the loans would be repaid with 1 percent interest as soon as the republican government was restored and the economic conditions allowed. However, these promises were not kept, for reasons including the reorganization and divisions within the liberal party, external factors that affected national politics, and the lack of money in the finances of the restored government.[19] From 1864 to 1867 Bustamante consolidated his authority as governor and military commander with the institutions under his authority. But his demise began in 1867 shortly after he was elected constitutional governor of the state.

Salazar Mendoza

In early May 1868 Governor Bustamante faced two attacks against him. The origin of these was the very core of the state congress. In the first attack he was accused of having overspent the budget; in the second, of having overstepped the power of the legislature. In fact, it was the legislature that had overstepped the governor's sphere. The state constitution provided that the governor prepare income and expense budgets, but despite what was legally established, the congressmen nevertheless prepared a budget that they then endorsed in a congressional session. In this clash between the legislative and executive powers, the congressmen took it upon themselves during the period between the ordinary and extraordinary congressional sessions, to put together a solid file against Bustamante. While an earlier similar file had failed to garner enough strength to sway viewpoints, the second file was effective. Notwithstanding Bustamante's strong defense and pleas, in September 1868 he was forced to request a leave of absence for a period of six months.[20]

After several months, in early 1869, Juan Bustamante returned to San Luis Potosí. His followers, according to one Potosino historian, advised him to take up arms. The pronunciamiento took several months to plan. On 20 August 1869 Bustamante initiated the pronunciamiento in Villa de Cedral, a town located in the northern plateau of the state of San Luis Potosí. Followers began to pronounce in towns across the region: Ahualulco, Guadalcázar, and Charcas. There were also echoes of the pronunciamiento in the eastern part of the state, known as the middle zone, primarily in the Rioverde region, and followers in the Huasteca region were mainly in the southern towns of Tancanhuitz and Tamazunchale.

Juan Bustamante may have thought the number of followers would grow as the movement went forward; but this was not the

case. An estimate of the number of *pronunciados* revealed roughly 340 men, civilians and soldiers—a significant number but not
large enough to reinstate Bustamante as governor.[21]

Whether or not the estimate of supporters is accurate, the mobilization of the pronunciados throughout the state stirred up fear
and uncertainty in the populace. Julius Noureau, United States
consul in San Luis Potosí, expressed this fear in a letter dated September 1869 and addressed to W. Hunter, second assistant secretary of state.[22] Along with the consular information, he explained
in detail his view of the pronunciamientos as:

> a thing hardly describable in our language, but of very frequent oc-
> currence here, as anyone who can raise and arm a small number of
> men bid open defiance to law and order [illegible] during a while
> and upon being prosecuted by the troops, disbands his crowd and
> disappears for a while only to return shortly afterwards without be-
> ing held to account for his former misdeeds.[23]

He describes the pronunciamiento as an anarchical movement
intended to destabilize. A situation like this was neither convenient nor profitable for men like the consul, who was also a United States commercial broker. Noureau went on to describe how
he saw his business being affected by the pronunciamento: "The
pronunciados [unlike the General Government] have imposed
very heavy taxes in all they got to [sic], and in fact, are living entirely on the country they have occupied."[24]

Praise for Miguel Hidalgo y Costilla;
Criticism of Juan Bustamante

Each September the official newspapers normally published several pages notifying their readers of various aspects and activities

of the Independence Day celebrations, such as the program, the *bando* (edict), the civic speeches, and event reviews. In September 1869, however, things were different; the newspaper *La Sombra de Zaragoza* published only one article about the celebrations, as the remaining pages were filled with news on the pronunciamiento.[25]

The civic speeches given on this particular anniversary were also in part dedicated to the pronunciamiento. The speeches were presented by Fortunato Nava and Benigno Arriaga, both of whom shared an idealized characterization of the figure of Miguel Hidalgo and stressed Bustamante's undemocratic behavior.[26] Nava's speech is characterized by its conciliatory tone, but Arriaga's is aggressive, particularly when referring to Bustamante. Arriaga clearly perceived himself as an agent of progress and saw the others, the pronunciados, as obstructing progress in the democratic life of San Luis Potosí.

Both authors complied with the order issued by Governor Tovar to prepare a speech in which the plan of the pronunciados was refuted. Furthermore, Nava was asked to deliver a speech in which the democratic benefits of Carlos Tovar's government were emphasized, and Arriaga was asked both to emphasize the democratic benefits of Tovar's government and to spotlight Bustamante's "unconstitutional and antidemocratic" behavior.

On the night of 15 September 1869 Fortunato Nava delivered his civic speech, subtly underlining the internal divisions between the liberal *potosinos* and extending an invitation to those who had been "misled" to reunite with the government institutions. Nava did not waver in his support of Tovar's government and the stability it provided or his rejection of the pronunciados' undemocratic practices. He believed that the Mexicans of the 1860s had journeyed happily toward freedom thanks to Miguel Hidalgo y

Costilla, the "apostle of freedom, prophet of our destinies, social philosopher, heroic warrior, . . . eminent liberator and . . . martyr of patriotic love," who sacrificed himself for this purpose.[27] Nava saw Hidalgo as the "providential patriarch of Mexico," not only for having planted the seeds of Independence but also because he endured all the hardships of "the relentless persecution of the inquisitors."[28]

On this commemorative night Nava assured his audience that "the great Hidalgo" had reached his goal, despite the lack of "people, weapons, resources, [and] organized troops."[29] Could people in their right mind be bold enough to tread on the invaluable legacy of the priest of Dolores? Yes, the foolish Juan Bustamante, who did so while defying democratic principles and institutions. Reading between the lines, Nava was declaring that this pronunciado, unlike Hidalgo, was incapable of undertaking a crusade to uphold the principles of freedom and democracy and that, quite the contrary, he was destroying the very things that the father of the nation had fought so hard to build.

Finally, Nava sent Bustamante and his followers a direct message of reconciliation: "We must see each other as nothing less than brothers, as dignified members of the great Mexican family, born of a kind mother and driven by the same interests, moved only by the desire of our venture, let us renew our oaths to ensure the future destiny of an independent Mexico, before the venerable altar of the nation [illegible] of our cherished freedom."[30]

Nava fulfilled his responsibilities on that 15 September night by acting as the intermediary between the authorities, the pronunciados, and the audience, and as the messenger capable of quieting the frenzy of the pronunciados. We do not, however, know the effect of the message on the audience; it may have had a positive impact and transformed the views of those members of the audience who had considered joining the pronunciamiento.

The following night, 16 September, Benigno Arriaga took to the stage temporarily set up along the tree-lined avenue, to become, in his own words, the "interpreter" of the feelings of his fellow patriots. His words focused on exalting the benefits of the "promised land of progress and freedom."[31] His speech overflowed with scholarly words that were probably incomprehensible to most in his audience. He praised or criticized the national heroes, depending on the case: he eulogized Morelos, Bravo, Guerrero, Victoria, Zaragoza, and even Porfirio Díaz. Arriaga included the names of Bolívar and Washington, to embrace Hidalgo in a more cosmopolitan agenda and place him on the same scale as the other continental heroes. Arriaga ridiculed characters such as Santa Anna and Arista: "the tyrannical and ridiculous like Santa Anna; now liberal and mean-spirited, like the illustrious General Arista."[32]

There is a third character in Arriaga's speech, who is not identified or personified in an obvious fashion. We can conclude that this personage is meant to be Juan Bustamante, the local troublemaker at the time. In his speech Arriaga claims that this third person attempted to silence the criticism and requests for accountability of his political adversaries, and "it would be necessary to suppress the man because no one can avoid the progress that leads to democracy; because democracy and progress are the inevitable destiny of humankind."[33] Arriaga saw Bustamante's movement as an act of aggression against progress and therefore against democracy. Furthermore, his attempts to silence his critics did nothing to further the democratic wishes of potosino society.

Arriaga, who took office as legislator in the state congress the day prior to his Independence Day speech, was convinced that a pragmatic, equitable, and democratic policy should prevail and that the disorder caused by the pronunciados contravened this. Carlos Tovar's government, he believed, was a guarantee that

> equality, order, morality, respect for the law, fraternity, love of work, freedom of conscience, of teaching, the emission of ideas, words, written or printed, the right of association, of inviolable property, an electoral [system] that renews and regenerates all of the powers; and that there are just as many other agents of public happiness, that offer the emigrant, the professor, the apostle, the muses, the capitalist, and the citizen, a good that would otherwise be impossible to know, democracy . . . is its true meaning, the practice of all of the social and political virtues.[34]

In short, Arriaga was convinced that the behavior of Bustamante and his pronunciados was incorrect. He exhorted those who had been misled to join instead the efforts to preserve freedom and defend progress; the door leading to the correct path was open, and it was up to them to make the right decision. Finally, Arriaga repeated that as legislators, he and his colleagues had a sacred mission to preserve peace and explained that "our fathers took up weapons to give us a nation; we take up instruments of industry and work and proclaim forgetfulness . . . we must join fraternally under the shield of the law to give our children true democracy and true freedom."[35] What Arriaga meant was that there was no room for pronunciamientos.

Final Considerations

Juan Bustamante's pronunciamiento was contested in different ways. On the one hand, he and his followers were persecuted by the government authorities' resorting to military force; on the other hand, the Independence festivities were used to transmit a message to the audience stressing the undemocratic and anti-progressive features of Bustamante's pronunciamiento. In this chapter I have described how the pronunciamiento was condemned in the Independence Day celebrations and how the civic speeches by Nava and Arriaga, ordered by Carlos Tovar via the Junta Patriótica, were aimed at tarnishing Bustamante's image and his movement. Both speeches reveal that the authors fulfilled their part of the bargain, although we cannot be sure of the effect on the audience. We know that Bustamante's movement failed, and perhaps the speeches of condemnation contributed to a general lack of enthusiasm for the pronunciamiento.

To conclude, I wish to comment on a contemporary article with a title that is perhaps the only phrase eloquently capturing the events of the 1869 Independence Day celebrations: "El 16 de septiembre: Indiferencia." The editor complained about the poor behavior of some "bad Mexicans" who protested silently during the celebration — it seems possible they were in sympathy with the pronunciados. Furthermore, he accused the "bad Mexicans" of adopting antipatriotic behavior that offended the "patriotism of the majority." From his point of view, the silent manifestation had been an anomaly because Mexicans "simply cannot accept the possibility of being indifferent to the celebrations respectfully dedicated to the memory of the heroes."[36] The article is relevant because it constitutes tacit acknowledgement by those in power that expressions of discontent were a reality in certain groups or members of society. The frustration must have been great when the authorities were unable to penalize the "bad Mexicans" because no crime had actually been committed, as they had not even taken up arms to express their discontent over Carlos Tovar's government. The "bad Mexicans" merely demonstrated their opposition in a hidden and passive way. The speeches by Nava and Arriaga may not have contributed at all to bringing the pronunciamiento to an end, yet there remains a possibility that they may have helped persuade the audience about the undemocratic and anti-progressive elements of such an unconstitutional movement.

Notes

I wish to thank Marisela Espinosa Villanueva, Claudia Ávila Salazar, Julio César Medina, and Rafael Mora, who helped me find information in the local historical archive. I would also like to thank Oscar G. Chávez for having provided me with two original texts on Juan Bustamante from his private library and for sharing information on *Cvadrante*.

1. Fowler, "El pronunciamiento mexicano," 9. Fowler considers the pronunciamiento was a "versatile, dynamic and fluid practice . . . a de facto legitimate means, albeit illegal, of inducing changes and reforms in government policies at the state and national levels," 12.

2. McDonald, "Los inicios del pronunciamiento," 48–49. The following papers have been written about the pronunciamiento carried out by Antonio López de Santa Anna in San Luis Potosí in 1823: Fowler, "Santa Anna y el Plan"; Avalos Calderón and Salazar Mendoza, "El Santa Anna de San Luis Potosí"; Leija Irurzo and Salazar Mendoza, "San Luis Potosí a la sombra"; Morales and Salazar Mendoza, "San Luis Potosí escenario."

3. Archivo Histórico del Estado de San Luis Potosí (henceforth cited as AHESLP), Congreso del Estado (henceforth CE), Actas de Congreso, Libro 7, sesión del 3 de agosto de 1869.

4. Only two (Román Fernández Nava and Julián de los Reyes) of the twelve congressmen who formed part of the legislature maintained their unconditional support of Bustamante during the entire judicial process started in the State Supreme Tribunal against him. The accusation was based on infractions termed "official and common crimes" and "sedition and falsehood." In Julián de los Reyes's opinion the case against Bustamante "*was not of a criminal nature but rather political,*" AHESLP, CE, Actas de Congreso, Libro 5, sesión del 9 de enero de 1869 (emphasis mine). The alleged infractions in the view of Fernández Nava and De los Reyes were not serious. Concerning the judicial charges

against Bustamante, see AHESLP, CE, Actas del Congreso, Libro 4, sesión ordinaria del 27 de diciembre de 1868; Libro 6, sesión del 29 de abril de 1869; Libro 6, sesión del 30 de abril de 1869.

5. The constitutional congress of the state decreed in Article 1: "Carlos Tovar has been named substitute governor of the state through a leave of absence of six months granted to the proprietary governor so he may separate himself from this station." AHESLP, Secretaría del Gobierno General (henceforth cited as SGG), La Sombra de Zaragoza, no. 168, 3 October 1868.

6. Governor Carlos Tovar must have believed that negotiating with the pronunciados would dent his authority; therefore he proceeded to calculate a series of strategies to maintain control, which certainly must have seemed weakened.

7. The political plan can be found in Manuel Muro's Historia de San Luis Potosí, 570–75, and in La Sombra de Zaragoza, no. 262, 29 August 1869. Of the six points described, I emphasize three: (1st) The people of San Luis Potosí refuse to recognize and declare void and of no value some of the acts of the state legislature; (3rd) they declare the permanence of Carlos Tovar to be arbitrary and illegal and his appointment clearly anti-constitutional; and (5th) the people of San Luis Potosí, despite refusing to acknowledge the so-called powers of the state, blindly follow the dispositions emanating from the supreme powers of the union, as it is not the aim, even remotely, to sever ties with the general government, but only to overthrow a band of traitors and enemies of progress, who have taken over public offices in a way grievous to the state and the entire nation.

8. Both Arriaga, "Discurso," and Nava, "Discurso pronunciado," are included in the 1869 compilation Discursos y composiciones poéticas, to be found in the Latin American Collection, University of Texas at Austin. The references for the present article are taken from a modern electronic version that I prepared.

9. To learn more about Bustamante's properties, see Herrera Facundo, "El proceso de desamortización," 114, 132, 140–45.

10. Rodríguez Barragán, "Don Juan Bustamante," 92.

11. Rodríguez Barragán, "Don Juan Bustamante," 88–89.

12. It was published under this name on 5 January 1867; the publisher Román Fernández Nava was appointed by Juan Bustamante. In September of that year Fernández Nava was elected congressman (1867–69). As already mentioned in note 4, the editor intervened in favor and in the defense of his friend Bustamante.

13. AHESLP, SGG, La Sombra de Zaragoza, no. 249, 31 July 1869 (emphasis mine). The signatories of the pronunciamiento agree that it began in Villa

de Cedral on 20 August 1869; they omitted, however, the site where they were based: El Salado, property of Bustamante. This location can be considered the epicenter.

14. On occasion, Muro expressed his disapproval of Bustamante by not attending the sessions in which the judicial and political situation of the republican was discussed. On other occasions, his participation was lukewarm. See, for example, AHESLP, CE, Actas de Congreso, Libro 4, sesión ordinaria del 27 de diciembre de 1868. In this assembly, local congressman Isidoro Bustamante—a raging adversary of Juan—denounced Bustamante for official and common offenses. Muro did not attend because he had asked for a leave of absence.

15. See Velázquez, *Historia de San Luis Potosí*, 3:115–16; 118–20; 124–27.

16. Lorena Herrera Facundo, in her study on the disentailment of church properties from 1856 to 1867, provides evidence demonstrating the fact that Juan Bustamante awarded himself some of the expropriated ecclesiastical goods. Herrera also demonstrates that Bustamante possessed some financial capital during the 1860s because of his involvement in trade that occurred prior to his political career; however, as governor, "he appropriated several country estates and capital in accordance with disentailment and nationalization laws." Furthermore, in his own interest, "he established himself as a guarantor of credit of other grantees who also benefited from these laws." Herrera Facundo suggests the possibility that the public servant obtained "privileged or reserved information regarding the estates about to be sold at a bargain." Herrera Facundo, "El proceso de desamortización," 115; 140–45.

17. Muro holds that Juárez decided Bustamante should replace Colonel Lorenzo Vega because Vega was not efficient at sending news and because "he believed it was more convenient for good public service and better success for the campaign, for the government and military command to recommend another person." Muro, *Historia de San Luis Potosí*, 425.

18. What Nereo Rodríguez Barragán means is that Bustamante personally purchased in the United States 600 rifles, 4,000 swords, 1,000 guns, 18,000 rounds of ammunition, and 500 sacks of gunpowder. He does not state, however, the source of the funds. He may have received them from the financial power groups of San Luis Potosí. Rodríguez Barragán, "Don Juan Bustamante," 83.

19. Brian Hamnett in his article on regional politics and the national project during the Restored Republic analyzes three problems that liberals faced in several regions throughout Mexico: presidentialism, centralism, and re-electionism. Juárez led the antidemocratic practice of perpetuating his stay in power

and Juan Bustamante emulated him in San Luis Potosí. The tension among the liberals with the vertical policies of Juárez and Lerdo increased between 1868 and 1870. Hamnett, "Liberalism Divided," esp. 673–84.

20. For more information, refer to Quezada Torres, "De la Reforma a la República," 138–41. Juan Bustamante asked José M. Lozano to be his attorney in suing the statet legislature. Bustamante and Lozano printed a document that would allow him to become better known, particularly among those who could give him the benefit of the doubt. Lozano, *Alegato de buena prueba*, 36.

21. The detail of the numbers is as follows: 100 men — or more — of General Pedro Macías in El Salado; 100 men of General Jesús Martel in Tamazunchale; 100 of Coronel Guillermo Vasqueti in Rioverde; and 40 of Martín Flores. The numbers may vary since the official sources may have reduced them. See AHESLP, SGG, *La Sombra de Zaragoza*, no. 262, 29 August; no. 266, 8 September 1869; no. 271, 23 September 1869; no. 276, 4 October 1869; no. 283, 20 October 1869; and Muro, *Historia de San Luis Potosí*, 569–76.

22. "At present I consider San Luis Potosi to be my permanent residence, being engaged in business here." Dispatches from United States consuls in San Luis Potosí, 1869–1886, microfilm, Geisel Library, University of California, San Diego (henceforth cited as UCSD). Noureau was born in Germany, reached the state of Texas in 1851, and became a U.S. citizen in 1856. He was appointed consul of the United States in San Luis Potosí on 28 September 1869. Noureau had been resident in the city of San Luis before he was appointed consul due to his activities as trade agent.

23. Dispatches from United States consuls in San Luis Potosí, 1869–1886, Geisel Library, UCSD.

24. Dispatches from United States consuls in San Luis Potosí, 1869–1886, Geisel Library, UCSD.

25. It was a top priority for the authorities to emphasize the political turbulence and the effects of the "bad Mexicans" on everyday life. For more information, see AHESLP, SGG, *La Sombra de Zaragoza*, no. 266, 8 September 1869; no. 271, 23 September 1869; no. 276, 4 October 1869; and no. 283, 20 October 1869.

26. On 15 September the Third Constitutional Legislature (1869–71) was installed. It was formed by eleven congressmen, among whom Benigno Arriaga stands out. This session is of extreme importance for the Law Project presented by local congressman Miguel María Esparza, who stated in his proposal: "All of those individuals involved in the mutinies promoted in the dispute between the state authorities, whatever their rank, who present themselves to

local political authorities within 15 days of the publication of this writ, may return to their families with no further probing for past actions." Another point raised in the session is the conciliatory proposal of Esparza regarding Juan Bustamante and his pronunciados: "It is impossible to forget that those who call themselves dissenters are our brothers; who profess the same political principles; and that there are many among them who fought in the same battlefields against the foreign intervention in the struggle for our nation's Independence." His proposal turned from a hostile to a conciliatory one, which meant a radical change in the discourse. AHESLP, CE, Actas de Congreso, Libro 7, Diputación Permanente, sesión del 15 de septiembre de 1869.

27. Nava, *Discurso*, 7.

28. Nava, *Discurso pronunciado*, 7.

29. Nava, *Discurso pronunciado*, 7.

30. Nava, *Discurso pronunciado*, 15–16.

31. Arriaga, *Discurso*, 1.

32. Arriaga, *Discurso*, 10.

33. Arriaga, *Discurso*, 7.

34. Arriaga, *Discurso*, 14.

35. Arriaga, *Discurso*, 10.

36. AHESLP, SGG, *La Sombra de Zaragosa*, no. 271, 23 September 1869.

WILL FOWLER

Eleven. "As Empty a Piece of Gasconading Stuff as I Ever Read": *The Pronunciamiento through Foreign Eyes*

The purpose of this final essay is to explore how the *pronunciamiento* phenomenon was represented in the writings of foreigners who visited Mexico during what Stanley Payne defined (for Spain) as the "era of the pronunciamiento."[1] Complementing Melissa Boyd's review in chapter 7 of the verdicts of Mexican intellectuals and reluctant *pronunciados*, I am concerned with how northern European and U.S. travelers regarded the pronunciamientos they witnessed — the views of British, French, German, and U.S. diplomats, diplomats' spouses, businessmen, scientists, writers, and artists.[2]

In looking more closely at descriptions arising when the "Western gaze" fell on the pronunciamiento, my hope is to explore an understanding of the practice that may be significantly different from Mexican views. By concentrating on foreigners' representation of the pronunciamiento, we can appreciate aspects of the phenomenon that we may have overlooked when concentrating on how Mexicans engaged with and understood it. It also becomes possible to see which aspects are noted by both Mexican and non-Mexican eyes, strengthening our evolving interpretation of the pronunciamiento's dynamics, uses, and political and cultural significance. This is an exercise that necessarily explores how the pronunciamiento was exploited to confirm northern European and

U.S. prejudices about the people of Mexico. Moreover, an analysis of the extent to which this form of insurrectionary politics was depicted humorously in foreign accounts should serve to make us rethink the pronunciamiento (as a farcical and theatrical endeavor), and consider European and U.S. prejudices toward Mexico at the time, and assess how these perspectives may have contributed to the formation of the "chaos school" of historiographical interpretation of independent Mexico.[3]

This essay is to a degree impressionistic. In part this is because the survey of travelogues and correspondence on which my analysis is based is by no means exhaustive, systematic, or comprehensive. I have read and reread a random sample of texts—some of them well-known favorites (like Fanny Calderón de la Barca's 1843 *Life in Mexico*), others fairly obscure—and noted when they made mention of pronunciamientos and what they said. Impressionism also stems from the fact that the nationalities of the foreign observers are far from homogeneous. The views of a Frenchman like nineteenth-century archeologist Claude Joseph Le Desiré Charnay Forets are scarcely representative of the same foreign gaze as those proffered by the penniless Prussian scientist Karl Bartholomeus Heller or U.S. prisoner of war William W. Carpenter. Further, the foreign writers studied here were not writing for the same audience. In some instances, their "foreign" representation of the pronunciamiento featured in travelogues written for a growing readership interested in exciting tales from remote and exotic lands, and the accounts very obviously catered for that audience's expectations, highlighting if not exaggerating the dangers the author had to overcome (tropical diseases, beasts, and lawlessness). Other accounts, however, figured in private letters addressed to specific individuals or were jotted down in personal diaries; in other words, the views were not always meant for public consumption.

I mention this not as an excuse but to stress the problems faced in attempting to offer a coherent or meaningful concept of "Western" foreignness that may be used to present an arguably consistent vision differing from or colluding with that of the Mexican "other." It may be worthwhile reminding ourselves of the kinds of issues we need to consider when using travel writing, in this case travel writing outside Europe in the nineteenth century, as a window into Mexico's turbulent past. What are the problems posed by using foreignness to interpret a given political custom—in the context of the nineteenth century?

The prolific fin de siècle author and traveler Mrs. Alec Tweedie would have us think that foreignness endowed her interpretation of Mexico with impartiality: "Whether my judgment be right or wrong, that judgment is at least honest. This book is an account of '*Mexico as I saw it*,' and no one and no consideration has swayed my judgment. I do not possess a single share in railway or mine, I have no interest whatever in Mexico—I wish I had, for commerce promises well—and therefore the opinions expressed in these pages are unbiased, even if they be wrong!"[4] Mrs. Tweedie's claim to objectivity notwithstanding, most of the research that has been dedicated to nineteenth-century travel writing has reached the conclusion that far from being detached and objective, it was characterized by rampant imperialism.

Certainly most of the texts studied here were produced at a time when, as Roy Bridges reminds us, "travel writing became increasingly identified with the interests and preoccupations of those in European societies who wished to bring the non-European world into a position where it could be influenced, exploited or, in some cases, directly controlled."[5] Or, as noted by Nigel Leask, a time when "the new travelogues were motivated by sensationalism and commercial greed rather than curiosity."[6] Does this mean, however, that we should disregard our travelers' accounts as being entirely unreliable because their northern European or U.S. prejudices impaired their vision?

One must be careful about generalizing. In an article I published in 2007 on Fanny Calderón de la Barca and British perceptions of mid-nineteenth-century Mexican society, I argued that the "Western gaze" required qualification, in that instance by taking into consideration issues of gender as well as Fanny's own special circumstances—she was Scottish rather than British, had been educated in the United States, and was a Catholic married to a Spaniard. With Fanny (and her depiction of banditry in Mexico) I found that the longer she stayed in Mexico, the fonder she became of the country and its people, and the more subtle and perceptive became her observations of Mexican society. Like that of so many other British travelers, Fanny's propensity to overplay her depictions of criminal behavior, in part because it makes for a more exciting or dramatic text, probably did have sinister consequences. At one level she conformed with a prejudiced tradition, repeated the expected mantra, and in so doing perpetuated an understanding of Mexican society that was mistrustful of its perceived innate criminal tendencies. And yet on the other hand, she distanced herself from a distinctly British overview through her Scottish references, came to stress a profound affection for the Republic, and eventually admitted not only that her first impressions had been hasty, and consequently inaccurate and misleading, but that the rumors of banditry were generally exaggerated, imaginary, or fanciful. I noted then that it is this paradoxical and ambivalent aspect of her travelogue that deserves further thought, as it hints at the problems of embracing too generalized an understanding of Western travel writing. Not all Britons who went to or wrote about Mexico saw the country in terms of filth, defilement, and immorality. Some were capable of questioning their prejudiced generic judgments even as they formulated these and, in so doing, recognized that there was prejudice, that the tendency to debase Mexican culture was misguided as well as ill-informed, and that were Mexico to enjoy a period of peace and stability, its people would no longer have to resort to crime to survive.[7]

In my earlier study of British Vice-Consul Joseph Welsh's coverage of and eventual participation in the 2 January 1832 pronunciamiento of Veracruz, it also became apparent that being a foreigner did not stop one from feeling strongly about the political situation of the country in which one lived; Welsh ended up spending the rest of his life in Mexico.[8] As has been demonstrated recently by Matthew Brown, significant numbers of British adventurers (as he would like us to think of them, rather than as mercenaries) who crossed the Atlantic to fight in the Spanish American wars of independence then stayed on, adopting the independent nations that emerged thereafter as their new patrias.[9]

Rosie Doyle made excellent use of British Minister Plenipotentiary Percy Doyle's correspondence with the earl of Malmesbury on the 1852 Blancarte pronunciamiento series in Jalisco to provide an insightful anatomy of a pronunciamiento cycle.[10] Michael Costeloe similarly made excellent use of Fanny's *Life in Mexico* and her correspondence to study the workings of a pronunciamiento, with specific reference to the Mexico City pronunciamiento of 15 July 1840.[11]

In other words, foreignness or the Western gaze was not inherently prejudiced; not all foreigners depicted Mexicans with contempt. Alternative interpretations and useful lessons may indeed be drawn from travelers' accounts of nineteenth-century Mexico. However, most of the travelogues I outline in the following pages were "greedy" and "sensationalistic," to return to Leask's view, and as a subject in northern European and U.S. texts, the pronunciamiento was more often than not used to illustrate nineteenth-century Mexican barbarism and the Mexicans' inability to govern themselves.

This becomes particularly obvious when we realize that as the nineteenth century unfolded, the Mexican travelogue became a genre in its own right, with its own generic expectations. With travel writers having read each other's work before writing their own accounts, certain themes began to recur; nay, they became an expected and integral part of this incipient genre. After reading and rereading more than twenty such travelogues one after another, there comes a point when they do start to sound the same. One would be disappointed when reading a nineteenth-century travelogue about Mexico if there were no mention of the Aztec past, violence and banditry, lawlessness and corruption, a semi-barbarous people, sombreros, *pistolas*, burros, cactus, pyramids and churches, *pulque*, bullfights and cruelty to animals, disease and heat, fiestas — and what concerns us here, revolutions. There is certainly evidence that early twentieth-century travel writers had read the accounts of their predecessors. One example is Rodney Gallop's *Mexican Mosaic* (London: Faber and Faber, 1939), in which he quotes Fanny Calderón de la Barca several times (e.g., see pp. 27, 36, 37, 93, 94) and refers to D. H. Lawrence's *The Plumed Serpent* (pp. 48, 69, 237, 238). The very titles of the following three canonical foreign texts about Mexico could not be more eloquent in highlighting our travelers' obsession with Mexico's inherent barbarism and criminality: John Kenneth Turner, *Barbarous Mexico* (1911); Graham Greene, *The Lawless Roads* (1939); Evelyn Waugh, *Robbery under Law: The Mexican Object-Lesson* (1939).[12]

As may be seen by analyzing a sample of travelogues written about Mexico during the long nineteenth century, with some notable exceptions, the pronunciamiento would generally be equated with a revolution of sorts, one that was recurrent and representative of Mexico's lawlessness and political instability, and yet one that was also in a sense farcical, comical, worthy of being used as a joke. The pronunciamiento, through foreign eyes, was therefore seldom depicted as a serious revolution: rather it was a ridiculous game, which, sadly, could result in plunder, acts of cruelty, and endemic instability. To return to the "impartial" Mrs. Tweedie (and her adoration of the hero of 2 April studied in chapter 9, Porfirio Díaz): "Mexico, with her fifteen millions of people, was in a terrible condition. One hundred and fifty different languages and dialects were spoken by the various Indian tribes. There had been fifty-two Presidents, Dictators, and Emperors in fifty-nine years, and disorder and revolution prevailed from end to end of the land."[13] As Michel Chevalier, the French engineer who coined the term "Latin America," would have us believe, writing during the French Intervention (1862–67): "Under the name of the Republic, Mexico has been kept in deplorable anarchy. . . . The number of men who in turn have occupied the presidency, and have overthrown one another, is almost indefinite, especially within the last six years. Doubt and despair consume the souls of good citizens."[14]

The Travelers' Definitions of the Pronunciamiento

For the majority of our travelers, one thing was certain: the pronunciamiento was a revolution of sorts, as the following sample of foreign definitions confirms. Fanny Calderón de la Barca noted in her famous 1843 *Life in Mexico*: "Revolution in Mexico! Or *Pronunciamiento*, as they call it."[15] U.S. Minister Plenipotentiary Waddy Thomson likewise stated in his 1847 *Recollections of Mexico*: "[Santa Anna] pronounced (that is the Mexican word for commencing a revolution) against Bustamante."[16] Similarly, British traveler Charles Kingsley, referring to Porfirio Díaz's pronunciamiento of October 1871, noted that he "consented to put himself at the head of a revolutionary movement, and, as they say here, 'pronounced' against the Government."[17]

This view would be reiterated well into the twentieth century, where one can find travelers like Charlotte Cameron, who noted in her 1925 "account of an English woman's experiences and adventures in the land of revolution" that there were rumors of "a revolution (or pronunciamiento, as they call it)."[18] U.S. ambassador John W. Foster in his 1910 Diplomatic Memoirs did not even bother defining or explaining the term *pronunciamiento* when he used it, although it becomes apparent that he considered it an unpeaceful and unconstitutional method: "The most fruitful source of the revolutions which have marked the independent existence of the Latin American States has been the effort of the public men of those countries to continue themselves in power or to attain the Presidency by other than peaceful and constitutional methods. This has been preëminently the case in the history of Mexico, and proved true in the epoch under review. The re-inauguration of Juarez was followed by a pronunciamiento by Diaz."[19]

Some foreign observers, however, did note that a pronunciamiento was not just a revolution. Like many Mexicans who similarly equated pronunciamientos with revolutions, the more perceptive foreigners observed certain aspects of the practice that qualified their representation of it. In this sense we are dealing with "a revolution *of sorts*." Prussian scientist Karl Heller, who witnessed some of the celebrations studied in Pedro Santoni's chapter on the pronunciamientos of the U.S.-Mexican War (1846–48), noted the processional/ritualistic aspect of the practice, paired with the importance of the military and the mobilization of the *populacho*: "Finally, on December 23 [1845] the revolution broke out in Veracruz. One made what is here called a pronunciamiento, namely, a procession in the street, which proclaims the change of administration and to which, as everywhere, a mob of the lowest rabble attaches itself. The city, whether it wanted to or not, had to adhere to the new plan, since the revolution emanated from the real ruler, the military."[20]

U.S. ambassador and artist David Hunter Strother (aka Porte Crayon), who was in Mexico from 1879 to 1885, captured aspects of the dynamics of a pronunciamiento, such as the manner in which news of one spread: "The Pronunciamiento of Negrete is on the Bulletin Boards & surrounded by a permanent Crowd. The Government seems to have been reassured on that Subject."[21] Referring to the 1841 Triangular Revolt or Revolución de Jalisco, Fanny noted the gamelike nature of the practice, in which threats and "gestures of rebellion" were made to force change or negotiation, without actually provoking a revolutionary bloodbath or necessarily engaging the participation of the populacho: "This revolution is like a game at chess, in which kings, castles, knights, and bishops, are making different moves, while the pawns are looking on or taking no part whatever."[22]

Santanista politician José María Tornel y Mendívil lamented the indifference of the people ("The people were silent and obeyed, as they have obeyed and been silent always, without there being a single stimulus that could shake them out of that cold indifference with which they observe so many revolutions pass by, one after another.")[23] In the same way Fanny would be struck by how unperturbed they were during the pronunciamiento of 15 July 1840, which saw the pronunciados seize the National Palace in Mexico City: "The tranquility of the sovereign people during all this period, is astonishing. In what other city in the world would they not have taken part with one or other side? Shops shut, workmen out of employment, thousands of idle people, subsisting, Heaven only knows how, yet no riot, no confusion, apparently no impatience. Groups of people collect in the streets, or stand talking before their doors, and speculate upon probabilities, but await the decision of their military chiefs, as if it were a judgment from Heaven, from which it were both useless and impious to appeal."[24] The question of popular participation (i.e., how representative was a pronunciamiento and how truthful was its claim to represent the "general will"?) certainly comes under scrutiny when reading Fanny's eyewitness account.[25] She also makes us consider in the same passage whether the pronunciamiento was an elite-driven practice aimed at forcing negotiation in a contained fashion that avoided bloodshed or major revolutionary upheaval. As we have seen in Shara Ali's chapter on the Santiago Imán pronunciamiento, there certainly was a tendency among certain sectors of the elite to see pronunciamientos as "their" means to effecting political change; as if the pronunciamiento were an acceptable way to misbehave among gentlemen — or *hombres de bien* — but not for people below their station, like Imán.

The English anthropologist Edward Tylor, writing in 1861 about mid-1850s Mexico, would offer an equally insightful account of a typical pronunciamiento cycle. He wrote from the perspective of a foreign merchant in siege-prone Puebla, with a view to highlighting how these recurrent "revolutions of sorts" or "curious episodes," as he termed them, had a particularly damaging impact on trade. The relevant passage in his *Anahuac: Or Mexico and the Mexicans, Ancient and Modern* is worth quoting in full, for it draws our attention to a number of important features. Among these are how news of a pronunciamiento circulated, how it tended to involve both army and volunteers, what motivated the pronunciados to join the revolution ("hope of pillage" or promotion) or to oppose it, how the violence was contained yet disruptive, how the process involved a certain amount of waiting—captured here through the eyes of a "typical" bored yet worried merchant); and how it ended with "pompous speeches" and enforced celebrations:

> Revolutions and sieges form curious episodes in the life of the foreign merchants in the Republic. . . . All at once there is a pronunciamiento. The street-walls are covered with proclamations. Half the army takes one side, half the other; and crowds of volunteers and self-made officers join them, in the hope of present pillage or future emolument. Barricades appear in the streets; and at intervals there is to be heard the roaring of cannon, and desultory firing of musketry from the flat roofs, killing a peaceable citizen now and then, but doing little execution on the enemy.
>
> Trade comes to a dead stop. Our merchant gets his house well furnished with provisions, shuts the outer shutters, locks up the great gates, and retires into seclusion for a week or a fortnight, or a month or two, as may be. At the time we were there he used to run no great

risk, for neither party was hostile to him; and if a stray cannon-ball did hit his house, or the insurgents shot his cook going out on an expedition in search of fresh beef, it was only by accident.

Having no business to do, the counting-house would probably take stock, and balance the books; but when this is finished there is little to be done but to practice pistol-shooting and hold tournaments in the court-yard, and to teach the horses to rayar; while the head of the house sits moodily smoking in his arm-chair, reckoning up how many of his debtors would be ruined, and wondering whether the loaded mules with his goods had got into shelter, or had been seized by one party or another.

At last the revolution is over. The new president is inaugurated with pompous speeches. The newspapers announce that now the glorious reign of justice, order, and prosperity has begun at last. If the millennium had come, they could not make much more talk about it. Our unfortunate friend, coming out of his den only to hear dismal news of runaway debtors and confiscated bales, has to illuminate his house, and set to getting his affairs into something like order again.[26]

Tylor would also observe how pronunciamientos seldom resulted in clashes of arms or revolutionary violence, although he also noted how they created a context where banditry was rife: "Cheap as Mexican revolutions are in actual bloodshed, we must recollect what they bring with them. Thousands of deserters prowling about the country, robbing and murdering, and spreading everywhere the precious lessons they have learnt in barracks."[27]

Like a number of nineteenth-century Mexican intellectuals (as discussed in chapter 7), in his 1857 *Le Mexique* Matthieu de Fossey, who emigrated to Mexico in 1831 with a group of French colonists, blamed the army for the Mexicans' addiction to "pronouncing":

Fowler

"The army makes the revolutions, and the revolutions give the army more power: that is the source of the continuous troubles. Every colonel wants to have a green sash, pronounces [*se prononce*], in other words refuses to obey the government and proclaims the principles of the opposition." He blamed the army and the fact that nobody was ever punished for having pronounced: "Impunity encourages the revolutionary spirit in this republic."[28] This latter point is certainly one worthy of further study and consideration, since it may well be the case, as was noted recently by Linda Arnold, that the way most pronunciados in independent Mexico were amnestied, forgiven, or at worst exiled for a brief spell meant that there was no serious deterrent to put off restless armed men from pronouncing.[29] What was the worst could happen to them? It is worth noting that in Spain pronunciados were regularly executed, and even this did not serve as a deterrent. As noted by Spanish compulsive pronunciado General Juan Prim, it was a case of "la caja" (the coffin) or "la faja" (the sash of the victorious/promoted officer).[30]

However, the most salient aspect of our travelers' depictions of the pronunciamiento was its association with Mexican barbarism and the Mexicans' inability to govern themselves *comme il faut*. To quote William Carpenter, Kentucky volunteer and veteran of the Mexican-American War, captured by the Mexican forces following the battle of Monterrey: "That they are incapable of governing themselves, their past history plainly shows, and they have still nearly an annual revolution." Like Fossey, Carpenter blamed the army: "The people have no sectional jealousies — nothing to cause these frequent *pronunciamientos*. They are the result of having so many restless, turbulent spirits commanding the armies. So long as these are suffered to dictate to the civil rulers, as they often do, so long will they have an unsettled and unstable government." Unlike Fossey, however, Carpenter's speculation about how much better Mexico would be if annexed by the United States hinted at a mistrust of the Mexicans' ability to overcome their inherent shortcomings: "When speaking on this subject, I have heard eminent men say that they really hoped the whole country would come under the jurisdiction of the United States, for then they would have a strong and vigorous government, capable of carrying out its measures with energy. Of this they had ocular demonstration during the [Mexican-American] war."[31]

The Barbaric Pronunciamiento and Western Imperialism

Numerous are the depictions of Mexico as a lawless country inhabited by "a half barbarous set" of people, to quote Susan Shelby Magoffin, one of the first U.S. women to travel the Santa Fe trail.[32] Similarly, numerous are the instances where U.S. travelers in the 1840s went from commenting on the Mexicans' barbarism to discussing how things might be different were the United States to annex the whole of the country.[33] Due to obvious constraints of space, I will not dwell on the many ways in which the Western imperialist gaze displayed contempt for all things Mexican. To illustrate what I mean, suffice it to quote D. H. Lawrence's sendup of a Mexican bureaucrat in "See Mexico After, by Luis Q": "Ay-de-mi! That's how one sighs in Spanish. I am sighing because I am Mexican, for who would be a Mexican?"[34]

Bearing this in mind, it is not surprising that the imperialist gaze on the pronunciamiento ultimately equated this practice with lawlessness. Porte Crayon was adamant that a pronunciamiento was nothing other than an excuse to rob and plunder.

Writing on 26 January 1883, he noted: "As far as I have observed every pronunciamiento which has occurred since I came to Mexico, has been nothing more respectable, than an attempt to plunder, under a very thin political pretext. That which was so tragically suppressed in Vera Cruz, before it had declared itself may have had some other motive—but it is evident that here as elsewhere most of the great political revolutions are nothing more than schemes for plunder and power."[35]

Kingsley, traveling in the early 1870s, would also highlight how pronunciamientos resulted in widespread robberies: "For between eight and nine months the whole country has been overrun with guerrilla bands, who make the revolution an excuse for wholesale highway robbery and murder, besides requisitions on every state for food, forage, arms, and money."[36] French *abbé* Emmanuel Domenech, on the other hand, would quite simply define the pronunciamiento in 1867 as an exercise in plunder, noting that only when a Mexican colonel became "more of a general than ever, and when he is in possession of one or several millions of francs, does he stop carrying those plunders called pronunciamientos; he compromises with the government and becomes governor of a province."[37]

Humor and the Pronunciamiento

Perhaps where this sense of Western imperialist superiority over the Mexican people is most obvious is in the way the pronunciamiento was depicted humorously. Joseph Conrad, in his great 1904 novel *Nostromo* about late nineteenth-century Latin America, shared our travelers' vision of the region being one of frequent political upheaval and repeated revolutions, yet unlike in the travelers' accounts that follow, Conrad conveyed a poignant sense of tragedy. In *Nostromo* the contempt felt by some of his foreign characters is invariably presented alongside the pain of the inhabitants of the imaginary Republic of Costaguana. When Mrs. Gould finds "the continuous political changes, the constant 'saving the country,' . . . a puerile and bloodthirsty game of murder and rapine played with terrible earnestness by depraved children," Conrad has her husband Charles Gould note: "My dear, you seem to forget that I was born here."[38]

Part of the humor clearly stemmed from the regularity and frequency of this occurrence; of how often Mexicans "pronounced." As Bostonian author and artist Susan Hale would have us know, following independence, "'Plans,' pronunciamientos, revolutions, restorations, followed each other in quick succession. Generals, dictators, presidents, sprang from the soil ready-made, to exercise for a few days their brief authority, and vanish as quickly. . . . In their wild merry-go-round they seem to have lost sight of the value of the position itself, which made the object of their revolutions."[39] Fanny equated the eruption of pronunciamientos with eclipses that could even be predicted before they took place: "Another [*pronunciamiento*] is predicted for next month, as if it were an eclipse of the sun. In nineteen years three forms of government have been tried and two constitutions, the reform of one of which is still pending in the Chambers. *'Dere is notink like trying!'"*[40]

One of the most humorous accounts is from Claude Joseph Le Desiré Charnay Forets in his 1863 travelogue and concerns the pronunciado's motivation:

We all have an idea of what a pronunciamiento is. I lose my job and, naturally, the government does not suit me anymore: I pronounce. I am on half a salary: I pronounce. I am a disgruntled colonel, a retired general, a dismissed minister, a president-in-waiting: I pronounce, I pronounce, I pronounce. I then issue a plan, surround myself with a few disgruntled employees, gather around me some beggars, create a nucleus, stop a stagecoach, impose myself upon some poor village, take over an hacienda by force: I am pronounced. I act for the greater good of the republic. What do you have to say about this? I create a faction, laziness allows my followers to grow in number, but I am a good reader, fortune smiles on me, and I find myself, a little surprised I confess, [sitting] in the presidential chair.[41]

Kingsley's account of what one needed to do to "raise a body of pronunciados," is equally telling. In his 1874 travelogue he recorded his Mexican military host saying: "I have only to go out on market or fiesta day, and call the people round me, and say, 'Now you shall have as much *pulque* as you like and I will give you your four reals a day if you will pronounce for me'; and then I give them *pulque*, and they all get drunk, and then I draw my sword and I make them a speech about '*la Patria*' and '*Libertad*,' and they all pronounce, and then there is a revolution."[42]

Porte Crayon, quoted already, focused—in between his regular consumption of toddy—on the language and rhetoric that characterized the pronunciamiento texts, to display his own humorous take on the practice. Writing about an 1879 pronunciamiento, he tells us: "An Extra Republican gives news of a Pronunciamiento by Genl Miguel Negrete at Monte Alto. It is as empty a piece of Gasconading Stuff as I ever read—the Spanish language being adapted to that style."[43] The point was that it was a farcical practice: "The Pronounciamiento a farce on paper."[44]

There is certainly a sense of the absurd in a number of foreign depictions, with the officers clowning about at one end, in what one Mexican described as their very particular "circo revolucio-nario," while the majority either look on indifferent or make the most of the situation and party.[45] In Fanny's words: "Mexico looks as if it had got a general holiday. Shops shut up, and all business is at a stand. The people, with the utmost apathy, are collected in groups, talking quietly; the officers are galloping about; generals, in a somewhat party-coloured dress, with large gray hats, striped pantaloons, old coats, and generals' belts, fine horses, and crimson-coloured velvet saddles."[46]

Heller was particularly struck by the manner in which pronunciamientos resulted in fiestas: "Naturally, Toluca, which through this revolution [August 1846] once more acquired the right of the capital of the province of Mexico, quite happily attached itself to the new movement, and on the morning of August 5 the dignitaries of the city marched through the streets and proclaimed their support for the new government, with a military band leading the way. They were followed by a mob of poor folk, who incessantly broke out with the cry, "Viva Santa Anna y la Federación, muera Paredes!" Few individuals opposed this new order. As soon as the procession had abandoned the street, everything was once again quiet as if nothing had happened."[47] Pronunciamientos were therefore pointless. They changed nothing. They merely served as an excuse for the dignitaries to process, for the local band to come out and play, for the poor folk to shout and drink, and for everybody to have a mindless party.

Conclusion

As we have seen in chapters 6 and 7, Mexicans were equally capable of laughing about the pronunciamiento syndrome. However-er, there is a difference between laughing at oneself or one's own cultural idiosyncrasies and laughing at someone else's or at a different group's cultural practices. When applying Leticia Neria's theory of humor to the case at hand, we could argue that while among those Mexicans who mocked their addiction to pronouncing it was a case of "relief theory" (i.e., laughing as a release mechanism, as a form of social and psychological relaxation, a defense or a safety valve for our fears and repressions), among our travelers it was more a case of "superiority theory," which, to quote Sigmund Freud, "is not laughter at power, but the powerful laughing at the powerless." According to Neria, "you are not only what you eat, you're also what you laugh at. . . . We laugh at people who are not like us because we find their differences funny. . . . This is why humor can tell us something about who we are and where we belong, because in what we find funny we discover what we consider to be inferior, ridiculous, different, stupid, or unlikable."[48]

The key question here is: what is missing from the foreigners' accounts? Bar the noted exceptions, the answer is: any sense that these pronunciamientos might be have been contributing to improving the Mexican state, saving the constitution, or rectifying the abuses of those in power. The sense of honor, glory, and patriotic endeavor so evident in the pronunciamiento texts themselves — and in their celebration — was not given any serious consideration whatsoever by the foreign observers reviewed here. Unlike the ambivalent Mexican accounts analyzed in this volume, capable of praising as well as criticizing these "revolutions of sorts," our foreign travelers found in them nothing redeemable or admirable or worthy of celebration.

However, the most obvious and damaging impact these humorous and ultimately exaggerated depictions of the pronunciamientos had is that they trivialized the practice and, in so doing, contributed to the formation of the school of chaos interpretation of nineteenth-century Mexico. Humor fails to recognize the fact that many pronunciados cared about their country and were celebrated and commemorated accordingly — men like Miguel Hidalgo, Rafael del Riego, Agustín de Iturbide, José Márquez, Santiago Imán, Ignacio Comonfort, Juan Bustamante, or Porfirio Díaz, whose veneration and damnation have been examined in this volume.

As was demonstrated by Shara Ali in 2010 — and in several contributions addressing motivations of individual pronunciados in my edited volume *Malcontents, Rebels, and Pronunciados* — although driven by personal goals and circumstances (and indulging in the occasional act of plunder), pronunciados were capable of doing so while striving to improve the lives of their countrymen *at the same time*.[49] To turn the pronunciamiento into a joke amounted to saying that Mexicans in the nineteenth century were a joke. It made understanding Mexican politics impossible and not worthy of study; impossible to understand because Mexico's politicians and "revolutionists" were all clowns and the people just passive and stupid; and not worthy of study because in being a joke, the subject did not merit our serious consideration.

It is therefore greatly rewarding that at the end of the three-year research project that gave rise to *Forceful Negotiations*, then *Malcontents, Rebels, and Pronunciados*, and now this third and final edited volume on the practice, we are much closer to understanding what the pronunciamiento was about, what it entailed, why men adopted it to address their grievances (and so did women, in the case of one pronunciamiento the research team discovered to have taken place in Zacatlán de las Manzanas, Puebla, on 29 July 1833). We are likewise closer to understanding why, however funny a pronunciamiento may have appeared to our arrogant travelers, it was far from a laughing matter for those communities who joined or were affected by an insurrectionary practice that was as much about restoring order, patching up the flaws and failures of the country's early constitutions and weak institutions, and addressing injustice as it was a force of disruption, violence, and instability.

In essence the pronunciamiento was the Mexicans' imperfect answer to the problems posed by a period of great upheaval and uncertainty. Studying this practice closely — exploring its origins, how it evolved and developed, its dynamics, the context in which it became so widespread, who pronounced, where, when, and why, and how Mexicans saw fit to celebrate it — has allowed us to move away from the "chaos school" interpretation of nineteenth-century Mexico with its emphasis on anarchy, barbarism, and pointless revolutions, and has enabled us to appreciate the incredibly complex choices Mexicans had to make following the consummation of independence. The pronunciamiento was the product of a society in transition, of unstable and unclear legitimacies, in economic disarray, where no single constitution was in place for long enough to give the country institutions that actually worked; a country, moreover, that had emerged from an eleven-year-long revolution of independence in which violence or the threat of violence had proved a determining factor in settling long-term disputes.

The pronunciamiento was, in a sense, a form of political vigilantism. In the same way that vigilantes take the law into their own hands because they believe justice will not otherwise be done — because the forces of law and order are corrupt or ineffective, and because the threat posed by the criminals waiting outside is very real indeed—the pronunciados took politics into their own hands. Mexicans pronounced because they believed the constitution did not work or was not being allowed to work; because the government or political class was corrupt, ineffective, or despotic; and because the threat posed to them by their political enemies (including other pronunciados) was very real as well. Needless to say, many used the act of pronouncing to further their career prospects, improve their lot, and indulge in the occasional act of robbery. But it is important not to ignore the pronunciamiento's bureaucratic nature: its claim to represent the "will of the nation," its dependency on receiving the support of constellations of *pronunciamientos de adhesión*, and its propensity to avoid bloodshed where possible, seeking to resolve problems through (forceful) negotiation. Contained within its insurrectionary drive was a strong belief in giving the pronunciamiento's demands a definite constitutional or institutional legitimacy.

Yes, the numerous waves of pronunciamientos that spread across Mexico throughout the nineteenth century made governance extremely difficult. Yes, in some cases they degenerated into conflicts characterized by appalling levels of violence. But, paradoxically, they spread because there was no government that succeeded in making good use of power for any significant period of time until, arguably, 1876.

Of course Mexicans celebrated this form of insurrection. The Egyptian people rejoiced in the same way after peacefully (and forcefully) occupying Tahrir Square in Cairo for eighteen days and forcing Hosni Mubarak to step down on 11 February 2011. Each time Mexicans pronounced, the hope was that they would solve once and for all the context of injustice or constitutional failure that had pushed them into pronouncing in the first place. They wanted to "solemnify" their achievement with *refrescos, iluminaciones, Te Deums, salvas, cañonazos,* and *repiques,* and thus call it a day, joyfully marking the end of that period of acute instability and the beginning of what should have been a time of peace, order, and prosperity.

Studying the pronunciamiento and its celebration has taught us that nineteenth-century Mexicans took their politics extremely seriously: that is why they were driven to meet in garrisons, town council rooms, and parish churches to discuss the remedies; it is why they were prepared to go out into the streets and embrace insurrection and pronounce. That they celebrated their political achievements with gusto is evidence, in itself, of how strongly the pronunciamientos they welcomed with church bells, music, and fireworks mattered to them. The foreigners surveyed in this chapter may have mocked the celebrations marking the end of each "revolution," the new president's inaugural "pompous speeches," and "the glorious reign of justice, order, and prosperity" that the newspapers announced "had begun at last," and they may have resented being told to illuminate their houses, but as several essays in this volume eloquently show, the truth is that Mexicans of the nineteenth-century took their political festivities and ceremonies seriously, and they did so because politics was important to them and the pronunciamiento was an integral component.

However, given that the government changed hands frequently until 1876, generally because of pronunciamiento pressure, it remains the case that the glorious pronunciados of one period invariably became the despicable outlaws of the next, as one faction replaced another and sought to impose its own historical narrative with its own pantheon of heroes and calendar of memorable and celebrated dates. As we have seen, Riego, Iturbide, Márquez,

Gárate, Imán, Paredes y Arrillaga, Santa Anna, Comonfort, Díaz, and Bustamante were both venerated and damned. The pronunciamientos of Cabezas de San Juan, Iguala, Jalisco, San Luis Potosí, Valladolid, the Ciudadela, Ayutla, Tacubaya, and Villa de Cedral studied in this volume, together with the action of 2 April 1867, were likewise commemorated and later deliberately forgotten. The fact that prior to the pronunciamiento of Tuxtepec (10 January 1876) no single pronunciamiento cycle succeeded in forging a stable political system with an enduring government prevented the pronunciamiento and its flawed heroes, however much they were celebrated in their day, from leaving a lasting legacy. Even Porfirio Díaz's heroic action of 2 April would cease to be commemorated, despite his steering the country through three decades of comparative stability from 1876 to 1910, as the politicians and historians of post-revolutionary Mexico (from 1917 onward) rewrote the country's *historia patria*.

The reasons why the insurrectionary movements and pronunciados studied in this volume were celebrated and condemned, commemorated and forgotten, and depicted in ambivalent terms as a necessary evil have been amply explained here. To foreigners like Porte Crayon, their pronunciamientos may have appeared farcical, the pronunciados little more than plunderers in disguise. In the end, though, the pronunciamiento was the way most nineteenth-century Mexicans addressed their political problems. To understand why they pronounced and how they celebrated and commemorated their pronouncements at the time represents a major step toward appreciating the immense problems Mexicans had to overcome in order to build a nation-state, and how the pronunciamiento, with all its faults, was an integral if flawed part of that process.

Notes

1. Payne, *Politics and the Military*, 18.

2. I am particularly concerned with the accounts of foreigners from countries where such a practice did not exist (i.e., not Spain). However, it would be *very* interesting to see if Spanish travelers made a distinction between the pronunciamientos of their homeland and those that erupted with equal consistency in Mexico.

3. Alongside the "chaos school" of scholarship, Timothy E. Anna listed "the 'disintegration school,' and the 'caudillo school,' (we will not mention the 'Mexicans were congenitally incapable of self-government school')," as well as "the 'regionalism makes things too murky for words school,'" as proof of the fact that historians found it hard to understand the imperfect process of "defining, creating, building nationhood." See Anna, "Demystifying Early Nineteenth-Century Mexico," 122. For the concept of the Western gaze (i.e., a northern European and American imperial view of its Orientalist other) see Said, *Orientalism*.

4. Tweedie, *Mexico as I Saw It*, 84.

5. Bridges, "Exploration and Travel," 53.

6. Leask, *Curiosity*, 299.

7. Fowler, "British Perceptions."

8. Fowler, "Joseph Welsh."

9. Brown, *Adventuring through Spanish Colonies*.

10. Doyle, "'The Curious Manner in which Pronunciamientos are Got Up in this Country.'"

11. Costeloe, "A Pronunciamiento in Nineteenth Century Mexico."

12. Turner, *Barbarous Mexico*; Greene, *Lawless Roads*; Waugh, *Robbery under Law*. This tradition remains very much intact to this day, even if the bandidos of the nineteenth and first half of the twentieth century have become drug-barons and traffickers in twenty-first century accounts. As an example, see Grant, *God's Middle Finger*.

13. Tweedie, *Mexico as I Saw It*, 121.

14. Chevalier, *Mexico, Ancient and Modern*, 2:77.

15. Calderón de la Barca, *Life in Mexico*, 226.

16. Thomson, *Recollections of Mexico*, 64.

17. Kingsley, *South by West*, 302.

18. Cameron, *Mexico in Revolution*, 92.

19. Foster, *Diplomatic Memoirs*, 74.

20. Heller, *Alone in Mexico*, 57.

21. Stealey (ed.), *Porte Crayon's Mexico*, 72.

22. Calderón de la Barca, *Life in Mexico*, 412.

23. Tornel y Mendívil, *Breve reseña*, 12.

24. Calderón de la Barca, *Life in Mexico*, 246.

25. For a discussion of the relation between elections, pronunciamientos, and the "will of the nation," see Fowler, "Entre la legalidad y la legitimidad."

26. Tylor, *Anahuac*, 282–83.

27. Tylor, *Anahuac*, 114.

28. Fossey, *Le Mexique*, 265, 264.

29. Arnold, "José Ramón García Ugarte."

30. Busquets, *Pronunciamientos y golpes*, 31.

31. Carpenter, *Travels and Adventures*, 253.

32. Magoffin, *Down the Santa Fe Trail*, 130.

33. For example, Waddy Thomson does precisely this in his *Recollections of Mexico*, p. 204.

34. Lawrence, "See Mexico After," 167.

35. Stealey (ed.), *Porte Crayon's Mexico*, 529.

36. Kingsley, *South by West*, 302–3.

37. Domenech, *Le Mexique tel qu'il est*, 153–54.

38. Conrad, *Nostromo*, 49.

39. Hale, *Mexico*, 272.

40. Calderón de la Barca, *Life in Mexico*, 351.

41. Forets, *Ciudades y ruinas*, 52–53 (my translation).

42. Kingsley, *South by West*, 243.

43. Stealey (ed.), *Porte Crayon's Mexico*, 70.

44. Stealey (ed.), *Porte Crayon's Mexico*, 72.

45. José Ignacio Gutiérrez, *Manifiesto de José Ignacio Gutiérrez*, 19 November 1844, in Zoraida Vázquez (ed.), *Planes en la nación*, 233–34.

46. Calderón de la Barca, *Life in Mexico*, 413.

47. Heller, *Alone in Mexico*, 121.

48. Leticia Neria's ideas and quotes are taken from a draft chapter of hers, written as part of her doctoral research program on humor and politics in 1970s Mexico, under my supervision. The quote from Sigmund Freud that Neria includes in her discussion of theories of humor and the nature of political humor is taken from *Jokes and their relation to the unconscious* (1905). See Neria, "Humour as Political Resistance."

49. Ali, "Origins of the Santiago Imán Revolt."

Bibliography

Abbreviations

AGEY	Archivo General del Estado de Yucatán
AHDF	Archivo Histórico del Distrito Federal
AHESLP	Archivo Histórico del Estado de San Luis Potosí
AMG	Archivo Municipal de Guadalajara
ASLP	Archivo del Ayuntamiento de San Luis Potosí
BPEJ	Biblioteca Pública del Estado de Jalisco
CE	Congreso del Estado de San Luis Potosí
CONACULTA	Consejo Nacional para la Cultura y las Artes
CPD	Colección Porfirio Díaz
INEHRM	Instituto Nacional de Estudios Históricos de la Revolución Mexicana
Instituto Mora	Instituto de Investigaciones Dr. José María Luis Mora
SGG	Secretaría del Gobierno General
UNAM	Universidad Nacional Autónoma de México
UASLP	Universidad Autónoma de San Luis Potosí

Libraries, Archives, and Collections

Britain

Public Record Office, Foreign Office Papers, London

Mexico

Archivo del Congreso del Estado de Jalisco
Archivo General del Estado de Yucatán, Mérida
Archivo Histórico del Distrito Federal, Guadalupe Hidalgo Festividades
Archivo Histórico del Distrito Federal, Mexico City Actas de Cabildo
  Historia—Monumentos

Archivo Histórico del Estado de San Luis Potosí

    Secretaría del Gobierno General

Archivo Municipal de Guadalajara

Archivo del Ayuntamiento de San Luis Potosí

Biblioteca Crescencio Carrillo y Ancona, Mérida

Biblioteca Nacional de México, Colección José María Lafragua, Mexico City

Biblioteca Nacional, Hemeroteca, Mexico City

Biblioteca Óscar G. Chávez, San Luis Potosí

Biblioteca Pública del Estado de Jalisco

Centro de Apoyo a la Investigación Histórica de Yucatán, Mérida

Colección Porfirio Díaz, Universidad Iberoamericana

Congreso del Estado de San Luis Potosí

United States

Geisel Library, University of California, San Diego Dispatches from United
    States consuls in San Luis Potosí, 1869–1886.

Nettie Lee Benson Latin American Collection, University of Texas at Austin

Bancroft Library, University of California at Berkeley

Books, Pamphlets, and Articles

2 [dos] de abril: periódico ilustrado. Ed. Macario González Pérez; director
    José Carrasco. Mexico City: Tipografía O'Farril, 1893.

Abrassart, Loïc. "El pueblo en orden. El uso de las procesiones cívicas y su
    organización por contingentes en las fiestas porfirianas. México, 1900–
    1910." *Historias* 43 (mayo–agosto 1991): 51–63.

Acereto, Albino. *Evolución histórica de las relaciones políticas entre México y
    Yucatán.* Mexico City: 1907.

Acle Aguirre, Andrea. "Ideas políticas de José Bernardo Couto y José
    Joaquín Pesado, 1801–1862." Unpubl. BA honors thesis, El Colegio de
    México, 2006.

Alamán, Lucas. *Historia de Méjico, desde los primeros movimientos que pre-
    pararon su independencia en el año de 1808 hasta la época presente.* Vol. 5.
    Mexico City: Imprenta de J. Mariano Lara, 1852.

Alatriste, Sealtiel. DE MEMORIA, "El héroe en cuestión." *Reforma,* 10 abril
    2010.

Ali, Shara. "The Origins of the Santiago Imán Revolt, 1838–1840: A Reas-
    sessment." In Will Fowler (ed.), *Forceful Negotiations: The Origins of the*

Pronunciamiento in Nineteenth-Century Mexico. Lincoln: University of
Nebraska Press, 2010. 143–61.

———. "The Pronunciamiento in Yucatán (1821–1840): From Independence to Independence." Unpubl. PhD diss., University of St. Andrews,
2011.

Amador Zamora, Rubén. "El manejo del fusil y la espada: Los intereses par-
tidistas en la formación de la guardia nacional en la ciudad de México,
agosto–octubre 1846." unpubl. ba thesis, Universidad Nacional Autónoma de México, 1997.

Ancona, Eligio. *Historia de Yucatán, desde la época más remota hasta nuestros
días*. 4 vols. Mérida: Imprenta de M. Heredia Argüelles, 1879.

Anna, Timothy E. *The Mexican Empire of Iturbide*. Lincoln: University of
Nebraska Press, 1990.

———. "Demystifying Early Nineteenth-Century Mexico." *Mexican Stud-
ies/Estudios Mexicanos* 9, no.1 (Winter 1993): 119–37.

———. *Forging Mexico, 1821–1835*. Lincoln: University of Nebraska Press,
1998.

———. "Iguala: The Prototype." In Will Fowler (ed.), *Forceful Negotiations:
The Origins of the Pronunciamiento in Nineteenth-Century Mexico*. Lincoln: University of Nebraska Press, 2010. 1–21.

Archer, Christon I. "Death's Patriots—Celebration, Denunciation, and
Memories of Mexico's Indepedence Heros: Miguel Hidalgo, José María
Morelos, and Agustín de Iturbide." In Lyman L. Johnson (ed.), *Death,
Dismemberment, and Memory: Body Politics in Latin America*. Albuquer-
que: University of New Mexico Press, 2004. 63–104.

Arnold, Linda. "José Ramón García Ugarte: Patriot, Federalist, or Malcon-
tent?" In Will Fowler (ed.), *Malcontents, Rebels, and Pronunciados: The
Politics of Insurrection in Nineteenth-Century Mexico*. Lincoln: University
of Nebraska Press, 2012. 91–110.

Arrangoiz, Francisco de Paula de. *México desde 1808 hasta 1867*. 1871–72; reprint, Mexico City: Porrúa, 1968.

Arriaga, Benigno. "Discurso pronunciado en el templete de la Alameda, la
noche del 16 de septiembre de 1869, por el C. Benigno Arriaga." In *Discursos y composiciones poéticas, que se leyeron en las festividades cívicas del 15
y 16 de septiembre del presente año por disposición de la junta patriótica*. San
Luis Potosí: Tipografía de Vélez, 1869.

Artola, Miguel. *La España de Fernando VII*. Madrid: Espasa, 1999.

Avalos Calderón, Denis, and Flor de María Salazar Mendoza. "El Santa
Anna de San Luis Potosí: Pronunciamiento santanista 1823." In *Memoria
Electrónica del 10 Verano de la Ciencia de la Región Centro*. San Luis Poto-
sí: UASLP, 2008. 1–5.

Avitia Hernández, Antonio. *Corridos de la capital*. Mexico City: CONACUL-
TA, 2000.

Báez Macías, Eduardo. "Pintura militar: Entre lo episódico y la acción de
masas." *Anales del Instituto de Investigaciones Estéticas* 23, no. 78 (primav-
era 2001): 133–34.

——. *La pintura militar de México en el siglo XIX*. Mexico City: Secretaría
de la Defensa Nacional, 2008.

Baker, Shannon, "Antonio López de Santa Anna's Search for Personalized
Nationalism." In Samuel Brunk and Ben Fallaw (eds.), *Heroes and Hero
Cults in Latin America*. Austin: University of Texas Press, 2006. 58–82.

Baqueiro, Serapio. *Ensayo histórico sobre las revoluciones de Yucatán desde el
año de 1840 hasta 1864*. Ed. Salvador Rodríguez Losa. Originally publ.
1865–66; Mérida: Ediciones de la Universidad Autónoma de Yucatán,
1990.

Baquer, Miguel Alonso. *El modelo español de pronunciamiento*. Madrid: Ri-
alp, 1983.

Bárcena, Manuel de la. "Manifiesto al Mundo." In Jaime Olveda (ed.), *Los
discursos opuestos sobre la independencia de la Nueva España*. Aranjuez:
Fundación Mapfre, Doce Calles, 2006.

Baz, Juan José. *Manifiesto que hace al público el C. Juan José Baz contradici-
endo las calumnias que respecto a él se han vertido en ocasión del pronunciamiento conocido con el nombre de Golpe de Estado*. Morelia: Tipografía de
Octaviano Ortiz, 1859.

Beezley, William H. *Mexican National Identity: Memory, Innuendo, and Popular Culture*. Tucson: University of Arizona Press, 2008.

——. "New Celebrations of Independence: Puebla (1869) and Mexi-
co City (1883)." In William H. Beezley and David E. Lorey (eds.), *¡Viva
México! ¡Viva la Independencia! Celebrations of September 16*. Wilmington
DE: Scholarly Resources, 2001. 131–40.

Beezley, William H., and David E. Lorey. "Introduction: The Functions of
Patriotic Ceremony in Mexico." In William H. Beezley and David E. Lorey (eds.), *¡Viva México! ¡Viva la Independencia! Celebrations of September
16*. Wilmington DE: Scholarly Resources, 2001. ix–xviii.

Beezley, William H., and David E. Lorey (eds.) *¡Viva Mexico! ¡Viva la Independencia! Celebrations of September 16.* Wilmington DE: Scholarly Resources, 2001.

Beezley, William H., and Colin M. Maclachlan. *El Gran Pueblo: A History of Greater Mexico.* 3rd ed. New York: Prentice Hall, 2003.

Beezley, William H., Cheryl English Martin, and William E. French (eds.). *Rituals of Rule, Rituals of Resistance: Public Celebrations and Popular Culture in Mexico.* Wilmington DE: Scholarly Resources, 1994.

Beltrán, Rosa. *La corte de los ilusos.* Mexico City: Planeta, 1995.

Benjamin, Thomas, and Marcial Ocasio-Meléndez. "Organizing the Memory of Modern Mexico: Porfirian Historiography in Perspective, 1880s–1980s." *Hispanic American Historical Review* 64, no. 2 (1984): 323–64.

Benson, Nettie Lee. *The Provincial Deputation in Mexico.* Austin: University of Texas Press, 1992.

Bioy Casares, Adolfo. *Descanso de caminantes: Diarios íntimos.* Buenos Aires: Editorial Sudamericana, 2001.

Blanco Valdés, Roberto L. *Rey, cortes y fuerza armada en los orígenes de la España liberal, 1808–1823.* Madrid: Siglo XXI de España–Institució Valenciana d'Estudis i Investigació, 1988.

Briceño Senosiáin, Lilian, Laura Solares Robles, Laura Suárez de la Torre (eds.). *José María Luis Mora: Obras Completas.* Vol. 8. Mexico City: Instituto Mora, CONACULTA, 1986.

———. *Valentín Gómez Farías y su lucha por el federalismo, 1822–1858.* Mexico City: Instituto Mora, Gobierno del Estado de Jalisco, 1991.

Bridges, Roy. "Exploration and Travel outside Europe (1720–1914)," in Peter Hulme and Tim Youngs (eds.), *The Cambridge Companion to Travel Writing.* Cambridge: Cambridge University Press, 2002. 53–69.

Brown, Matthew. *Adventuring through Spanish Colonies: Simón Bolívar, Foreign Mercenaries and the Birth of New Nations.* Liverpool: Liverpool University Press, 2006.

Brunk, Samuel, and Ben Fallaw (eds.) *Heroes and Hero Cults in Latin America.* Austin: University of Texas Press, 2006.

Brushwood, John S. *Mexico in Its Novel: A Nation's Search for Identity.* Austin: University of Texas Press, 1966.

Bulnes, Francisco. *El verdadero Díaz y la Revolución: Rectificaciones y aclaraciones a las memorias del general Porfirio Díaz.* Mexico City: Instituto Mora, 2008.

Busquets, Julio. *Pronunciamientos y golpes de estado en España*. Barcelona: Planeta, 1982.

Bustamante, Carlos María de. *Apuntes para la historia del gobierno del general don Antonio López de Santa Anna, desde principios de Octubre de 1841 hasta el 6 de Diciembre de 1844, en que fue depuesto del mando por uniforme voluntad de la nación*. 1845; reprint, Mexico City: Fondo de Cultura Económica, 1986.

———. *Cuadro histórico de la revolución mexicana*. 8 vols. 1844; reprint, Mexico City: Fondo de Cultura Económica, 1985.

———. *El nuevo Bernal Díaz del Castillo, o sea, historia de la invasión de los anglo-americanos en México*. 2 vols. 1847; reprint, Mexico City: INEHRM, 1987.

Calderón de la Barca, Madame. *Life in Mexico*. London: Century, 1987.

Callcott, Wilfrid Hardy. *Santa Anna: The Story of an Enigma Who Once Was Mexico*. Norman: University of Oklahoma Press, 1936.

Cámara y Zavala, Felipe de la, *Memorias*. N.p., 1836–41.

Cameron, Charlotte. *Mexico in Revolution: An Account of an English Woman's Experiences and Adventures in the Land of Revolution, With a Description of the People, the Beauties of the Country and the Highly Interesting Remains of Aztec Civilisation*. London: Seeley, Service and Company, 1925.

Campa, Gustavo E. *Himno sinfónico, arreglado a 4 manos por Ricardo Castro*. Mexico City: Lit. Em. Moreau y Hno., [1884].

Canción patriótica la niña bonita. Mexico City: Oficina de Ontiveros, 1820.

Cañedo Gamboa, Sergio Alejandro. "The First Independence Celebrations in San Luis Potosí, 1824–1847." In William H. Beezley and David E. Lorey (eds.), *¡Viva México! ¡Viva la Independencia! Celebrations of September 16*. Wilmington DE: Scholarly Resources, 2001. 77–87.

Carpenter, William W. *Travels and Adventures in Mexico: In the Course of Journeys of Upward of 2500 miles, Performed on Foot, Giving an Account of the Manners and Customs of the People, and the Agricultural and Mineral Resources of the Country*. New York: Harper and Brothers, 1851.

Carr, Raymond. *Spain 1808–1939*. Oxford: Clarendon Press, 1966.

Casasola, Gustavo. *Biografía ilustrada del general Porfirio Díaz, 1830–1965*. Mexico City: Ediciones Gustavo Casasola, 1970.

———. *Seis siglos de historia gráfica de México, 1325–1900*. Vol. 3. Mexico City: Ediciones Gustavo Casasola, 1966–69.

Cepeda Gómez, José. *Los pronunciamientos en la España del siglo XIX.* Madrid: Arco, 1999.

Chartier, Roger. *Espacio público, crítica y desacralización en el siglo XVIII: Los orígenes culturales de la Revolución francesa.* Barcelona: Gedisa, 1995.

———. *Sociedad y escritura en la edad moderna.* Mexico City: Instituto Mora, 1995.

Chevalier, Michel. *Mexico, Ancient and Modern.* Trans. Thomas Alpiss. Vol. 2. London: John Maxwell and Company, 1864.

Coerver, Don M. *The Porfirian Interregnum: The Presidency of Manuel González of Mexico, 1880–1884.* Fort Worth: Texas Christian University Press, 1979.

Colección de decretos correspondiente al año de 1829. Xalapa: Tipografía del Gobierno del Estado [de Veracruz], 1904.

Colección de decretos y ordenes de la Primera Legislatura Constitucional del Estado de San Luis Potosí. San Luis Potosí: Impresa de Ladislao Vildosola, 1829.

Comellas, José Luis. *Los primeros pronunciamientos en España 1814–1820.* Madrid: Consejo Superior de Investigaciones Científicas, 1958.

Conrad, Joseph. *Nostromo: A Tale of the Seaboard.* London: J. M. Dent and Sons, 1958.

Corbett, Barbara M. "Republican Hacienda and Federalist Politics: The Making of 'Liberal' Oligarchy in San Luis Potosí 1787–1853." Unpubl. PhD diss., Princeton University, 1997.

Correspondencia privada del Dr. José María Mata con Don Melchor Ocampo. Morelia: Edición del gobierno del Estado, 1959.

Cortés, José María. *Discurso pronunciado en la Alameda de esta ciudad el 11 de abril de 1867 en la solemnización de la toma de Puebla, por el comisionado J.M.C.* Oaxaca: Impreso por M. Rincón, 1867.

Cosío Villegas, Daniel. *Historia moderna de México.* 7 vols. Mexico City: Hermes, 1955–72.

Costeloe, Michael P. "16 de septiembre de 1825: Los orígenes del día de la independencia de México." In Luis Jáuregui and José Antonio Serrano Ortega (eds.), *Historia y nación II: Política y diplomacia en el siglo XIX mexicano.* Mexico City: Colegio de México, 1998. 263–79.

———. *The Central Republic in Mexico, 1835–1846: Hombres de Bien in the Age of Santa Anna.* Cambridge: Cambridge University Press, 1993.

———. "Church-State Financial Negotiations in Mexico during the American War, 1846–1847." *Revista de Historia de América* 60 (July–December 1965): 91–123.

———. "The Junta Patriótica and the Celebration of Independence in Mexico City, 1825–1855." *Mexican Studies/Estudios Mexicanos* 13, no. 1 (Winter 1997): 21–53.

———. "The Mexican Church and the Rebellion of the Polkos." *Hispanic American Historical Review* 46, no. 2 (May 1966): 170–78.

———. *La primera república federal de México (1824–1835): Un estudio de los partidos políticos en el México independiente.* Trans. Manuel Fernández Gasalla. Mexico City: Fondo de Cultura Económica, 1975.

———. "A Pronunciamiento in Nineteenth-Century Mexico: 15 de julio de 1840." *Mexican Studies/Estudios Mexicanos* 4, no. 2 (Summer 1988): 245–64.

Cressy, David. "National Memory in Early Modern England." In John R. Gillis (ed.), *Commemorations: The Politics of National Identity.* Princeton: Princeton University Press, 1994. 61–73.

Cuevas, Luis Gonzaga. *Porvenir de México.* 2 vols. Mexico City: Imprenta de Ignacio Cumplido, 1852; reprint, Colección CIEN de México. Mexico City: CONACULTA, 1992.

Curcio-Nagy, Linda. *The Great Festivals of Mexico City: Performing Power and Identity.* Albuquerque: University of New Mexico Press, 2004.

Decreto núm. 117 [para la premiación de los ciudadanos que lucharon contra las tropas francesas el 2 de abril de 1867]. Puebla: Imprenta del Hospicio, 1869.

Defensa del inmortal D. Rafael Riego. Mexico City: Oficina de J. M. Benavente y Socios, 1820.

DePalo, William A. Jr. *The Mexican National Army, 1822–1852.* College Station: Texas A&M University Press, 1997.

Díaz, Porfirio. *Memorias del gral. Porfirio Díaz.* Introd. Matías Romero. Mexico City: Biblioteca de Omega, 1892.

Diccionario Porrúa: Historia, biografía y geografía de México. 2nd ed. Mexico City: Porrúa, 1964.

Di Tella, Torcuato S. *National Popular Politics in Early Independent Mexico, 1820–1847.* Albuquerque: University of New Mexico Press, 1996.

Domenech, Emmanuel. *Le Mexique tel qu'il est: La vérité sur son climat, ses habitants et son gouvernement.* Paris: E. Dentu Libraire, 1867.

Doyle, Rosie. "'The Curious Manner in which Pronunciamientos are Got

Up in this Country': The Plan of Blancarte of 26 July 1852." In Will
Fowler (ed.), *Forceful Negotiations: The Origins of the Pronunciamiento in
Nineteenth-Century Mexico*. Lincoln: University of Nebraska Press, 2010.
203–25.

——. "The Pronunciamiento in Nineteenth-Century Mexico: The Case
of Jalisco (1821–1852)." Unpubl. PhD diss., University of St. Andrews,
2012.

Ducey, Michael T. "Municipalities, Prefects, and Pronunciamientos: Pow-
er and Political Mobilizations in the Huasteca during the First Federal
Republic." In Will Fowler (ed.), *Forceful Negotiations: The Origins of the
Pronunciamiento in Nineteenth-Century Mexico*. Lincoln: University of
Nebraska Press, 2010. 74–100.

Duncan, Robert H. "Embracing a Suitable Past: Independence Celebrations
under Mexico's Second Empire, 1864–6." *Journal of Latin American Studies* 30, no. 2 (May 1998): 249–77.

——. "Political Legitimation and Maximilian's Second Empire in Mexico, 1864–1867." *Mexican Studies/Estudios Mexicanos* 12, no. 1 (Winter
1996): 27–66.

Echanove Trujillo, Carlos A. *La vida pasional e inquieta de don Crecencio Rejón*. Mexico City: Talleres Gráficos Laguna, 1941.

El Centinela de Noche-Bea. Mexico City: Oficina de D. Alejandro Valdés,
1820.

*Enciclopedia Yucatenense: Patrocinada por el gobierno del estado de Yucatán, a
cargo del Dr. Francisco Luna Kan*. 12 vols. Mexico City: Edición oficial del
gobierno de Yucatán, 1977.

Escalante Gonzalbo, Fernando. *Ciudadanos imaginarios. Memorial de los af-
anes y desventuras de la virtud y apologia del vicio triunfante en la República Mexicana: Tratado de moral pública*. Mexico City: El Colegio de México, 1992.

Esparza Liberal, María José. "Abraham López, un calendarista singular." In
Anales del Instituto de Investigaciones Estéticas 84 (Spring 2004): 5–52.

Esposito, Matthew D. "Death and Disorder in Mexico City: The State Fu-
neral of Manuel Romero Rubio." In William H. Beezley and Linda A.
Curcio-Nagy (eds.), *Latin American Popular Culture: An Introduction*
(Wilmington DE: Scholarly Resources, 2000. 87–103.

F. V. *La Espada de la Justicia*. Mexico City: Oficina de D. Juan Bautista de
Arizpe, 1820.

Fernández, Justino. *El arte del siglo XIX en México*. Mexico City: UNAM, Instituto de Investigaciones Estéticas, 1967.

Fernández de Lizardi, José Joaquín. *Amigos, enemigos y comentaristas (1810–1820)*. Mexico City: UNAM, 2006.

———. *Contestación de el Pensador a la carta que se dice dirigida a él por el Coronel don Agustín de Iturbide*. Mexico City: Oficina de D. J. M. Benavente y Socios, 1821.

———. *Obras IV—Periódicos*. Mexico City: UNAM, 1970.

———. *Obras X—Folletos (1811–1820)*. Mexico City: UNAM, 1981.

———. *Obras XI—Folletos (1821–1822)*. Mexico City: UNAM, 1991.

Fernández Sebastián, Javier. "La crisis de 1808 y el advenimiento de un nuevo lenguaje político. ¿Una revolución conceptual?" In Alfredo Ávila and Pedro Pérez Herrero (comps.), *Las experiencias de 1808 en Iberoamérica*. Mexico City: Universidad de Alcalá, UNAM, 2008. 105–33.

Fontana, Josep. "Prólogo." In Irene Castells, *La utopia insurreccional del liberalismo: Torrijos y las conspiraciones liberales de la década omniosa*. Barcelona: Editorial Crítica, 1989.

———. *La quiebra de la monarquía absoluta, 1814–1820*. Madrid: Ariel, 1971.

Forets, Claude Joseph Le Desiré Charnay. *Ciudades y ruinas americanas*. Mexico City: CONACULTA, 1994.

Fossey, Matthieu de. *Le Mexique*. Paris: Henri Plon, 1857.

Foster, John W. *Diplomatic Memoirs*. Vol. 1. London: Constable and Company, 1910.

Fowler, Will. "British Perceptions of Mid-Nineteenth Century Mexican Society: The Topos of the Bandit in Madame Calderón de la Barca's *Life in Mexico* (1843)." *Septentrión* 1 (enero–junio 2007): 65–87.

———. "Civil Conflict in Independent Mexico, 1821–57: An Overview." In Rebecca Earle (ed.), *Rumours of Wars: Civil Conflict in Nineteenth-Century Latin America*. London: Institute of Latin American Studies, 2000. 49–86.

———. "Entre la legalidad y la legitimidad: Elecciones, pronunciamientos y la voluntad general de la nación, 1821–1857." In José Antonio Aguilar Rivera (ed.), *Las elecciones y el gobierno representative en México (1810–1910)*. Mexico City: FCE, IFE, CONACYT, CONACULTA, 2010. 95–120.

———. "Fiestas santanistas: La celebración de Santa Anna en la villa de Jalapa, 1821–1855." *Historia Mexicana* 52, no. 2 (October–December 2002): 391–447.

———. "Introduction: The Nineteenth-Century Practice of the Pronunciamiento and Its Origins." In Will Fowler (ed.), *Forceful Negotiations: The Origins of the Pronunciamiento in Nineteenth-Century Mexico*. Lincoln: University of Nebraska Press, 2010. xv–xxxix.

———. "'I Pronounce Thus I Exist': Redefining the *Pronunciamiento* in Independent Mexico, 1821–1876." In Will Fowler (ed.), *Forceful Negotiations: The Origins of the Pronunciamiento in Nineteenth Century Mexico*. Lincoln: University of Nebraska Press, 2010. 246–65.

———. "Joseph Welsh: A British Santanista (Mexico, 1832)." *Journal of Latin American Studies* 36 (2004): 29–56.

———. *Mexico in the Age of Proposals, 1821–1853*. Westport, CT: Greenwood Press, 1998.

———. "Rafael del Riego and the Spanish Origins of the Nineteenth-Century Mexican *Pronunciamiento*." In Matthew Brown and Gabriel Paquette (eds.), *Connections after Colonialism: Europe and Latin America in the 1820s*. Tuscaloosa: University of Alabama Press, in press.

———. "El pronunciamiento mexicano del siglo XIX: Hacia una nueva tipología." *Estudios de Historia Moderna y Contemporánea de México* 38 (julio–diciembre 2009): 5–34.

———. "The Pronunciamientos of Antonio López de Santa Anna, 1821–1867." In Will Fowler (ed.), *Malcontents, Rebels, and Pronunciados: The Politics of Insurrection in Nineteenth-Century Mexico*. Lincoln: University of Nebraska Press, 2012. 205–35.

———. "Santa Anna y el Plan de San Luis Potosí, 1823." In Flor de María Salazar Mendoza and Carlos Rubén Ruíz Medrano (coords.), *Capítulos de la Historia de San Luis Potosí siglos XVI al XX*. San Luis Potosí, México: UASLP–AHESLP, 2009. 137–60.

———. *Santa Anna of Mexico*. Lincoln: University of Nebraska Press, 2007.

———. *Tornel and Santa Anna: The Writer and the Caudillo (Mexico 1795–1853)*. Westport CT: Greenwood Press, 2000.

Fowler, Will (ed.). *Forceful Negotiations: The Origins of the Pronunciamiento in Nineteenth-Century Mexico*. Lincoln: University of Nebraska Press, 2010.

———. *Malcontents, Rebels, and Pronunciados: The Politics of Insurrection in Nineteenth-Century Mexico*. Lincoln: University of Nebraska Press, 2012.

Frasquet, Ivana, and Manuel Chust. "Agustín de Iturbide: From the Pronunciamiento of Iguala to the Coup of 1822." Trans. Kim Lauren Gillespie.

In Will Fowler (ed.), *Forceful Negotiations: The Origins of the Pronunciamiento in Nineteenth-Century Mexico*. Lincoln: University of Nebraska Press, 2010. 22–46.

Galeana de Valdés, Patricia (coord.), *José María Lafragua*. Mexico City: Serie Los Senadores, LIII Legislatura, Senado de la República, 1987.

García Barragán, Elisa. "El arquitecto Lorenzo de la Hidalga." *Anales del Instituto de Investigaciones Estéticas* 80 (Spring 2002): 101–28.

García Cubas, Antonio. *El libro de mis recuerdos*. 7th ed. 1904; Mexico City: Editorial Porrúa, 1978.

García, Genaro (ed.). *Documentos inéditos o muy raros para la Historia de México publicados por Genaro García: La Revolución de Ayutla según el archivo del General Doblado*. Vol. 26. Mexico City: Vda. de C. Bouret, 1909.

Garner, Paul. *Porfirio Díaz*. Harlow: Pearson Education, 2001.

———. *Porfirio Díaz. Del héroe al dictador: Una biografía política*. Mexico City: Editorial Planeta, 2003.

Gil Novales, Alberto. *Rafael del Riego: La Revolución de 1820, día a día*. Madrid: Tecnos, 1976.

Giron, Nicole (ed.), *Ignacio Manuel Altamirano: Obras completas, XIX Periodismo Político 2*. Mexico City: CONACULTA, 1989.

Goldman, Noemí. "Legitimidad y deliberación: El concepto de opinión pública en Iberoamérica, 1750–1850." In Javier Fernández Sebastián (dir.), *Diccionario político y social del mundo iberoamericano: La era de las revoluciones, 1750–1850*. Madrid: Fundación Carolina, Sociedad Estatal de Conmemoraciones Culturales, Centro de Estudios Políticos y Constitucionales, 2009. 981–98.

Gómez Haro, Eduardo. *El héroe del 2 de abril: Episodio en un acto y tres cuadros inspirados en un hecho de la vida militar del señor general Porfirio Díaz, verso de Eduardo Gómez Haro; música de Carlos Samaniego*. Mexico City: El Fénix, 1905.

González y Obregón, Luis. *Las calles de México: Leyendas y sucedidos*. 4th ed., 2 vols. Mexico City: Ediciones Botas, 1936.

Granados, Luis Fernando. "Pequeños patricios, hermanos mayores: Francisco Próspero Pérez como emblema de los *sans-culottes* capitalinos hacia 1846–1847." *Historias* 54, no. 1 (January–April 2003): 25–37.

Grant, Richard. *God's Middle Finger: Into the Lawless Heart of the Sierra Madre*. New York: Free Press, 2008.

Greene, Graham. *The Lawless Roads.* Harmondsworth: Penguin, 1976.

Gruening, Ernest. *Mexico and Its Heritage.* New York: Century, 1928.

Guerra, François-Xavier. "Mexico from Independence to Revolution: The Mutations of Liberalism." In Elisa Servín, Leticia Reina, and John Tutino (eds.), *Cycles of Conflict, Centuries of Change: Crisis, Reform and Revolution in Mexico.* Durham: Duke University Press, 2007. 129–52.

————. "El pronunciamiento en México: Practices e imaginarios." *Travaux et Recherches dans les Amériques de Centre* 37 (Juin 2000): 15–26.

Gutiérrez de Estrada, José María. "La monarquía como posibilidad." In Álvaro Matute, *Lecturas Universitarias, Antología. México en el Siglo XIX: Fuentes e interpretaciones históricas.* Mexico City: UNAM, 1992.

Guzmán, Mariano (ed.). *Corona cívica a los héroes del 2 de abril de 1867.* Mérida: Imprenta de J. D. Espinosa é hijos, 1868.

Hale, Charles A. "The Civil Law Tradition and Constitutionalism in Twentieth-Century Mexico: The Legacy of Emilio Rabasa." *Law and History Review* 18, no. 2 (2000): 257–79.

Hale, Susan. *Mexico.* London: T. Fisher Unwin, 1891.

Hamnett, Brian R. "Liberalism Divided: Regional Politics and the National Project during the Mexican Restored Republic, 1867–1876." *Hispanic American Historical Review* 76, no. 4 (1996): 659–89.

Handelman, Don. *Models and Mirrors: Towards Anthropology of Public Events.* Cambridge: Cambridge University Press, 1990.

Heller, Karl Bartolomeus. *Alone in Mexico: The Astonishing Travels of Karl Heller, 1845–1848.* Trans. and ed. Terry Rugeley. Tuscaloosa: University of Alabama Press, 2007.

Herrera Facundo, Lorena. "El proceso de desamortización de los bienes eclesiásticos en la capital de San Luis Potosí, 1856–1867: Consecuencias, tensiones y especulaciones." Unpubl. BA thesis, Universidad Autónoma de San Luis Potosí, 2008.

Herrera Serna, Laura. "La guerra entre México y Estados Unidos en los calendarios de mediados del siglo XIX." *Boletín del Instituto de Investigaciones Bibliográficas* 5, no. 1–2 (First and second semester, 2000): 149–206.

Hobsbawm, Eric. "Introduction: Inventing Traditions." In Eric Hobsbawm and Terence Ranger (eds.), *The Invention of Tradition.* Canto edition. Cambridge: Cambridge University Press, 1996. 1–15.

Huxley, Aldous. *Beyond the Mexique Bay.* London: Chatto and Windus, 1934.

Imán, Santiago. *Alocución de Santiago Imán*. Valladolid, 12 February 1840. Mérida: Imprenta de Lorenzo Segui, 1840.

Iniciativa a las cámaras de la unión de la II Legislatura de SLP, sobre el Gral. Bustamante y sus Ministros. Mexico: Impreso por Ignacio Cumplido, Calle de Zuleta N.14, 1833.

Iturbide, Augustin de. "Don Agustin de Iturbide, Continued." *Records of the American Catholic Historical Society* 27, no. 1 (March 1916): 16–44.

———. "Don Agustin de Itubide." *Records of the American Catholic Historical Society* 26, no. 4 (December 1915): 289–310.

Jarman, Neil. *Material Conflicts: Parades and Visual Displays in Northern Ireland*. Oxford: Berghan Books, 1998.

Jáuregui, Luis, and José Antonio Serrano Ortega (eds.). *Historia y nación II: Política y diplomacia en el siglo XIX mexicano*. Mexico City: Colegio de México, 1998.

Johnson, Lyman L. "Why Dead Bodies Talk: An Introduction." In Lyman L. Johnson (ed.), *Death, Dismemberment, and Memory: Body Politics in Latin America*. Albuquerque: University of New Mexico Press, 2004. 1–26.

Kant, Immanuel. "An Answer to the Question: 'What Is Enlightenment?'" Konigsberg, Prussia: 1784.

Kelly, Francis Clement. *Blood-Drenched Altars*. Milwaukee: Bruce Publishing Company, 1935.

Kertzer, David I. *Rituals, Politics, and Power*. New Haven: Yale University Press, 1988.

Kingsley, Charles. *South by West or Winter in the Rocky Mountains and Spring in Mexico*. London: W. Isbister and Company, 1874.

Knight, Alan. "The Several Legs of Santa Anna: A Saga of Secular Relics." *Past and Present*, supplement 5 (2010): 227–55.

———. *The Mexican Revolution*. 2 vols. Cambridge: Cambridge University Press, 1986.

Koselleck, Reinhart. *The Practice of Conceptual History: Timing History, Spacing Concepts*. Trans. Todd Samuel Presner. Stanford CA: Stanford University Press, 2002.

Koselleck, Reinhart, and Michael Jeismann (eds.). *Der politische Totenkult: Kriegerdenkmaler in der Moderne*. Munich: Wilhelm Fink, 1994.

Krauze, Enrique, and Fausto Zerón-Medina. *Porfirio: La guerra (1854–1867)*. Vol. 2. Mexico City: Editorial Clío, 1993.

Krauze, Enrique. *Místico de la autoridad: Porfirio Díaz*. Biografía del poder, vol. 1. Mexico City: Fondo de Cultura Económica, 1987.

La gratitud del ayuntamiento constitucional de la villa de Coyoacán le mueve a dirigir al pueblo esta proclama. Mexico City: Oficina de D. Alejandro Valdés, 1820.

La visita del señor presidente de la República, general Porfirio Díaz a la ciudad de Monterrey, en diciembre de 1898. Monterrey, Nuevo León: Imprenta y Litografía de Ramón Díaz, 1899.

Lacey, Elaine. "The 1921 Centennial Celebration of Mexico's Independence: State Building and Popular Negotiation." In William H. Beezley and David E. Lorey (eds.), *¡Viva Mexico! ¡Viva La Independencia! Celebrations of September 16*. Wilmington DE: Scholarly Resources, 2001. 199–232.

Lafragua, José María. *Memoria de la primera secretaría de estado y del despacho de Relaciones Interiores y Exteriores de los Estados Unidos Mexicanos, leída al soberano Congreso constituyente en los dias 14, 15 y 16 de diciembre de 1846, por el ministro del ramo, José María Lafragua*. Mexico City: Imprenta de Vicente García Torres, 1847.

———. *Miscelánea de política*. Mexico City: INEHRM, 1987.

Las lágrimas del egoísmo. Mexico City: Oficina de D. Mariano Ontiveros, 1820.

Las zorras de Sansón. Mexico City: Imprenta de Alejandro Valdés, 1820.

Lawrence, D. H. "See Mexico After, by Luis Q." In D. H. Lawrence, *Mornings in Mexico and Other Essays*. Cambridge: Cambridge University Press, 2009. 165–72.

Leask, Nigel. *Curiosity and the Aesthetics of Travel Writing, 1770–1840*. Oxford: Oxford University Press, 2002.

Leija Irurzo, Edgardo, and Flor de María Salazar Mendoza. "San Luis Potosí a la sombra del general Antonio López de Santa Anna: Avenencias y desavenencias políticas, 1822–1823." In *Memoria Electrónica del 10 Verano de la Ciencia de la Región Centro*. San Luis Potosí: UASLP, 2008), 1–5.

Lemoine, Ernesto. *La revolución de independencia, 1808–1821, Testimonios*. Tomo 2, en *La República Federal Mexicana: Gestación y Nacimiento, Volumen IV*. Mexico City: Departamento del Distrito Federal, 1974.

Lerdo de Tejada, Miguel. *Marcha Polka al gran presidente Porfirio Díaz*. Casa Wagner y Levin, n.d.

Les arbres de la liberté. Paris: Publication de la Mission du Bicentenaire de la Révolution française et des droits de l'homme et du citoyen, 1989.

Lipset, Seymour Martin. *Political Man: The Social Bases of Politics.* London: Heineman, 1983.

López, Juan. *Guadalajara y sus mandatarios de 1532 a 1986.* Guadalajara: Gobierno de Jalisco, Secretaría General, Unidad Editorial, 1988.

López Cancelada, Juan. *El comercia de ambos mundos.* Cádiz, 1828–29; republished as *Sucesos de Nueva España hasta la coronación de Iturbide,* intro. Verónica Zárate Toscano, Mexico City: Instituto Mora, 2008.

Lorenzo, María Dolores. "Negociaciones para la modernización urbana: La demolición del mercado del Parián en la ciudad de México, 1843." *Estudios de Historia Moderna y Contemporánea de México* 38 (July–December 2009): 85–109.

Lozano, José M. *Alegato de buena prueba presentado por el C. Lis. José M. Lozano en representación del ciudadano gobernador constitucional Juan Bustamante, ante el C. Juez de Distrito en el juicio de amparo promovido por el primero contra el veredicto que pronunció la H. Legislatura del Estado, erigida en Gran Jurado, el 27 de diciembre de 1868.* San Luis Potosí: Tipografía de Exiga, plazuela de San Francisco, 1869.

Magner, James A. *My Faces and Places.* 3 vols. Palm Beach: Palm Press, 1990.

Magoffin, Susan Shelby. *Down the Santa Fe Trail and into Mexico: The Diary of Susan Shelby Magoffin, 1846–1847.* Ed. Stella M. Drumm with foreword by Howard R. Lamar. Lincoln: University of Nebraska Press, 1982.

Malo, José Ramón. *Diario de sucesos notables de Don José Ramón Malo (1832–1853).* 2 vols. Mexico City: Editorial Patria, 1948.

Matute, Álvaro. *Antología, México en el siglo XIX: Fuentes e interpretaciones históricas.* Mexico City: UNAM, 1981.

Mayo, C. M. *The Last Prince of the Mexican Empire.* Cave Creek AZ: Unbridled Books, 2009.

McCullough-Friend, Christine. "There's a Mexican Empress Buried at St. John's." *Catholic Standard and Times,* 6 May 1999.

McDonald, Kerry. "Los inicios del pronunciamiento en San Luis Potosí." In Flor de María Salazar Mendoza, *12 Ensayos sobre política y sociedad potosina durante la Independencia y la Revolución.* San Luis Potosí: Congreso del Estado de San Luis Potosí–UASLP–AHESLP, 2009. 47–53.

———. "The Experience of the Pronunciamiento in San Luis Potosí, 1821–1849." Unpubl. PhD diss., University of St. Andrews, 2011.

Mexico Bicentennial Commission. "Encabeza Presidente Homenaje a

Héroes de la Independencia." Accessed 6 August 2010. http://www.bicentenario.gob.mx/.

Meza, Rafael. "Pedro Silva Meneses: Héroe anónimo." *El Sol de Tlaxcala*, 3 May 2010.

Monroy Castillo, María Isabel. *Sueños, tentativas y posibilidades: Extranjeros en San Luis Potosí, 1821–1845*. San Luis Potosí: El Colegio de San Luis–Archivo Histórico del Estado de San Luis Potosí, 2004.

Morales Córdova, David Aarón. "Agustin I." *Cuadernos Americanos*, Nueva Epoca, vol. 3, no. 121 (July–September 2007): 89–113.

Morales, Nydia Lissette Carmen, and Flor de María Salazar Mendoza. "San Luis Potosí escenario político del general Antonio López de Santa Anna para el pronunciamiento de 1823." In *Memoria electrónica del 10 verano de la ciencia de la región centro*. San Luis Potosí: UASLP, 2008. 1–5.

Moreno Gutiérrez, Rodrigo. "Nuestras ideas sobre la consumación: Recorrido historiográfico sobre el proceso de la consumación de la independencia de México." In Marta Terán and Víctor Gayol (eds.), *La corona rota: Identidades y representaciones en las independencias iberoamericanas*. Castelló de la Plana: Universitat Jaume I, 2010. 343–57.

Muir, Edward. "Images of Power: Art and Pageantry in Renaissance Venice." *American Historical Review* 84 (1979): 16–52.

Muría, José María. *El federalismo en Jalisco (1823)*. Mexico City: INAH, 1973.

Muro, Manuel. *Historia de San Luis Potosí*. 3 vols. San Luis Potosí: Sociedad Potosina de Estudios Históricos, Tallers Bloea de México, 1973.

Murray, Paul V. *The Catholic Church in Mexico: Historical Essays for the General Reader*. Vol. 1: *1519–1910*. Mexico City: Editoriales E.P.M, 1965.

Nava, Fortunato. "Discurso pronunciado por el C. Lic. Nava, en la festividad cívica de la noche del 15 de septiembre de 1869, en el Teatro Alarcón." In *Discursos y composiciones poéticas, que se leyeron en las festividades cívicas del 15 y 16 de septiembre del presente año por disposición de la junta patriótica*. San Luis Potosí: Tipgrafía de Vélez, 1869.

Neria, Leticia. "Humour as Political Resistance and Social Criticism: Mexican Comics and Cinema, 1969–1976." Unpubl. PhD diss., University of St. Andrews, 2012.

Niemeyer, E. V. Jr. "Anticlericalism in the Mexican Constitutional Convention of 1916–1917." *Americas* 11, no. 1 (July 1954): 31–49.

Nora, Pierre (ed.). *Realms of Memory: Rethinking the French Past*. English edition ed. and with foreword by Lawrence D. Kritzman; trans. Arthur Goldhammer. 3 vols. New York: Columbia University Press, 1996.

Noveno calendario de Abraham López, arreglado al meridiano de México y antes publicado en Toluca, para el año de 1847. 2nd ed. Mexico City: Imprenta del autor, calle de Donceles 18, n.d.

Ocampo, Melchor. *Textos políticos.* Mexico City: Colección SepSentas, Secretaría de Educación Pública, 1975.

Octavo calendario de Abraham López, arreglado al meridiano de México y antes publicado en Toluca, para el año de 1846. Mexico City: Imprenta del autor, calle de Donceles 18, n.d.

Olavarría y Ferrari, Enrique de. *México independiente.* Vol. 4 in Vicente Riva Palacio (ed.), *México a través de los siglos.* Mexico City: Editorial Cumbre, 1980. (See Riva Palacio.)

——. *Reseña histórica del teatro en México, 1538–1911.* 3rd rev. ed., 5 vols. Mexico City: Editorial Porrúa, 1961.

Olveda Legaspi, Jaime. *La política de Jalisco durante la primera época federal.* Guadalajara: Poderes de Jalisco, 1976.

Oración patriótica que en la plazuela principal de la Alameda de México pronunció J. M. Herrera el 16 de septiembre de 1829, aniversario del grito de Dolores. Mexico City: Imprenta del Águila, 1829.

Oronoz, Fray Luis Gonzaga. *A la nación española.* Mexico City: Imprenta de Ontíveros, 1820.

Pacheco Real, Antonio. *Discurso pronunciado por el ciudadano Antonio Pacheco Real.* Mexico City: Imprenta Ignacio Cumplido, 1835.

Palti, Elías José. *La invención de una legitimidad: Razón y retórica en el pensamiento mexicano del siglo XIX (Un estudio sobre las formas del discurso político).* Mexico City: Fondo de Cultura Económica, 2005.

——. *El tiempo de la política: El siglo XIX reconsiderado.* Buenos Aires: Siglo XXI, 2007.

Parra, Enrique Plasencia de la. *Independencia y nacionalismo a la luz del discurso conmemorativo (1825–1867).* Mexico City: CONACULTA, 1991.

Parsons, Wilfrid. *Mexican Martyrdom.* New York: Macmillan and Company, 1936.

Payne, Stanley. *Politics and the Military in Modern Spain.* Stanford CA: Stanford University Press, 1967.

Payno, Manuel. *Memoria sobre la revolución de 1857 y enero de 1858.* In *Memorias de México y el mundo.* Mexico City: CONACULTA, 2000. 33–96.

———. "Comonfort." In *El Libro Rojo*. Mexico City: Editorial del Valle de México, 1977. 513–26.

———. "Defensa que hace el ciudadano Manuel Payno en la causa que se la ha instruido por la sección del Gran Jurado del Congreso Nacional por el participio que tomó en los sucesos de diciembre de 1857." In *Memorias de México y el mundo*. Mexico City: CONACULTA, 2000. 97–112.

Paz, Octavio. *El laberinto de la soledad*. Ed. Anthony Stanton. Manchester: Manchester University Press, 2009.

———. *The Labyrinth of Solitude*. New York: Grove Press, 1985.

Pérez Toledo, Sonia. "Mobilización social y poder político en la ciudad de México en la década de 1830." In Brian F. Connaughton (coord.), *Prácticas populares, cultura política y poder en México, siglo XIX*. Mexico City: Universidad Autónoma Metropolitana, 2008. 335–93.

Pérez Verdía, Luis. *Historia particular del Estado de Jalisco*. Vol. 2. Guadalajara: Universidad de Guadalajara, 1988.

Piccato, Pablo. *City of Suspects: Crime in Mexico City, 1900–1931*. Durham: Duke University Press, 2001.

Plasencia de la Parra, Enrique. *Independencia y nacionalismo a la luz del discurso conmemorativo (1825–1867)*. Mexico City: CONACULTA, 1991.

Portilla, Anselmo de la. *Historia de la revolución de México contra la dictadura del general Santa Anna: 1853–1855*. 1856; Mexico City: Fundación Miguel Alemán, 1991.

———. *México en 1856 y 1857: Gobierno del General Comonfort*. 1858; Mexico City: INEHRM, 1987.

Presas, José. *Juicio imparcial sobre las principales causas de la revolución, y acerca de las poderosas razones que tiene la metrópoli para reconocer su absoluta independencia*. Bordeaux: Pedro Beaume, 1828.

Prieto, Guillermo. *Memorias de mis tiempos*. Paris 1906; reprint, Mexico City: Editorial Porrúa, 1985.

———. *Lecciones de historia patria*. Mexico City: CONACULTA, 1999.

Proclama dirigida al inmortal Quiroga, sacada de la Miscelánea de comercio, artes, y literatura número 66. Mexico City: Oficina de Alejandro Valdés, 1820.

Q. E. D., *Don Antonio siempre el mismo: Modos que se cumpla la ley queremos todos*. Mexico City: Oficina de don Alejandro Valdés, 1820.

Quezada Torres, María Teresa. "De la Reforma a la República Restaurada, 1856–1875." In *Cien años de vida legislativa. El Congreso del Estado de San*

Luis Potosí: 1824–1824. San Luis Potosí: El Colegio de San Luis–H. Congreso del Estado, 2000). 105–201.

Quinto calendario de Abraham López, arreglado al meridiano de México para el año de 1843, antes publicado en Toluca. Mexico City: I. Avilés, 1842.

Quiroga, Antonio. *Ejército nacional: Al ilustrísimo señor obispo de Cádiz.* Mexico City: Oficina de Alejandro Valdés, 1820.

———. *Exhortación hecha por el inmortal Quiroga en nombre de la Nación española, a los habitantes de ella.* Mexico City: Oficina de Alejandro Valdés, 1820.

Ramírez, José Fernando. *Mexico during the War with the United States.* Ed. Walter V. Scholes, trans. Elliott B. Scherr. Columbia: University of Missouri Press, 1950.

Reed, Nelson. *The Caste War of Yucatán.* Stanford CA: Stanford University Press, 2001.

Rejón, Manuel Crescencio. *Pensamiento político.* Mexico City: UNAM, 1996.

Reseña de las fiestas del 2 y 3 de abril de 1895 con motivo de las condecoraciones decretadas para los vencedores en el Sitio de Querétaro y asalto de Puebla en 1867. Mexico City: Imprenta Gutemberg, 1895.

Reyes, Bernardo. *El general Porfirio Díaz: Estudio biográfico con fundamento de datos auténticos y de las memorias del gran militar y estadista, de las que se reproducen los principales pasajes.* Mexico City: J. Ballesca, 1903.

Reyes de la Maza, Luis. *Cien años de teatro en México [1810–1910].* Mexico City: Colección SepSentas, Secretaría de Educación Pública, 1972.

Reyes Heroles, Jesús (coord.). *Mariano Otero: Obras.* 2 vols. Mexico City: Porrúa, 1967.

Riego, Rafael del, et al. *Representación hecha al rey y a las Cortes, por los generales del ejército de observación Rafael del Riego, Miguel López Baños y Felipe Arco-Agüero.* Mexico City: Oficina de J. M. Benavente y Socios, 1820.

Riva Palacio, Vicente (ed.). *México a través de los siglos: Historia general y completa del desenvolvimiento social, político, religioso, militar, artístico, científico y literario de México desde la antigüedad más remota hasta la época actual; obra única en su género.* 5 vols. 1: *Historia antigua y de la conquista,* 2: *Historia del virreinato,* 3: *La guerra de independencia,* 4: *México independiente*; 5: *La Reforma.* Mexico City: Ballescá, 1880–89; reprint, Mexico City: Editorial Cumbre, 1956, 1880. CD-ROM. Mexico City: Universidad Autónoma Metropolitana–Azcapotzalco, INAOE, El Colegio de Jalisco, 2007. Online at http://www.archive.org.

Rivera, Agustín. *Anales mexicanos. La Reforma y el Segundo Imperio.* Mexico City: UNAM, 1994.

Rivera Cambas, Manuel. "D. Ignacio Comonfort." In *Los gobernantes de México.* Mexico City: Transcontinental de ediciones mexicanas, 1989. 282–330.

———. *Historia de la intervención europea y norteamericana en México y del Imperio de Maximiliano de Habsburgo.* 1888–89; reprint, Mexico City: IN-EHRM, 1985.

Rodríguez Barragán, Nereo. "Don Juan Bustamante, Gobernador Liberal de San Luis Potosí." *Cvadrante Revista de Cultura* (San Luis Potosí), Año IV, 1956.

Rodríguez E., Jaime O. "Los caudillos y los historiadores: Riego, Iturbide y Santa Anna." In Manuel Chust and Víctor Mínguez (eds.), *La construcción del héroe en España y México (1789–1847).* Valencia: Universidad de Valencia, 2003. 309–35.

———. "The Origins of the 1832 Rebellion." In Jaime E. Rodríguez O. (ed.), *Patterns of Contention in Mexican History.* Wilmington DE: Scholarly Resources, 1992. 145–62.

Rodríguez Piña, Javier. "Conservatives Contest the Meaning of Independence, 1846–1855." In William H. Beezley and David E. Lorey (eds.), *¡Viva Mexico! ¡Viva La Independencia! Celebrations of September 16* (Wilmington DE: Scholarly Resources, 2001. 101–30.

Rodríguez-Moya, Inmaculada. "Agustín de Iturbide: ¿Héroe o Emperador?" In Manuel Chust and Víctor Mínguez (eds.), *La construcción del héroe en España y México (1789–1847).* Valencia: Universitat de València, 2003. 211–28.

Rovira, Guiomar. *¡Zapata vive! La rebelión indígena de Chiapas contada por sus protagonistas.* Barcelona: Virus Editorial, 1994.

Rugeley, Terry. "En busca de Santiago Imán." *Unicornio,* Suplemento Cultural de *Por Esto!,* 21 February 1999, 3–9.

———. *Rebellion Now and Forever: Mayas, Hispanics, and Caste War Violence in Yucatán, 1800–1880.* Stanford CA: Stanford University Press, 2009.

———. *Yucatán's Maya Peasantry and the Origins of the Caste War.* Austin: University of Texas Press, 1996.

Said, Edward W. *Orientalism.* London: Penguin, 2003.

Salazar Mendoza, Flor de María. *La junta patriótica de la capital potosina: Un espacio político de los liberals (1873–1882)*. San Luis Potosí: Ponciano Arriaga, 1999.

Santoni, Pedro. "The Failure of Mobilization: The Civic Militia of Mexico in 1846." *Mexican Studies/Estudios Mexicanos* 12, no. 2 (Summer 1996): 169–94.

———. "Lucas Balderas: Popular Leader and Patriot." In Jeffrey M. Pilcher (ed.), *The Human Tradition in Mexico*. Wilmington DE: Scholarly Resources, 2003. 41–56.

———. *Mexicans at Arms: Puro Federalists and the Politics of War, 1845–1848*. Fort Worth: Texas Christian University Press, 1996.

———. "Where Did the Other Heroes Go? Exalting the '*Polko*' National Guard Battalions in Nineteenth-Century Mexico." *Journal of Latin American Studies* 34, no. 4 (November 2002): 807–44.

Sater, William. "Review: Heroic Myths for Heroic Times." *Mexican Studies/ Estudios Mexicanos* 4, no. 1 (Winter 1988): 151–61.

Sierra, Justo, *Evolución política del pueblo mexicano*. Originally publ. 1900–1901 in *Mexico: Su evolución social*; reprint, Mexico City: UNAM, 1957.

Skinner, Quentin. "Algunos problemas en el análisis del pensamiento y la acción políticos." In Ambrosio Velasco Gómez (coord.), *Resurgimiento de la teoría política en el siglo XX: Filosofía, Historia y Tradición*. Mexico City: UNAM, 1999. 221–53.

Solares Robles, Laura. *La obra política de Manuel Gómez Pedraza 1813–1851*. 2 vols. Mexico City: Instituto Mora, Instituto Matías Romero, Acervo Histórico Diplomático de la Secretaría de Relaciones Exteriores, 1999.

Sordo Cedeño, Reynaldo. "El Congreso y la guerra con Estados Unidos de América, 1846–1848." In Josefina Zoraida Vázquez (coord.), *México al tiempo de su guerra con Estados Unidos (1846–1848)*. Mexico City: Secretaría de Relaciones Exteriores, El Colegio de México, y Fondo de Cultura Económica, 1997. 47–103.

Stealey, John E. III (ed.). *Porte Crayon's Mexico: David Hunter Strother's Diaries in the Early Porfirian Era, 1879–1885*. Kent: Kent State University Press, 2006.

Tanck de Estrada, Dorothy. "Los catecismos políticos: De la revolución francesa al México independiente." In Solange Alberro, Alicia Hernández Chávez, and Elías Trabulse (eds.), *La revolución francesa en México*. Mexico City: El Colegio de México, 1992. 65–80.

Tapia Méndez, Aureliano. *El diario de Ipandro Acaico.* Mexico City: Ed. Jus, 1988.

Tenembaum, Barbara A. "Streetwise History: The Paseo de la Reforma and the Porfirian State, 1876–1910." In William H. Beezley, Cheryl English Martin, and William E. French (eds.), *Rituals of Rule, Rituals of Resistance: Public Celebrations and Popular Culture in Mexico* Wilmington DE: Scholarly Resources, 1994. 127–50.

———. "'They Went Thataway': The Evolution of the *Pronunciamiento*, 1821–1856." In Jaime E. Rodríguez O. (ed.), *Patterns of Contention in Mexican History.* Wilmington DE: Scholarly Resources, 1992. 187–205.

Tenorio, Mauricio. "1910 Mexico City: Space and Nation in the City of the Centenario." In William H. Beezley and David E. Lorey (eds.), *¡Viva Mexico! ¡Viva la Independencia! Celebrations of September 16.* Wilmington DE: Scholarly Resources, 2001. 167–98.

Thomson, Waddy. *Recollections of Mexico.* New York: Wiley and Putnam, 1847.

Tornel y Mendívil, José María. *Breve reseña histórica de los acontecimientos más notables de la nación Mexicana.* Mexico City: INEHRM, 1985.

Tornel, José María. *Oración pronunciada por el Coronel José María Tornel.* Mexico City: Imprenta del Águila, 1827.

Torrente, Mariano. *Historia de la indepencia de México.* Ed. Ernesto de la Torre Villar. Mexico City: UNAM–Miguel Angel Porrúa, 1989.

Toscano, Carmen. *Memorias de un mexicano.* Filmed by Salvador Toscano. 1950; re-release (DVD), Mexico City: Fundación Carmen Toscano I.A.P., 2011.

Troncoso, Juan Nepomuceno. *Dar que van dando: Carta a un argelino residente en México y autor del papel titulado No rebuznaron en balde el uno y el otro alcalde.* Puebla: Imprenta Liberal, 1820.

———. *Pascuas a un militar.* Puebla: Imprenta Liberal de Troncoso Hermanos, 1821.

Turner, John Kenneth. *Barbarous Mexico.* Chicago: Charles H. Kerr, 1911.

Tweedie, Mrs. Alec. *Mexico as I Saw It.* London: Hurst and Blackett, 1902.

Tylor, Edward B. *Anahuac: Or Mexico and the Mexicans, Ancient and Modern.* London: Longman, Green, and Roberts, 1861.

Van Young, Eric. "Of Tempests and Teapots: Imperial Crisis and Local Conflict in Mexico at the Beginning of the Nineteenth Century." In Elisa Servín, Leticia Reina, and John Tutino (eds.), *Cycles of Conflict,*

Centuries of Change: Crisis, Reform, and Revolution in Mexico. Durham: Duke University Press, 2007. 23–59.

Vanderwood, Paul J. *The Power of God against the Guns of Government: Religious Upheaval in Mexico at the Turn of the Nineteenth Century*. Stanford CA: Stanford University Press, 1998.

Vázquez Mantecón, María del Carmen. "Las fiestas para el libertador y monarca de México Agustín de Iturbide, 1821–1823." *Estudios de Historia Moderna y Contemporánea de México* 36 (July–December 2008): 45–83.

Vázquez de Knauth, Josefina. *Nacionalismo y educación en México*. Mexico City: El Colegio de México, 1975.

————. "El modelo de pronunciamiento mexicano, 1820–1823." *Ulúa* 7 (enero–julio 2006): 31–52.

————. "Political Plans and the Collaboration between Civilians and the Military, 1821–1846." *Bulletin of Latin American Research* 15, no. 1 (January 1996): 19–38.

————. "Los pronunciamientos de 1832: Aspirantismo político e ideología." In Jaime E. Rodríguez O. (ed.), *Patterns of Contention in Mexican History*. Wilmington DE: Scholarly Resources, 1992. 163–86.

Vázquez, Josefina Zoraida (ed.). *Planes en la nación mexicana. Libro dos: 1831–1834*. Mexico City: Senado de la República–El Colegio de México, 1987.

————. *Planes en la nación mexicana. Libro cuatro: 1841–1854*. Mexico City: Senado de la República–El Colegio de México, 1987.

Velázquez, Primo Feliciano. *Historia de San Luis Potosí*. 4 vols. San Luis Potosí: Archivo Histórico del Estado y Academia de Historia Potosina, 1982.

Verdery, Katherine. *The Political Lives of Dead Bodies: Reburial and Postsocialist Change*. New York: Columbia University Press, 1999.

Vigil, José María. *La Reforma*. Vol. 5 in Vicenta Riva Palacio (ed.), *México a través de los siglos*. Mexico City: Editorial Cumbre, 1980. (See Riva Palacio.)

Warren, Richard A. *Vagrants and Citizens: Politics and the Masses in Mexico City from Colony to Republic*. Wilmington DE: Scholarly Resources, 2001.

Waugh, Evelyn. *Robbery under Law: The Mexican Object-Lesson*. London: Chapman and Hall, 1939.

Yturbide, Prince Agustin de. "Mexican Haciendas: The Peon System." *North American Review* 168, no. 509 (April 1899): 424–33.

————. "Mexico under President Diaz." *North American Review* 158, no. 451 (June 1894): 715–28.

Zamacois, Niceto. *Historia de Méjico.* 18 vols. Barcelona: J. F. Parres y cía, 1876–82.

Zamacona, Manuel María de. *Discurso pronunciado por el C. Lic. Manuel María de Zamacona, en el acto solemne de la inauguración de la penitenciaria de Puebla.* Puebla: Imprenta de la Escuela de Artes y oficios, 1891.

Zárate Toscano, Verónica. "Agustín de Iturbide: Entre la memoria y el olvido." *Secuencia* 28 (enero–abril 1994): 5–27.

————. "El papel de la escultura conmemorativa en el proceso de construcción nacional y su reflejo en la ciudad de México en el siglo XIX." *Historia Mexicana* 53, no. 2 (octubre–diciembre 2003): 417–46.

————. "El Paseo de la Reforma como eje monumental." In Carmen Collado (coord.), *Miradas recurrentes: La ciudad de México en los siglos XIX y XX.* Mexico City: Instituto Mora–UNAM Azcapotzalco, 2004. 62–83.

————. "Héroes y fiestas en el México decimonónico: La insistencia de Santa Anna." In Manuel Chust and Víctor Mínguez (eds.), *La construcción del héroe en España y México (1789–1847).* Valencia: Universitat de València, 2003. 133–53.

————. "Las conmemoraciones septembrinas en la ciudad de México y su entorno en el siglo XIX." In Verónica Zárate Toscano (ed.), *Política, casas y fiestas en el entorno urbano del Distrito Federal Siglos XVIII–XIX.* Mexico City: Instituto Mora, 2003. 129–97.

————. "Las pervivencias de Iturbide en el México de hoy." *Millars Espai i Història* (Universitat Jaume I, Castellón) 30 (2007): 105–122.

————. "San Ángel as the Site of National Festivals in the 1860s." In William H. Beezley and David E. Lorey (eds.), *¡Viva México! ¡Viva la Independencia! Celebrations of September 16.* Wilmington DE: Scholarly Resources, 2001. 87–101.

————. "Septiembre: Mes de la patria en la Ciudad de México y poblaciones aledañas en el siglo XIX (Parte primera)." *Jahrbuch für Geschichte Lateinamerikas* 38 (2001): 183–206.

Zárate Toscano, Verónica (ed.). *Política, casas y fiestas en el entorno urbano del Distrito Federal Siglos XVIII–XIX.* Mexico City: Instituto Mora, 2003.

Zavala, Lorenzo de. *Ensayo histórico de las revoluciones de México: Desde 1808 hasta 1830.* 2 vols. Mexico City: SRA, CEHAM, 1981.

Contributors

Shara Ali graduated from the University of St. Andrews in 2005 with an MA in Spanish. She completed an MA in Latin American Area Studies at the Institute for the Study of the Americas in London in 2006 before returning to St. Andrews, where she obtained her PhD in June 2011 after completing her dissertation "From Independence to Independence: The Pronunciamiento in Yucatán (1821–1841)," benefiting from a School of Modern Languages scholarship. She currently works as a lecturer in Spanish and Latin American Studies at the College of Science Technology and Applied Arts of Trinidad and Tobago.

Melissa Boyd graduated from the University of St. Andrews, where she was awarded an MA in Spanish and history in 2005. She obtained her PhD at the same institution in June 2012. Her research interests include Mexican liberalism, nineteenth-century political thought, norms and behavior, political history, and the history of ideas with particular reference to Mariano Otero.

Rosie Doyle obtained her PhD in June 2012 at the University of St. Andrews as part of the Arts and Humanities Research Council–funded project on the Pronunciamiento in Nineteenth-Century Mexico under the supervision of Will Fowler. Her area of research is the experience of the pronunciamiento in Jalisco. She has an MA in Latin American Studies from the Institute of Latin American Studies, University of London, where she studied development and Gender Studies and majored in human rights.

Will Fowler is professor of Latin American Studies at the University of St. Andrews. He is the author of *Mexico in the Age of Proposals, 1821–1853* (Westport CT, 1998), *Tornel and Santa Anna: The Writer and the Caudillo* (Westport CT, 2000), *Latin America since 1780* (London, 2002; 2nd edition, 2008), and *Santa Anna of Mexico* (Lincoln NE, 2007). He has published numerous articles on the early national period and edited twelve volumes on Mexican and Latin American political history, including *Gobernantes mexicanos*, 2 vols. (2008), *Forceful Negotiations* (2010), and *Malcontents, Rebels, and Pronunciados* (2012).

Kerry McDonald graduated from the University of St. Andrews with an MA in modern languages (German and Spanish) in 2003 and obtained a postgraduate degree in translation from Herriot-Watt University in 2004, working as a translator thereafter. She obtained her PhD in June 2011 after completing her dissertation on "The Experience of the Pronunciamiento in San Luis Potosí," benefiting from an Arts and Humanities Research Council grant.

Antonia Pi-Suñer Llorens obtained her doctorate in history from the Universidad Nacional Autónoma de México, where she is professor of Mexican history. Her research interests revolve around the Mexican nineteenth century, Mexican historiography, and diplomatic relations between Mexico and Spain. She is the author of *México y España durante la República Restaurada* (Mexico City, 1985); *El general Prim y la cuestión de México* (Mexico City, 1996); *Historiografía mexicana*, vol. 4: *En busca de un discurso* *integrador de la nación* (Mexico City, 1996); *Una historia de encuentros y desencuentros: México y España en el siglo XIX*, co-authored with Agustín Sánchez Andrés (Mexico City, 2001); and *La deuda española en México: Diplomacia y política en torno a un problema financiero* (Mexico City, 2006).

Flor de María Salazar Mendoza teaches at the Autonomous University of San Luis Potosí in the Coordinación de Ciencias Sociales y Humanidades. Her area of specialty is nineteenth-century Mexico. She is the author of *La junta patriótica de la capital potosina: Un espacio político de los liberales (1873–1882)* (San Luis Potosí, 1999) and *Dos estancias de Benito Juárez en San Luis Potosí 1863–1867* (San Luis Potosí, 2007). She has served as director of the Archivo Histórico del Estado de San Luis Potosí.

Rodrigo Moreno Gutiérrez is completing his PhD at UNAM, writing a thesis on political culture in Mexico following the achievement of Independence. He lectures in history at the Facultad de Filosofía y Letras in the same institution. He has published a book chapter in Alicia Mayer's *América en la cartografía: A 500 años del mapa de Martin Waldseemüller* (2010) and a study on the consummation of independence in the north of Mexico in Ana Carolina Ibarra's edited volume on *La independencia en el Septentrión de la Nueva España* (2010).

Pedro Santoni is professor of history at California State University, San Bernardino. His publications include *Mexicans at Arms: Puro Federalists and the Politics of War, 1845–1848*, and "Where Did the Other Heroes Go? Exalting the 'Polko' National Guard Battalions in Nineteenth-Century Mexico." In addition, he has edited *Daily Lives of Civilians in Wartime Latin America: From the*

Wars of Independence to the Central American Civil Wars (Westport CT, 2008), served as a member of the Board of Contributing Editors for the *Encyclopedia of War*, 5 vols. (Norton MA, 2011) and as an assistant editor for the *Encyclopedia of the Mexican-American War* (forthcoming). He has also served as president of the Southwestern Historical Association and as a consultant for historical projects sponsored by the Ford Foundation and the Texas Parks and Wildlife Department.

Richard A. Warren is associate professor of history at Saint Joseph's University in Philadelphia, Pennsylvania. He was awarded a BA cum laude in Social Studies from Harvard University and an MA and PhD in history from the University of Chicago. He has published widely on state formation in Latin America, most notably *Vagrants and Citizens: Politics and the Masses in Mexico City from Colony to Republic*, originally published in 2001 and reissued in paperback in 2007.

Verónica Zárate Toscano is a researcher at the Instituto de Investigaciones Dr. José María Luis Mora (Mexico City) and is president of the Mesa Directiva del Comité Mexicano de Ciencias Históricas. With a BA and an MA in history from UNAM (1981, 1986), she was awarded the title of doctor of history by the Colegio de México in 1992 for her thesis "Los nobles ante la muerte en México: Actitudes, ceremonias y memoria. 1750–1850." Her publications include *Gozos y sufrimientos en la historia de México* (Mexico City, 2007), co-edited with Pilar Gonzalbo Aizpuru; *Una docena de visiones de la historia: Entrevistas con historiadores americanistas* (Mexico City, 2004); *Política, casas y fiestas en el entorno urbano del Distrito Federal, siglos XVIII–XIX* (Mexico City, 2003); and *Los nobles ante la muerte en México: Actitudes,* *ceremonias y memoria, 1750–1850* (Mexico City, 2000). She has published numerous articles on rituals, ceremonies, fiestas, and Mexican sites of memory as well as editing *Orden, desorden y corrupción: El gobierno colonial 1802–1804 según un escritor anónimo 1802–1804* (Mexico City, 2000), and co-editing *La Ciudad de México: Antología de lecturas, siglos XVI–XX* (Mexico City, 1995). She is completing a monograph on fiestas and public celebrations in independent Mexico.

To order or obtain more information on these or other
University of Nebraska Press titles, visit www.nebraskapress.unl.edu.

www.ingramcontent.com/pod-product-compliance
Lightning Source LLC
Chambersburg PA
CBHW021808270326
41932CB00007B/96